MW01039700

REFLECTIONS
ON ISLAMIC ART

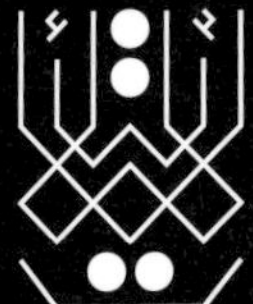

Edited by Ahdaf Soueif

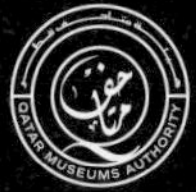

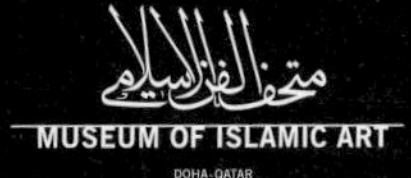

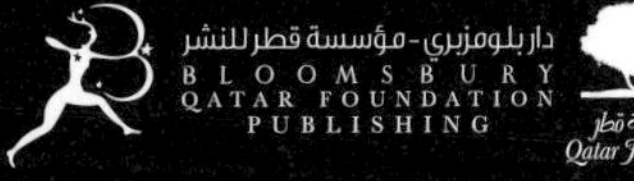

Qatar Museums Authority
would like to thank the following:
HE Sheikha Al Mayassa bint Hamad bin Khalifa Al Thani, Chair of QMA Board of Trustees;
and HE Sheikh Hassan bin Mohammed bin Ali
Al-Thani., Vice Chair of QMA Board of Trustees

Mark Fisher, former QMA Trustee
(who initiated this project); Abdulla Al Najjar, CEO, QMA;
and Roger Mandle, Executive Director, QMA

Oliver Watson, former Director, Museum
of Islamic Art; and Aisha Al Khater, Director, MIA

MIA Imaging Team
Marc Pelletreau (Photography, unless
indicated below);
Khalid Ali; Amin Diban; and Samar Kassab
MIA Curatorial Team
Michelle Walton and William Greenwood
MIA Conservation Team
Lisa Usman; Susan Rees; and Konstantinos Hatziantoniou
MIA Head of Galleries
Stephen Barclay

Additional Photo Credits
MIA: MS.2 (p.32); Hughes Dubois: JE.85 (p.168)
Nicolas Ferrando: MS.2 (pp. 35 and 37); PO.316 (p.60); MS.56 (p.218); Lois Lammerhuber: MIA architecture (pp. 59, 230, 234 and 237)

The MIA Imaging Team wishes to thank Virginia Commonwealth University in Qatar for their help in supporting the photography of this book.

QMA would also like to thank the following:
Nigel Newton, CEO, Bloomsbury Publishing; Kathy Rooney, Managing Director, Bloomsbury Information Publishing; and Anne Renahan, Managing Editor, Bloomsbury Qatar Foundation Publishing

First published in 2011 by
Bloomsbury Qatar Foundation Publishing
Qatar Foundation
Villa 3, Education City
PO Box 5825
Doha, Qatar
www.bqfp.com.qa

Hardback edition ISBN: 9789992142608
Paperback edition ISBN: 9789992142806

Design: Muiz Anwar
Design Consultant: Will Webb

Cover

Detail from Safavid Silk and Metal Bouclé Velvet Panel (pp. 114-5, 117, 251 and 256)

Back Cover

Natural Leaf (pp. 52 and 249). This is an invocation, inscribed in mirror-image *thuluth* script to 'the Generous, the Enricher, the Loving' – three of the ninety-nine names of God.

Contents

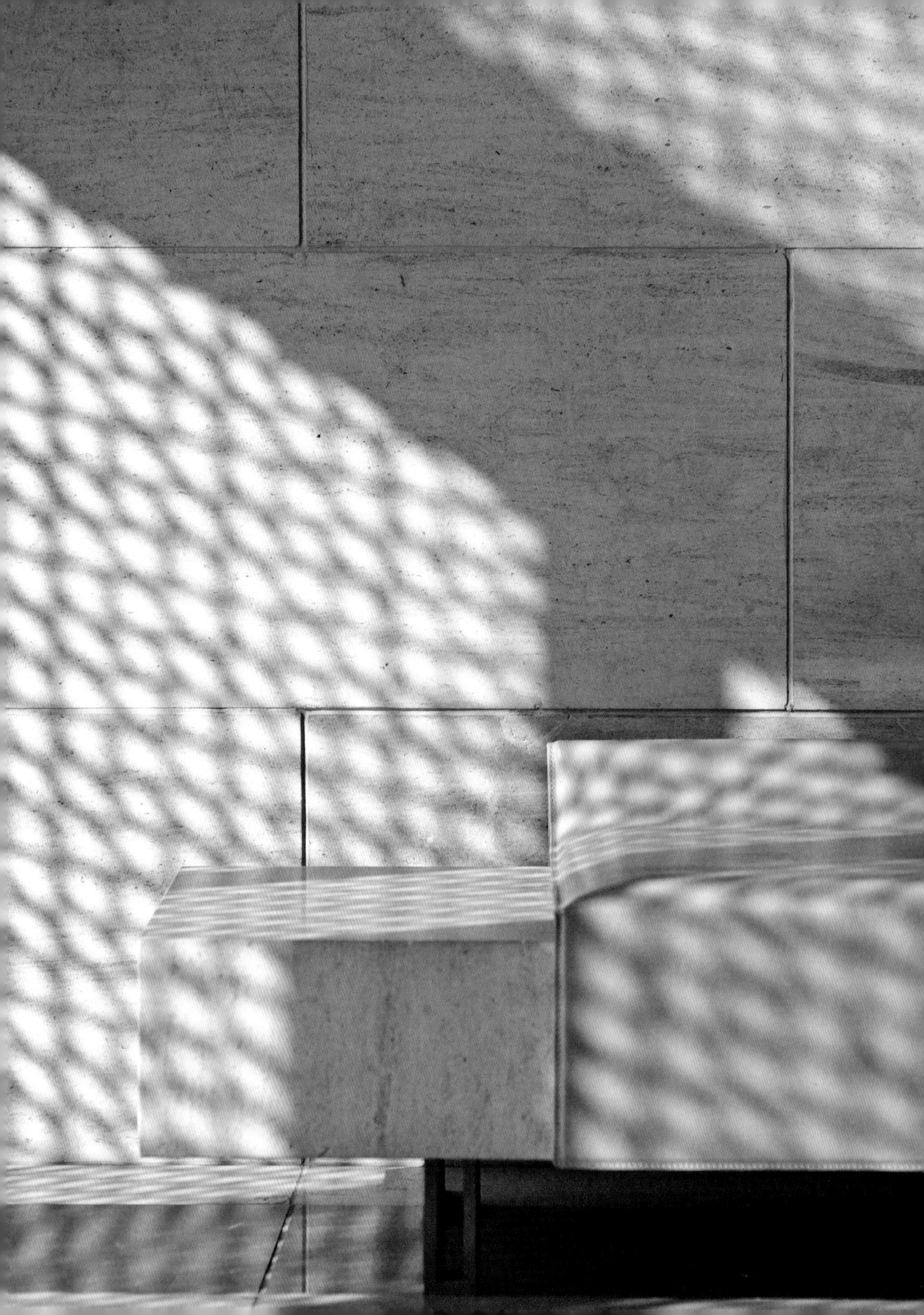

Foreword

Sheikha Al Mayassa bint Hamad bin Khalifa Al Thani

Museums are places of reflection. Museums are also contexts for viewing objects that people have thought important enough to save over time, arranged with other objects to tell stories. But museums are more than places in which to gather information from the visual narratives these objects provide. The works of art in museums have been called mirrors or lenses through which we can see ourselves or distant times quite clearly. In an attempt to demonstrate this principle across creative platforms, we have invited a distinguished group of writers to reflect upon objects within the Museum of Islamic Art in Doha. It has been our hope that these contemporary writers from a wide variety of cultural backgrounds would be inspired by an object in the collection to write a poem, story or essay.

I would like to thank Mark Fisher, a former Trustee of Qatar Museums Authority, the group that governs the museums of Qatar, including the Museum of Islamic Art, for initiating this project, which was developed in collaboration with the noted author, Ahdaf Soueif. It was their hope that this book would show the continuing relevance of beautiful objects from distant times in the history of the Islamic world. Our staff, working with Ms Soueif, has assembled this lovely group of writings that Bloomsbury Qatar Foundation Publishing has so handsomely produced in this book. Each object selected by an author is placed at the lead of their writing so that the reader can encounter it as the first words of these works are read. We hope that in this way, the combination of images and words will resonate and delight, and will demonstrate how works of art can be passages to some other place of peace and understanding.

I am grateful to all those who have worked on this project, in particular to the artists, craftspeople and writers who have given it the vitality we sought.

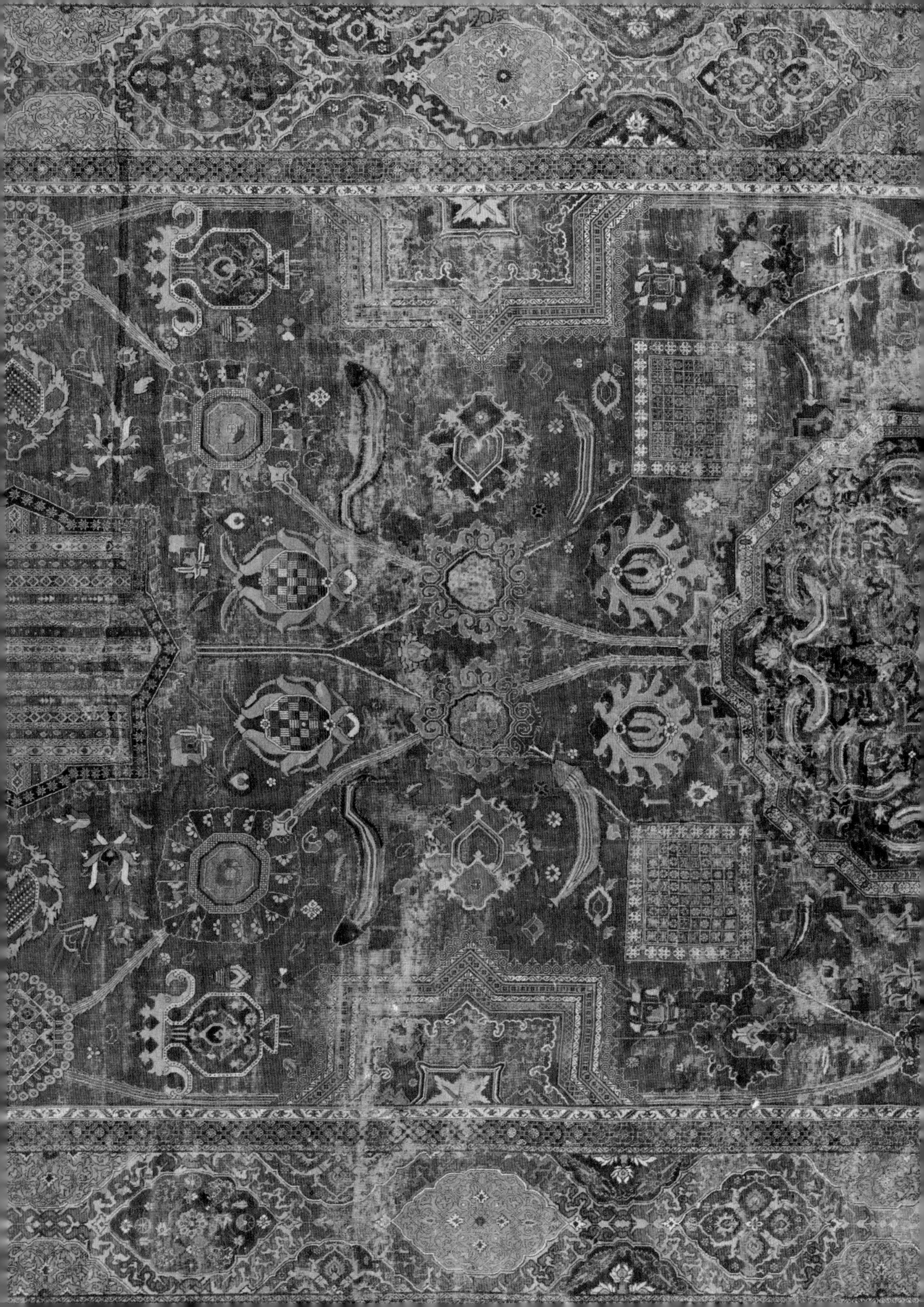

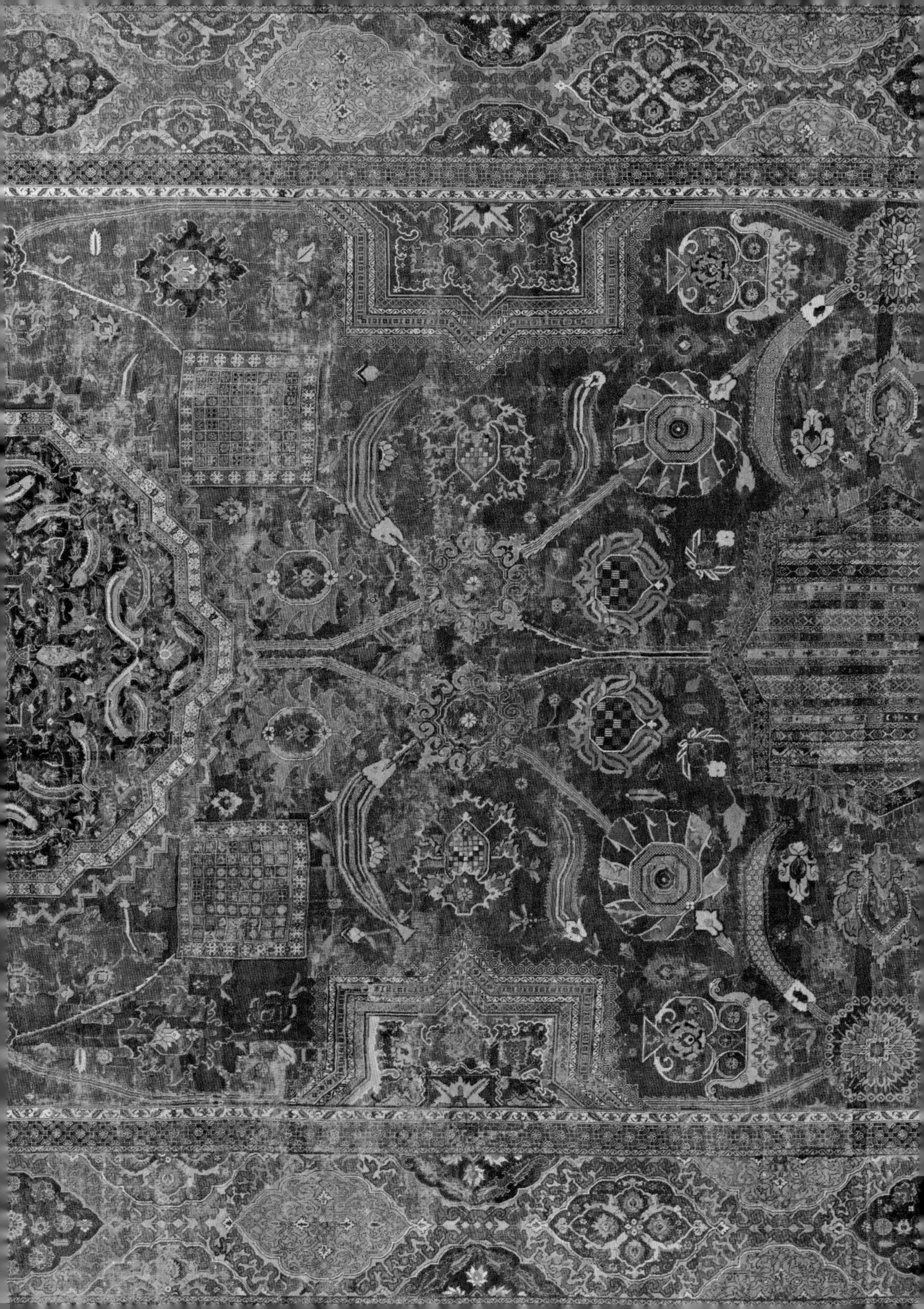

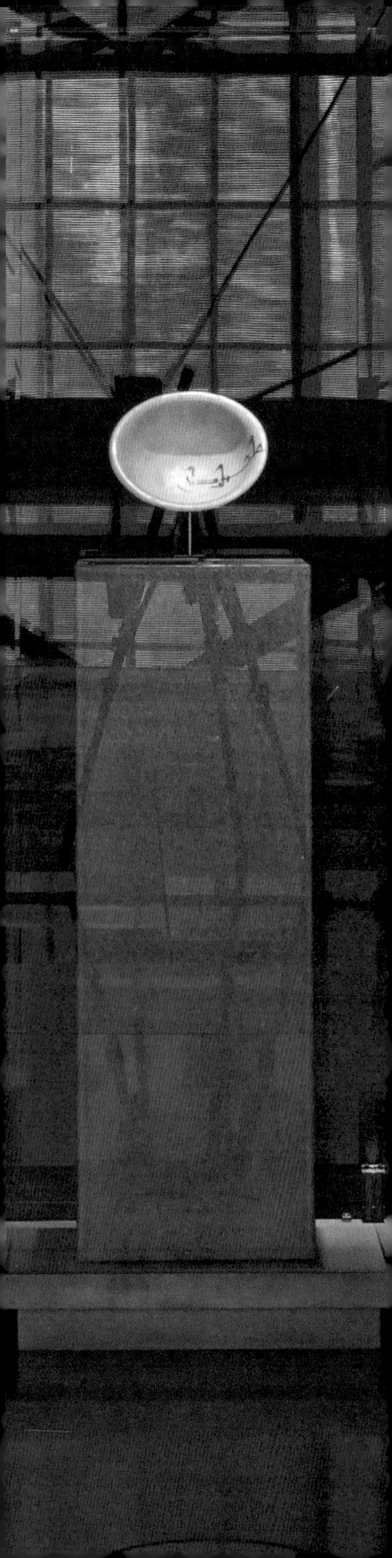

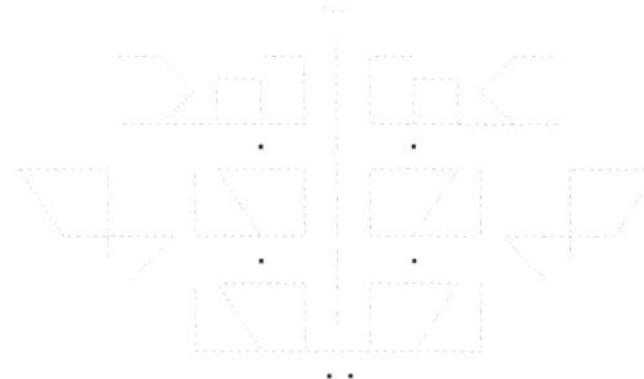

Introduction

Ahdaf Soueif

An austere off-white ceramic dish tilts on its granite stand. The blue markings extending from its right rim to its centre are almost Japanese in their spareness. This is Arabic calligraphy from tenth-century Baghdad: '*Ma 'umila saluha*'. What was made was made well.

On the wall behind it a massive wall-hanging, measuring – I'm guessing – maybe four metres by two and a half. It's a beautiful object: geometric designs frame arabesques and florals – and running through its borders are the repeats of four words: '*La ghaliba illa Allah*': No conqueror but God; the phrase of hope and confidence that brings sorrow rushing into our hearts – the motto of the last Arab kings of Granada.

By one of those quirky coincidences that seem to be telling you something, the Filipino driver who brought me here – and whose name I requested as I left the car – is Edgar Bobadillyo. I'm gazing at the wall-hanging and trying to tease out a coherent link between the crisp, contained, Mr. Bobadillyo and his tragic namesake, Abu Abdallah Muhammad XII, whose fate it was to go down in history as the king who lost Granada, the last Muslim sliver of al-Andalus, to Ferdinand of Aragon and Isabella of Castile in 1492 (897 AH). He left his beloved Alhambra while his workmen's chisels were still tap-tap-tapping at its walls: '*la ghaliba illa Allah la ghaliba illa Allah la ghaliba...*'

Ten years later the new rulers reneged on the city's terms of surrender: now Muslim and Jewish Granadans had to convert to Christianity – or leave. Citizens went into hiding. Others scattered.

And scattered with them were their carriable goods: their rugs and lamps and books and pots and pens and all the things we now know as objects of 'Islamic art'. Some of these objects are here. They hang on walls, or pose in polished glass display cases that play tricks on my eyes – send me their own messages. On this, my first visit, I sit and watch each object migrate from its case and multiply in ghostly reflections in others. They change colour and position. The horse-fountain (or is it a deer?) from tenth-century Córdoba (and there's another name to pluck at the heartstrings) with his fleur-de-lis decorations and his mane so finely plaited nudges the fourteenth-century incense burner of revolutionary Egyptian or Syrian design made for *'al-'alim, al-'amil, nasir al-dunya wa al-din al-Sultan Muhammad ibn Qalawun'*. They both glow with an incandescent, reddish hue, and above them details of a carpet float across a screen in a mesmerising loop.

I close my eyes, breathe, open. Straight ahead of me, in his case, the real bronze horse pulls back, permanently startled. His stubby little tail is curled, his ears prick forward. In front of his eyes, reflected on the glass of his case and on the wall next to the Andalusian tapestry and rivalling it in size, the vertical lines and horizontal walkways of the Museum form a grid, a scaffolding for the skyscrapers and towers of Doha, for the skyline that's sprung up here in the past few years; a skyline, a harbour front, its face to the sea, its back to the desert.

And on the border between the desert and the sea, this building.

In the last article in this book, Nasser Rabbat quotes I.M. Pei as saying he'd found his inspiration for Doha's Museum of Islamic Art in the *fawwarah* of the mosque of Ahmad ibn Tulun in Cairo. But every time I look at the Museum, the building that rises behind it like a prefiguring shadow is the Sultan Hasan Mosque – also in Cairo; monumental, majestic, original, and laying powerful claim to contemporary global attention as architecture and as icon.

I drove in from the airport in November 2009, and Mr. Bobadillyo/Buabdallah (whose name I did not yet know) pointed: that is the Museum. My gaze, following the trajectory of his hand, fell on the massive, blocked, geometric form bulking against the dark horizon: 'Of course,' I said. 'You have seen it before?'

Well, I hadn't – but I sort of had. I had seen it without knowing; in the way of such buildings, its shape, its weight, had somehow slipped into my landscape without my noticing. But what became clear to me in the few days that I spent in the city that is its home, was the extent to which the Museum provides a reference point, an anchor for the eye. As you come in from the airport, emerge from Souk Waqif, drive in from downtown, your eyes cast around for the familiar shape and, finding it, settle comfortably on its solidity. And as you get to know it there's pleasure also in sharing its mosque-like secret; that the solid, piled-up bulk embraces space in such a way that you experience stepping inside it as a liberation. Aloof and imposing, it becomes more and more dominant as you approach, its bulk and its details coming closer, then closer, occupying your horizon utterly until, at the moment of contact, of entry, it sets you free. And then it makes you an offering of its treasure of shapes and patterns and light and texture. And promises you more when you venture further, when you pass through the dark doorways into the galleries. It is no surprise how often the great atrium window makes an appearance in the pieces here: Riz Ahmed, Suad Amiry, Jamal Mahjoub, all mark it: a point of arrival, a point of departure, a point of view.

And it was by the atrium window that we always arranged to meet after the 'ramble-at-will' round the Museum. For that's how this book took shape: a collection of potential contributors invited to visit Doha for a couple of days, taken to the Museum, and turned gently loose into it. Their brief: to fall in love.

Some already had. Youssef Rakha, William Dalrymple and Nasser Rabbat all knew before they left home what they wanted to write about. Radwa Ashour too. On the phone she told me there was a penbox she visited every time she was in Doha; 'I walk round it,' she said, 'like a small pilgrimage.' Others, like James Fenton, had heard of an object and came to find it, and others yet wandered around the Museum until something – a buckle, an astrolabe, a book, a leaf – called out to them.

That first day as I sat in the Museum I had grieved for the objects; for the dishes banished for ever from the table, the lamps from the light, the fountainheads from the running water. Now, the collection started to speak to me; it told me what this book had to be: it would be a conversation. Liberated from East/West dichotomies, from Art/Science and Expert/Layman distinctions, it would be a space where we would hear the work of past artists speaking and being spoken to by their colleagues today. It would be the setting for a conversation taking place in a democracy of era, age, politics, gender, geography and genre. As it was with the collection of objects, so it would be with the collection of poets, artists, historians, scientists, essayists, designers and fictioneers who would together make this book.

It was an enterprise fraught with peril. What if everyone fell in love with the same piece? What if someone found nothing to like? What if...? But the perils were both hypothetical and insurmountable. We would see what happened.

The invited contributors were twenty-seven people whose work was consistently elegant and thought-provoking. At the same time many of them were people you would not normally see in the same newspaper, let alone the same book. The trait shared by every participant was professional excellence. Plus – as it turned out – a willingness to engage with the new and the different. The invitation was to visit the Museum, choose an object, and write a piece or a poem in response to it. 'The Museum,' I wrote, 'lends itself particularly well to the idea of this book: that there will be one piece that speaks to you, or a group of pieces that sets off a train of thought/feeling – and that out of this will come a response in words or images... Does this appeal?' It did. The responses were positive, intrigued, enthusiastic. As Eric Hobsbawm, Shirin Neshat, Pankaj Mishra said 'yes' I sensed the 'rightness' of the project. Its details were still hidden in the future, in the spark yet to be struck between writer and object, but I could already feel its spirit.

Muiz Anwar, the book's designer, elaborated it. The design, he proposed, would be like the Museum: spare and withheld; its aesthetic – inspired by the Islamic manuscript – simply to create the space to display each couple: the article and its object.

I will not, here, perform the usual editorial run-through of each item in the book. Let the pieces keep their right to surprise you. I'll just say that twenty-four people, unprompted, chose different objects – and their responses to them were as varied as the objects themselves.

Then three chose the same one: 'Portrait of St Jerome Representing Melancholy', by Farrukh Beg 1615-16 (1024 AH) after the engraving by Dürer. But Jabbour al-Douaihy, Adam Foulds and Raja Shehadeh each come to their choice from a very different place – and each one forms his own relationship with it. Their conclusions, as they contemplate this object in the moment of its transformation from a 'Christian' work to a 'Muslim' one, go to the heart of the question: 'What's 'Islamic' about Islamic art?'

Art, in the Muslim world, was part of daily life; the function of art – aesthetic pleasure, contemplation and commentary on the world – was also a function of items of familiar use. And, within that usefulness, an almost infinite diversity. In the Museum we see it in the great Andalusian carved beams and architraves, the impossibly delicate filigree filters of Syrian clay water jugs, the ascetic bowls of Iraq, the sumptuous jewellery of the Mughals. This was not a culture that tolerated difference; it rejoiced in it. In the days of its expansion, the new ideas and spirit of Islam had the ability, wherever they went, to energise the local culture, to prompt a re-engagement with its own arts and traditions and a re-fashioning of them into new and vibrant life.

From across a gallery I had recognised a length of white linen, as familiar as my own dresses. How many times had I seen that distinctive fabric on Egyptian temple walls? I knew, before I started walking across, that a border of turquoise and gold would run through it – and there it was. And on the label it said: 'Tiraz. Egypt. Early 11th C. Linen Silk.' And through the border ran the simple declaration, over and over, '*Al-mulk l-Illah*': Dominion is God's.

Seven years ago I wrote about what it was like to grow up in Egypt in the sixties, and how we believed we were living on a ground open and common to all cultures. I called this ground 'Mezzaterra': 'a fertile land; an area of overlap, where one culture shaded into the other, where echoes and reflections added depth and perspective, where differences were interesting rather than threatening because foregrounded against a backdrop of affinities'.[1] I wrote those words then both to record the retreat from – and to try to hold onto – this common ground.

Everywhere in the Museum we can see the common ground Islam created between the new and the old; that area of mutual overlap and influence, excavated and cultivated by artists of long ago

– and we can see that it was far richer than any isolated patch could ever be. And that perhaps a key feature of the attitude, the mindset, that sparked such creative wealth was its ability to hold contrasting points of view, together, in creative tension, 'as parts of a whole', Tash Aw notes, 'rather than opposite strands'.

And in the Sultan Muhammad ibn Qalawun inscription that spoke to me on my first day there's an example of that duality: '*al-'alim, al-'amil, nasir al-dunya wa al-din*' – no hint of difficulty here, rather the formulaic description insists that the ideal person is both a "*alim*', a man of thought, and – following that – a "*amil*', a man of action; an upholder (*nasir*) of the concerns of both this world (*al-dunya*) and the next.

Writing this introduction today, on my balcony in Cairo, it feels as though I can once again see the common ground, there, on the horizon. And that every word we say, every act we perform, pushes us to or away from it. And I consider again the messages I sensed on that November day in 2009.

This book, and the process that has given birth to it, has tried to *be* the ideals, the ambition, the glamour, the reach, the fecundity, the inclusiveness, of the Islamic culture; its ability, when at its best, to elicit the best from everyone living and working within it regardless of where they came from or what beliefs they held – this is what the collection of the Museum of Islamic Art in Doha demonstrates. And this is what these essays pick up again and again, whether in celebrating it or in mourning its temporary loss.

Only temporary loss. For Abu Abdallah of Granada has come back to the Arab world – in this instance as a migrant worker, chauffeuring in Doha, where the MIA stands between the desert and the sea; a lighthouse at the eastern tip of an Arab world that is rediscovering its potential and its spirit. The Museum's objects may be exiled from their place of birth, banished from their quotidian use, but their indispensable job now is to remind us of a central strand of the world's heritage: of an attitude of mind; of the genius of a culture that was able to combine differences, even opposites, and to hold them in a balance that constantly remade the world beautiful, useful, new.

Cairo, May 2011

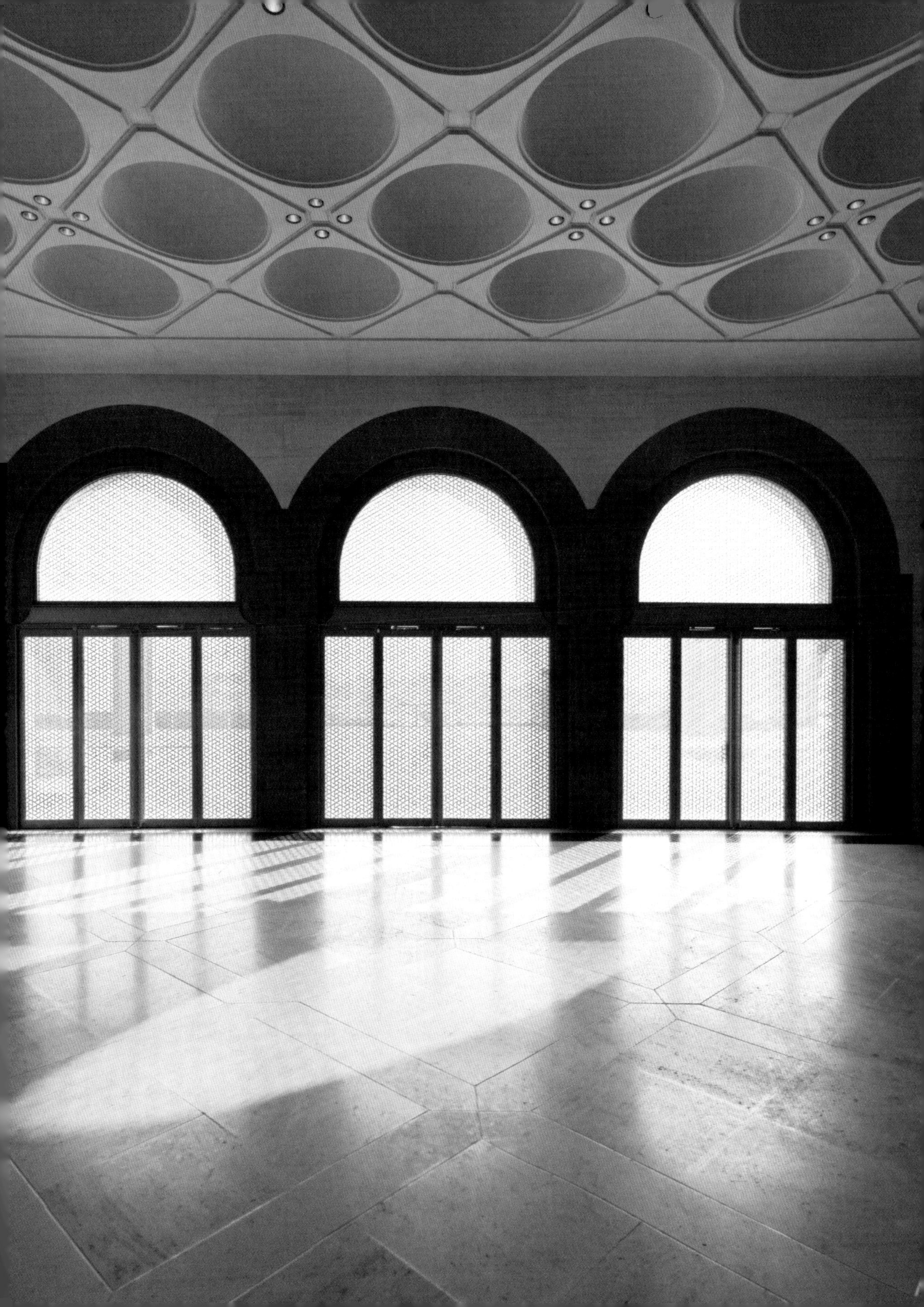

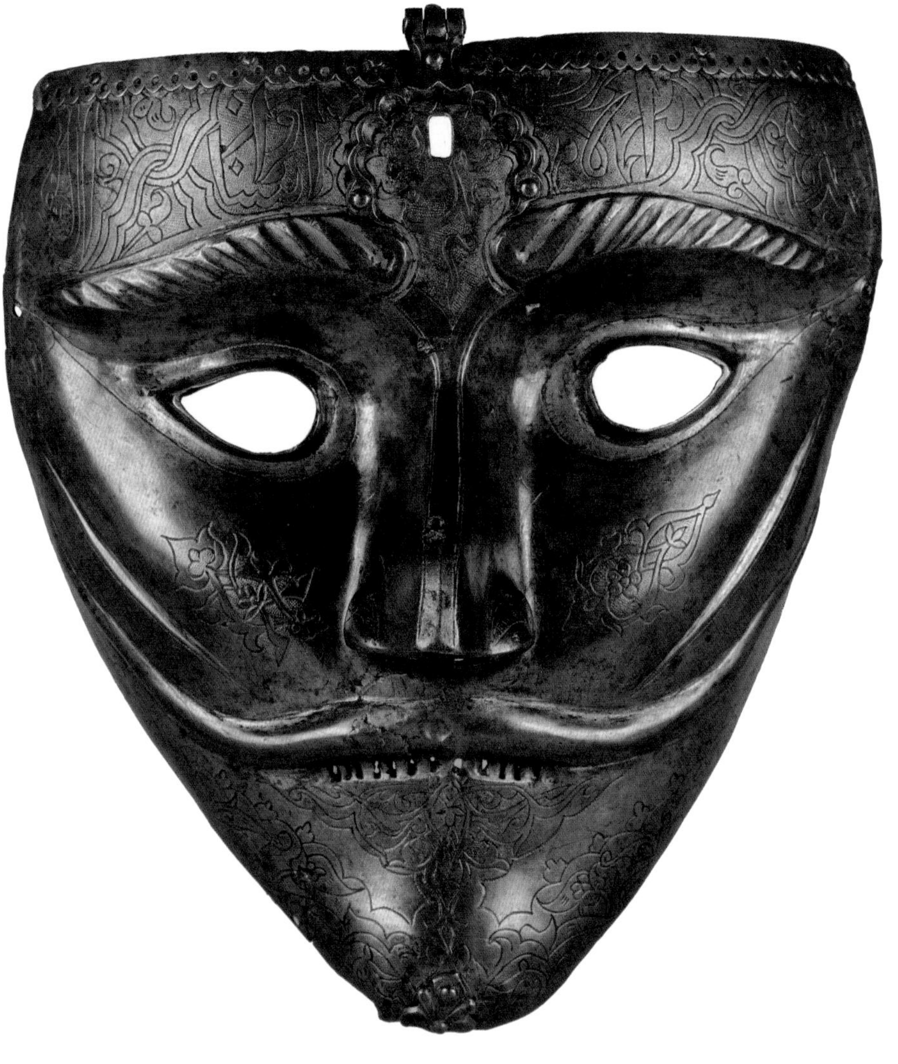

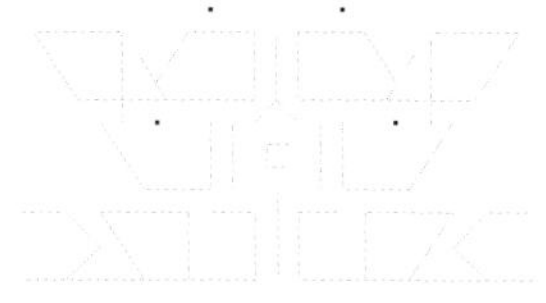

Grand-dad's Attic

Riz Ahmed

Grand-dad's attic is time travel.
A trove of cluttered war spoils
And golden dusted space.

He straddled the globe, you know.
A poet and doctor,
A hot-blood technician,
Precise imagineer.
A one-off, 'blue-sky' type.

His wit and muscle humbled me
Even as we buried him.

A home-team Goliath that fell,
His coffin still stretches my concept of domestic 'cos
Greatness smells so familiar up here.
As common as gutter scents and gutlessness outside,
So deeply shoved-up nose the brain is
Pickled into thinking this is
How it always was.

But beyond this dangling whiff of a god, is only indigestion.
No mouthfuls fit or sit in belly
Whether jaw snapped back or guts wrenched out.
None of this can leave with me and none of it will nourish.
So I scratch'n'sniff and taste for clues
In each angle of each picture frame,
Tongue outstretched.

'The ruins attest the monument was great' –
But brick-dust won't rebuild for me,
When 'Empire' means Darth Vader
And swords are for Orcs and Dwarves.

I'm a derivative, a speculation, a product of commodity
Hunting ghosts for scraps of glory gift-shop souvenirs.

Still waiting there for snow-flake crumbs
My stuck-out tongue dries out,
Just as a single tear appears and tickles down my face,
Splashing with drama on a rusted silver screen.
I swallow shut my gob, tuck in my shirt, feel like a knob.
'Well that's my contribution... Well done.'
I turn to go.

In the end,
Perhaps leaving this attic is the best.
The swirl of proud-ashamed smallness
Whirling in your chest, you face
A giant, skyward, window
Dreaming out its crystal view –
With his stories behind us,
The horizon invites us
To carve blue-skies anew.

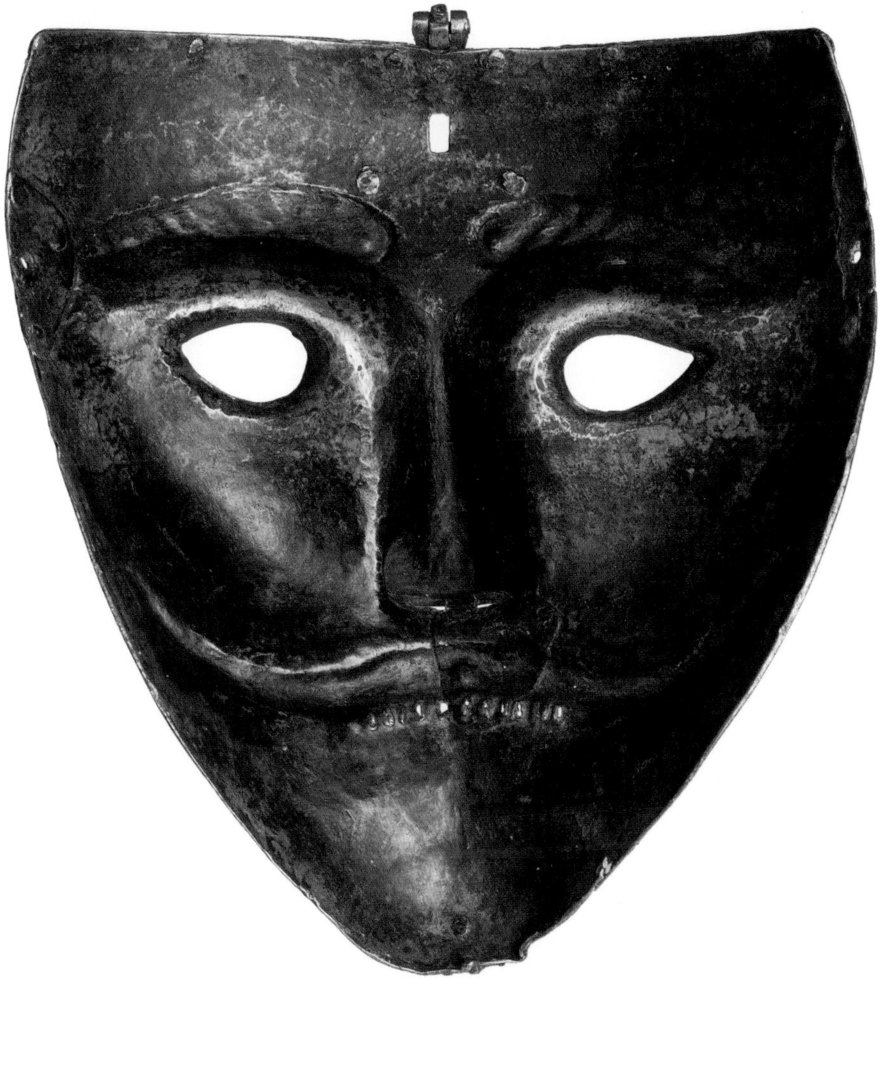

لا يمسه إلا المطهرون
تنزيل من رب العالمين

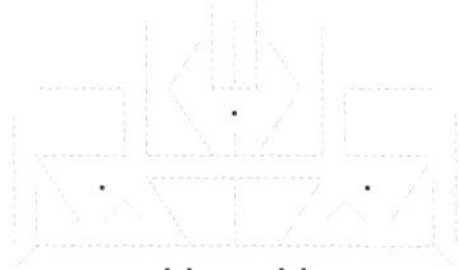

The Journey

Pankaj Mishra

There is a line from Ibn Battutah's *Rihlah* that has stayed with me, years after I first came across it during a prolonged stay in Pakistan. The fourteenth-century Moroccan globetrotter describes a caravan of *Hajj* pilgrims travelling at night with lighted torches through an area made hazardous by brigands. 'People travel,' he writes, 'as it were among wandering stars which illuminate the depth of the darkness and which enable the earth to compete in brightness with the stars of heaven.'

The simple words act on each other and conjure up a brilliant scene. You see the convoy snaking through the desert under a vast black dome; you feel the sandaled feet sinking into the sand and hear the tinkle of camel bells; you sense the boxed Qur'ans and the prayer mats rising and falling together in the camel saddlebags.

Here, from Doha's Museum of Islamic Art, is one such Qur'an, handily portable and, going by its condition, reverently handled over nearly a millennium. Dating back to tenth-century North Africa, it is in the Arabic script that bears the name of Kufah, now a little town in Iraq but once known as a centre of Islamic learning and as famous as the bazaar towns of Fustat and Basra in the 'Arab' Middle Ages.

The Moroccan binding with flap and gilt decorations is from a later period, most probably the fifteenth century. Its magnificence suggests a series of noble owners, and repeated pilgrimages to Makkah from one of the glittering cities (Baghdad, Damascus, Cairo) of the Middle East – and, who knows, even beyond: South-east Asia, China and Indonesia.

What strikes me most is the beautifully angular Kufic script. The vertical strokes are short and brisk; but there is latent ambition in its elongated strokes. It is said that the Kufic script actually shaped the early Qur'ans since its horizontal strokes needed a suitably wide page format. Certainly, these ligatures stretch and stretch, until they seem to be longing to meet some invisible horizon. A millennium later, it looks like the script of a people confident of taking their unique message to the remotest corners of the globe.

It is still astonishing to think of the successes they achieved. In 622 CE, the first year of the Islamic calendar, Muhammad and his band of followers established the first community of believers in a small town in Arabia. Less than a century later, Arab Muslims are in Spain – the contrast with Christianity, which remained a persecuted minority religion for centuries after the death of Christ, couldn't be greater. Great empires – Persian, Roman – fall before the energetically expanding community of Muslims. Islam quickly becomes the new symbol of authority from the Pyrenees to the Himalayas; and the order it creates isn't just political or military. The conquerors of Jerusalem, North Africa and India bring into being a fresh civilisation with its own linguistic, legal, administrative bases, its own arts and architecture, and standards of beauty.

Like all civilisations, the Islamic borrows from pre-existing ones – Indian, Sassanian, Hellenic – but what gives it a striking unity and wholeness is the Arabic language of the Qur'an, the classical language of doctrine as well as of law, prayer, history, poetry and beauty. Extensive mercantile networks and pilgrimage routes to Makkah from all corners of the world affirm the unity of *Dar al-Islam*. For a Muslim in Morocco, India or Java, history retains its moral and spiritual as well as temporal significance; it can be seen as a gradual working out of God's plan. The *Dar al-Harb* (land of infidels) exists on the unimportant and unknown periphery.

The invading Mongols break into this self-contained world in the thirteenth century, terminating the classical age of Islam. But within half a century the Mongols convert to Islam and become its most vigorous champions. Islam shows itself capable of innovations, such as the Sufi orders that spread across the Islamic world, sparking a renaissance of Islam, this time in non-Arab lands. For centuries, God's design for the world could seem to be empirically fulfilled.

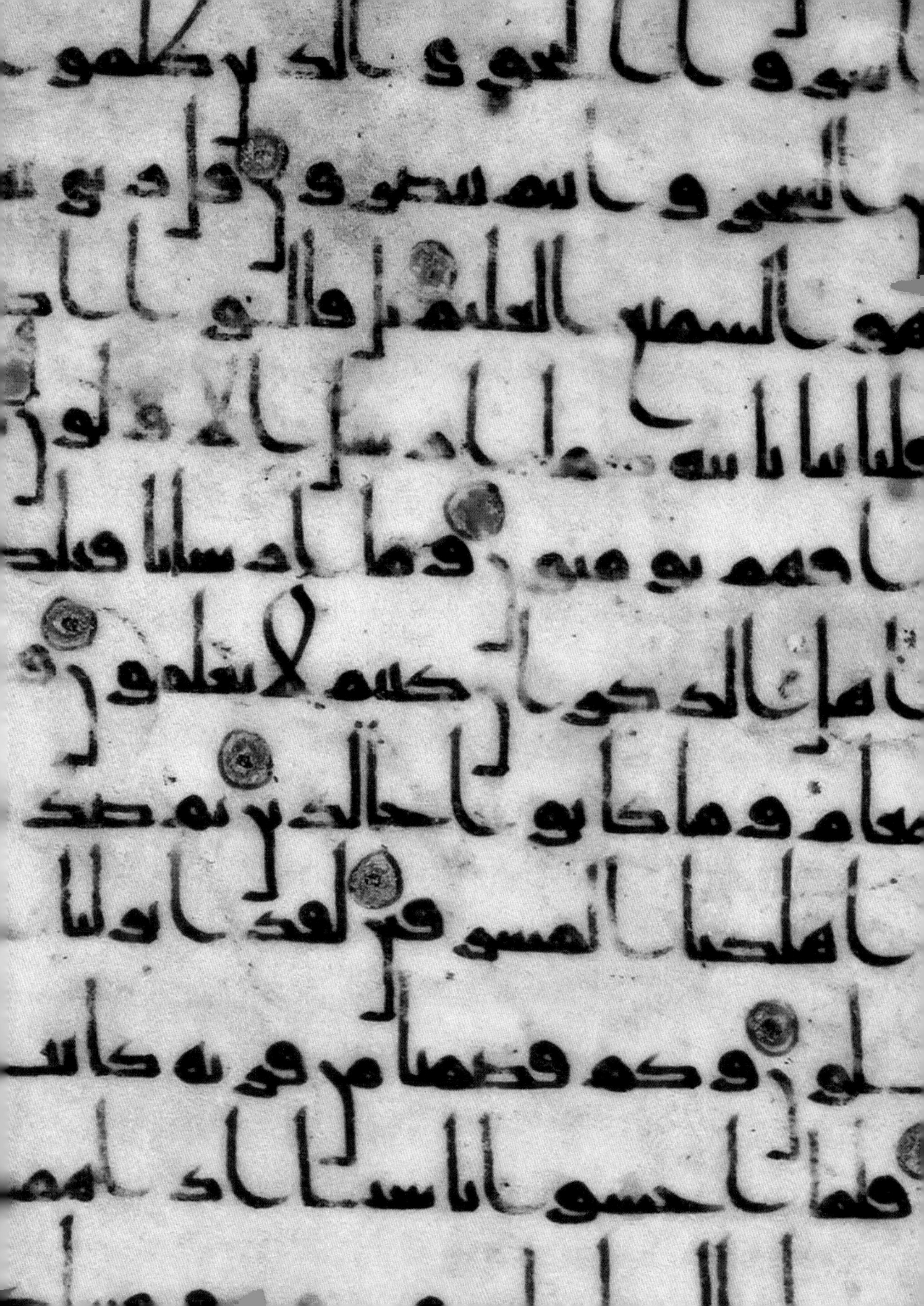

I knew little of this history when I first read Ibn Battutah. I was in Pakistan trying, like many journalists, to travel across the Khyber Pass to Afghanistan, where the Taliban were about to destroy the Bamiyan Buddhas. I had started writing a book about the Buddha, and had been reading with some fascination about the way merchant caravans had travelled with his ideas from North India to Central Asia. In Pakistan I had visited some of the sites where merchants had built great Buddhist monasteries; I was appalled and depressed by the possibility that the Bamiyan Buddhas, one of the antique sites of Buddhism's transmission to Central and East Asia, might be destroyed.

Peshawar itself had the effect of driving me back to my hotel and the book waiting for me in my room. The romance of the city that Western journalists had written about fifteen years ago, when the Soviet army was in Afghanistan, just forty miles away, propping up a communist government, and Peshawar was the frontline city for the jihad sponsored by the United States and its allies, the time when European and American journalists cosied up to their favourite 'Muj' (Mujahideen) and had photos taken of themselves lugging rocket-launchers or huge sacks of heroin – this degraded infatuation with danger at other people's expense wasn't for me.

I saw only the acrid smoke from the burning tyres that the Afghan refugees huddled around for warmth, the beggar children with startlingly green eyes, and the heroin addicts slumped on broken pavements. The backlash from the anti-Soviet jihad was still months from reaching the World Trade Center in New York. But Peshawar, with its destitute refugees, drug lords, addicts, criminals and fanatics who threw acid at unveiled women, was a microcosm of the large-scale devastation that had already occurred in Pakistan.

A few miles outside the city was the *madrasah* where many of the Taliban's leaders had been educated; it still supplied many of their foot soldiers. Here, boys as young as five, and from places as far off as Uzbekistan, sat in neat rows in a courtyard, committing the Qur'an to memory.

To learn all about the Qur'an and the life of the Prophet had always been necessary knowledge for salvation. 'The Qur'an,' Ibn Khaldun, Ibn Battutah's great contemporary, wrote in his *Muqadimmah*, 'has become the basis of instruction, the foundation of all habits that might be acquired later on.' At the same time, Islam had also emphasised the value of other kinds of learning – sciences, medicine and technology. Go to China, if need be, in search of knowledge, the Prophet had exhorted. 'Travelling in search of knowledge,' Ibn Khaldun had asserted, 'is absolutely essential for the acquisition of useful learning and of perfection through meeting authoritative teachers and having contact with scholarly personalities.' But these boys in the *madrasah* near Peshawar, offspring of destitute and/or devout families, were doomed to be nothing more than cannon fodder for other people's jihads.

So I withdrew deeper into my book. Here, in the pages of the *Rihlah*, was another world of Islam: confident of its completeness and triumphs. Growing up in India, where British imperialists had broken Muslim power in the nineteenth century, I had seen only aspects of its decay. In Pakistan, I could see a nihilistic defiance of all-encroaching Western power. And it was Ibn Battutah's book that now impressed upon me the fact that Islam once constituted a universalism no less vigorous and appealing than the one offered by the West in our own time.

Such was the unity and expanse of the Islamic world by the fourteenth century that Ibn Battutah found a shared central core of knowledge and religious duties wherever he went. Like a Harvard MBA today, he found himself employable in both West Africa and Delhi. In Granada, already overrun by the Christians, he met Indian Muslims. The verses of Sa'di were being sung in the Chinese city of Hangzhou. In Fuzhou, Ibn Battutah ran into a man from a town near Tangier.

Later, when I began to read more about Islamic history, it became clearer to me that Ibn Battutah himself stood at the beginning of a new revival and expansion of Islam. In Persia, Turkey and India, new culturally vigorous dynasties and empires would soon come to the fore; and these would exceed, in political vigour and aesthetic subtlety, even the glories of Baghdad and Damascus. Islam would travel even further east, this time through Sufi brotherhoods. Not just the *ulema*, but ordinary Muslims themselves would now transmit their knowledge to society at large and to the next generation, and to foreign lands. From Kufah to Kalimantan, the travelling scholar, the trader, and the Friday assembly would give Islam an easy new portability.

I also learned how quickly, after the centuries of cultural and technological backwardness, the West had caught up with, and then begun to politically subjugate, the Islamic world in the nineteenth and twentieth centuries. In 1929 (1347 AH), a North Indian poet and pilgrim to Makkah, Abdul Majid Daryabadi, recorded how the invincible modern civilization of the West, and the fundamentalist Muslim response to it, had impinged on even the holiest sites of Islam.

In 1916 (1334 AH) the pro-European Sharif Hussein controlled Makkah and the Marseillaise was played as pilgrims presented themselves at Mount Arafat. By 1925 (1343 AH), the Wahhabi family of the Sauds had assumed power in Arabia. But, as Daryabadi reported, British imperialists still controlled the land and sea routes to Arabia. They had helped dethrone the Ottoman Khalifah. The harsh Saudi Wahhabis had demolished sites sacred to Muslims from India; their bans on old customs divided the Muslim community. Meanwhile, goods of Western manufacture, even prayer mats and beads, had overwhelmed the markets of Madinah.

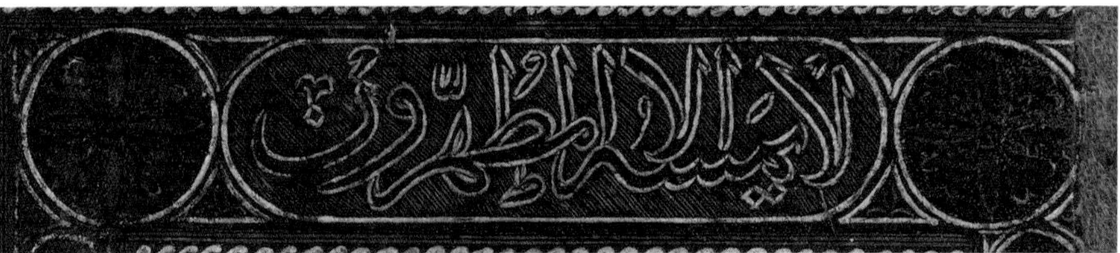

Between the descriptions of Ibn Battutah and Daryabadi lies a whole history, when the world suddenly seemed to work independently of the God of the Qur'an, shifting the balance of power drastically to the *Dar al-Harb*. By the mid-nineteenth century, Western nations dominated, as direct or indirect rulers, the remotest corners of the Muslim world: Indonesia as well as Central Asia.

It was then that many Muslims developed their sense of a world out of sync with God, of a glorious history gone terribly wrong, and the related suspicion that their failure to follow a 'true' path of Islam was to blame for their political setbacks. These have since become recurring notes in the modern history of Muslim countries, motivating many fundamentalist attempts to return to a purer form of Islam.

The political violence of some of these fundamentalists has spawned a cartoon version of Islam in the West, in which every *madrasah* is a nursery for suicide-bombers, and *Shari'a* law is all about stoning women to death. But such headline-generating ignorance obscures the continuing dynamism and vitality of Islam today – which is more often to be found among ordinary Muslims than among their political spokespersons.

Islam remains the fastest-growing religion in the world; and this is because of its little-remarked but astonishing flexibility, its ability to adapt to new conditions. The Hajj and *Umra* still affirm the form of universal sovereignty available to the *ummah*. The network of *madrasahs* and charitable outfits keeps expanding. New charismatic preachers and evangelists arise in even the seemingly inhospitable conditions of secular life in the West, often using the tools of modernity – first cassette tapes and now satellite TV and the internet – to convey their interpretation of the Qur'an. *Ijtihad* – that ongoing endeavour to work out interpretations of the Qur'an that address current needs – and which is debated endlessly by deskbound scholars, is flourishing on the airwaves. Meanwhile, the ideological fantasy that everyone will become blandly secular as they wear Western clothes and consume designer brand-names has been making its way to the trash-heap of history.

Certainly, one can never underestimate the power and appeal of folk Islam in its oldest centres. Sufis had been the most crucial bearers of the faith in places as distinct as North Africa, Anatolia, Bengal and Sumatra. They borrowed forms of devotion from other spiritual traditions; shrines that housed relics of saints and hairs from the Prophet's beard were the outposts of Islam. Hindus and Muslims commonly worshipped at each other's sites across the Indian subcontinent. One of my most intense childhood memories is of being immersed, by my Hindu Brahmin parents, into the ecstatic crowd at the great *dargah* (shrine) of the Sufi saint Moinuddin Chishti in Ajmer. And, visiting Pakistan last year, after almost a decade of the catastrophic war on terror, I was amazed to find myself in that old cosmopolitan world again.

According to near-hysterical Western politicians and journalists, the Taliban were within an inch of conquering Pakistan. But there was no hint of that at the shrine of Shah Hussein, a famous sixteenth-century poet, who lies buried with his close Hindu friend (possibly lover) on

وأبقى وأمر أهلك بالصلوة واصطبر عليها لا نسألك رزقا نحن نرزقك

والعاقبة للتقوى وقالوا لولا يأتينا بآية من ربه أولم تأتهم بينة

ما في الصحف الأولى ولو أنا أهلكناهم بعذاب من قبله لقالوا ربنا

لولا أرسلت إلينا رسولا فنتبع آياتك من قبل أن نذل ونخزى قل كل

متربص فتربصوا فستعلمون من أصحاب الصراط السوي ومن اهتدى

[illegible]

بسم الله الرحمن الرحيم اقترب للناس حسابهم وهم في غفلة

معرضون ما يأتيهم من ذكر من ربهم محدث إلا استمعوه وهم

يلعبون لاهية قلوبهم وأسروا النجوى الذين ظلموا هل هذا

إلا بشر مثلكم أفتأتون السحر وأنتم تبصرون قال ربي يعلم القول

في السماء والأرض وهو السميع العليم بل قالوا أضغاث أحلام

بل افتراه بل هو شاعر فليأتنا بآية كما أرسل الأولون ما آمنت

قبلهم من قرية أهلكناها أفهم يؤمنون وما أرسلنا قبلك إلا رجالا

نوحي إليهم فاسألوا أهل الذكر إن كنتم لا تعلمون وما جعلناهم

جسدا لا يأكلون الطعام وما كانوا خالدين ثم صدقناهم الوعد

فأنجيناهم ومن نشاء وأهلكنا المسرفين لقد أنزلنا إليكم كتابا

فيه ذكركم أفلا تعقلون وكم قصمنا من قرية كانت ظالمة وأنشأنا

بعدها قوما آخرين فلما أحسوا بأسنا إذا هم منها يركضون

لا تركضوا وارجعوا إلى ما أترفتم فيه ومساكنكم لعلكم

تسألون قالوا يا ويلنا إنا كنا ظالمين فما زالت تلك دعواهم حتى

Lahore's outskirts. Approached through a warren of sinisterly dark and empty lanes, the folk fair, which is the centrepiece of spring in Lahore, a testament to the city's long, pluralist past, came as an explosion of light, colour, and noise. The alleys leading to the tomb throbbed with groups of dancing young men in shalwar-kameezes, each whirling around their own frantic drummer; their perspiring faces gleamed in the light from the white bulbs that hung over stalls selling wooden toys, clay crockery, syrupy sweets, a pizza-shaped fried bread – and, yes, beautifully bound copies of the Qur'an.

The crowd of revellers was overwhelmingly lower-middle-class. My upper-class Pakistani companion was nervous among them. 'People in Pakistan are in denial about the Taliban,' he had despaired earlier that evening. 'We do not recognise what they are doing to Pakistan.' But here was a centuries-old celebration of a friendship between a Muslim and a Hindu, a manifestation of the inclusive nature of South Asian Islam. For once, I felt complacent, assured that while the old global civilisation of Islam was gone, its once-famous cities – Herat, Balkh, Baghdad – now in ruins, the religion still offered a compelling way of being in the world to its manifold and diverse adherents.

Who knows, we may well be on the verge of a new cosmopolitan era in Islam, one as significant as the Sufistic civilization that replaced the Caliphate destroyed by the Mongols. The long view may have been unavailable to the calligrapher(s) of this tenth-century Qur'an, or Ibn Battutah, travelling just decades after the Mongol invasions. But we who have arrived late in history – in time to witness even the all-powerful West in decline – know how fragile are the dominant verities and assumptions of our own age. Indeed, the rise of Asia and the unexpected emergence of new cities from Doha to Jakarta as centres of commerce and culture reminds us that the horizons once evoked by a script in tenth-century Mesopotamia have yet to be reached – or even clearly sighted. The vastness and diversity of the world this fourteen-centuries-old faith moves through are only beginning to come into view; and generations to come will no doubt possess even fuller evidence of the resilience and flexibility of Islam.

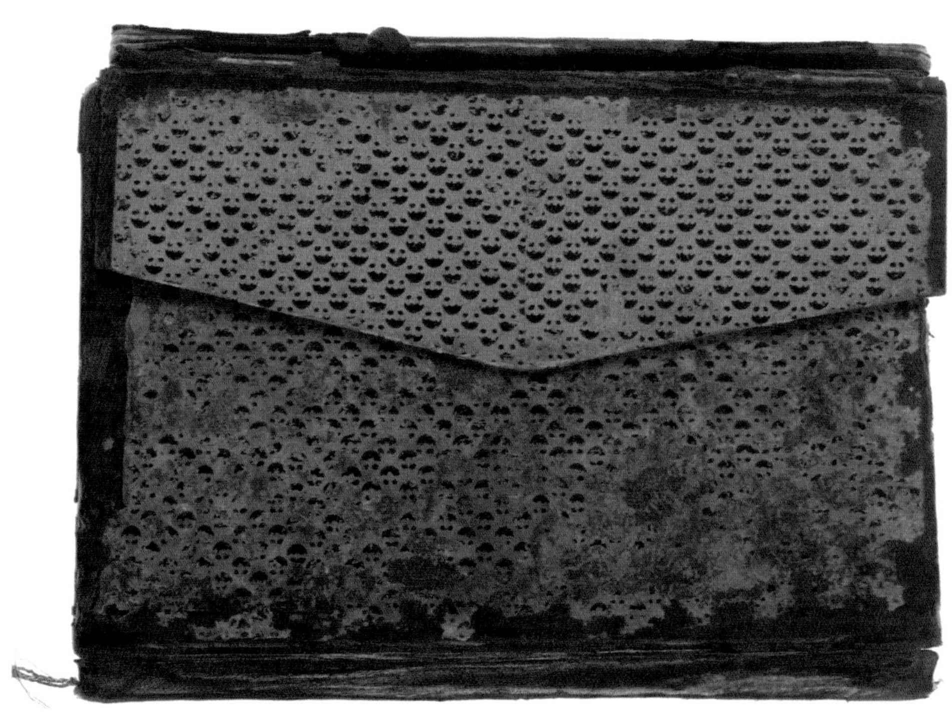

The Book of Fixed Stars

Tash Aw

School was not a great success for me. From the very earliest moments, I hated the regimentation, the learning by rote (Malaysia in the late 1970s was not a place of great experimentation), the bullying, the competitiveness. I spent much time gazing out of the windows, idly charting the shapes of the scrubby bushes and the deep monsoon drains that marked the boundaries of the playing fields and the suburbs beyond. Rainstorms were the best times: the noise of rain on the zinc roofs would be so loud that the teachers' voices could not be heard and the electricity would often trip following the first strike of lightning, and we would be left to our own devices, sketching racy drawings or trading football cards in the semi-darkness until the rains passed.

Primary school history was repetitive and taken for granted: the history of our country began with the founding of a Malay empire based in Malacca, midway between the trading routes linking Arabia and China; a melting pot of cultures was born of this exchange, enriched and complicated by the subsequent arrival of European cultures. These were the things that every child at every Malaysian state school learnt at the time. We grew up in a culture that arose from many other sources and did not question this heritage, nor were we remotely amazed by it. At that age, it was merely a drag. So, too, were the bi-weekly calligraphy lessons in *jawi*, the Arabic script. They were just something that one had to endure dutifully as all good Malaysian schoolchildren were expected to. I never once thought it surprising that I, an ethnic Chinese, should be writing in Arabic, for it was just something that everyone did. It was so imbued in the landscape of our history, this crazy tapestry of cultures with their interwoven threads, that we had lost all ability to see its colour.

In the thirty years that have passed since those primary school days, these threads have begun to unravel, just like so much else in the world around us. Differences between the individual cultures that formed my identity have become increasingly marked, fired by the flames of religion and money; it is not a problem that is uniquely Malaysian, for the world post-9/11 has, to me, seemed more aggressive in its readiness to see distinction between people rather than similarity. It is futile and Utopian, many argue, to seek to regain common ground, for the world is complex, and complexity requires conflict – even a small country like Malaysia is a vortex of competing interests, for goodness' sake. And yet occasionally something will remind me of the genesis of my country, the reason we all exist. And that reason was not conflict.

I have rarely seen a physical object which summarises the interflow of cultures as powerfully – and beautifully – as *Kitab Suwar al-Kawakib*, The Book of Fixed Stars. Dating from 1125 (518 AH), it is part of the famed tradition of Arab astronomy, the knowledge of fixed points and navigation that would eventually lead merchant sea traders to South-east Asia, where they would not only trade with but convert local Sultans to Islam and begin the foundations of a new country. When I first passed in front of the book what arrested my attention was not just its beauty but its familiarity. My knowledge of Persian illuminated manuscripts is sketchy, to say the least, but somehow I felt I knew this book – as if it had existed somewhere in the dusty recesses of my being. Maybe it was the fact that certain words in the description struck a chord within me ('stars,' 'exploration,' 'sea voyages'); or maybe it was the uncertain ethnic origin of the illustrated figure: Middle Eastern? Indian? Central Asian? Chinese?

Wandering through I.M. Pei's museum, I was beginning to suffer from Beauty Fatigue – an overkill of the sublime. It takes time just to get to grips with the building itself, a study in the possibility and perfection of light; a distillation of geometry. And then there is the adjustment one has to make upon entering the exhibition spaces – the sudden dilation of pupils to take in the darkened galleries, the pools of soft light falling on objects seemingly suspended in mid-air against the black background. Although the galleries, too, appear minimalist in their aesthetic, they are filled with textures that invite touch: what are the walls covered with? Metal? Rattan? Finely grained timber? And what of the floor, perfectly hard and smooth, neither shiny nor matt? These are things that weigh sneakily on the senses before one even begins to contemplate the objects.

I tried not to hurry as I stood before each object but it wasn't easy. Every time I paused before one display cabinet something else called out to me from the corner of my eye. After a few hours I realised that the concentration of this almost otherworldly beauty was too great for my mortal sensibilities, and I was becoming saturated by the rarest antiquities and some of the finest craftsmanship the world has ever seen. I waltzed past the twelfth-century Persian *mina'i* fritware bowl and barely registered the fourteenth-century illustration of *Feridoun Storming the Palace of Zahhak*; even the jar of white jade, commissioned by the Qing Emperor Qianlong, which might elsewhere have roused me from my stupor, appeared merely pretty in the cabinet of exquisite *objets d'art*. I would have a quick look at just one more gallery, I thought; I would have to return the following day, refreshed and more receptive. It was then that I saw the *Kitab*. I paused, drew breath and smiled. My notebook, in which I had been furiously scribbling notes, suddenly seemed superfluous. I thought: this is what I have come to see.

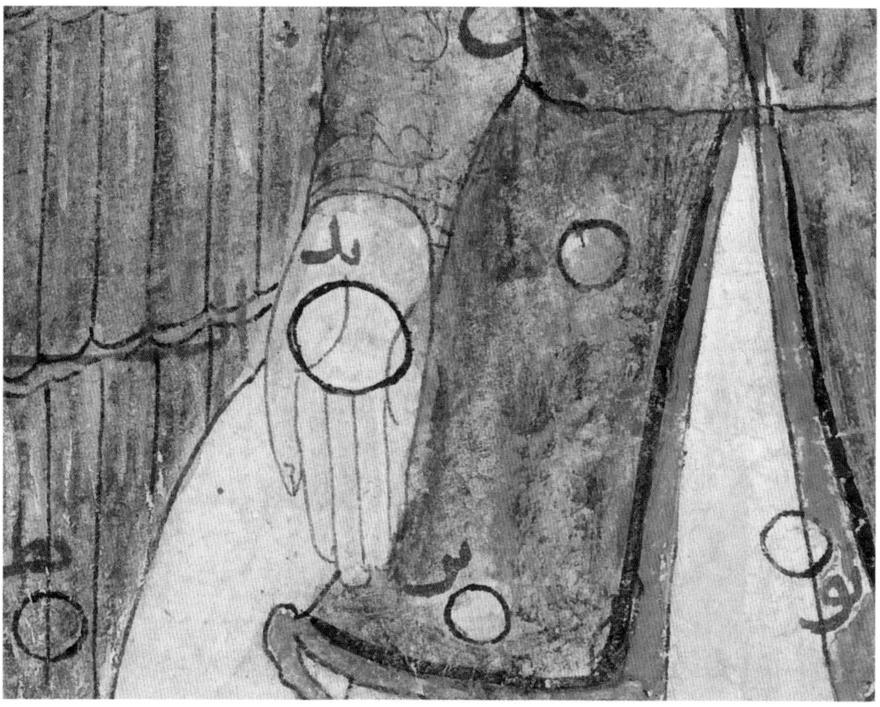

The book lies open on a page showing a winged figure – an angel, one presumes – dressed in a teal-green coat edged in red; a pale lavender-coloured headband sits across its forehead. Its hair falls in curls around its full plump cheeks, but it is the eyes that seize you: narrow, feline, mischievous. The clear round face and Eastern eyes do not immediately announce its provenance. The clothes probably hold obvious clues, even to the most amateur historian, but my gaze is held by its face; maybe I don't want to search for signs of its origin, maybe I want to be fascinated by its mysterious features – probably Near Eastern, I would say, that vast area that airline pilots casually call 'the Stans', where, even today, cultures and ethnic groups bleed into each other and borders have little meaning. Perhaps this is why I am attracted to this coy cherubic face: it could almost be someone I know (the precocious young son of a friend in Beijing comes to mind). The connection I make with it is personal and instinctive, beyond aesthetic appreciation. It feels as if it belongs somewhere in my own history.

Along the angel's head and body are alignments of stars; the biggest is on its palm. Its 'could-be-from-anywhere' self is the outline of a constellation. I make a quick check of the date once more: not long after the production of this manuscript, Arab traders were to reach the shores of South-east Asia – the first significant encounter that local cultures would have with major foreign influences, for it would result in the eventual conversion of the local population to Islam. I wonder how many of those voyages were undertaken using the stars mapped on the body of this green-coated guide.

Some other things I learn about the book: it was written in Arabic by a Persian who based it on the works of Ptolemy, combining them with Arab and Bedouin astronomical traditions. Because it is such an early work, the illustrated figures represent a range of features and styles of dress – some Hellenistic, some Arab, others oriental. Knowing this makes me frustrated that I am unable to reach into the glass cabinet and turn the pages of the book. What do the other figures look like? Will I find more Chinese-looking ones in beautiful foreign clothes? And what do the Hellenistic ones look like – will they be blond?

This is interesting to me because, spending most of the year in Europe, I have become aware of how closely the modern idea of Islam has become wedded to Arab countries, how it is perceived

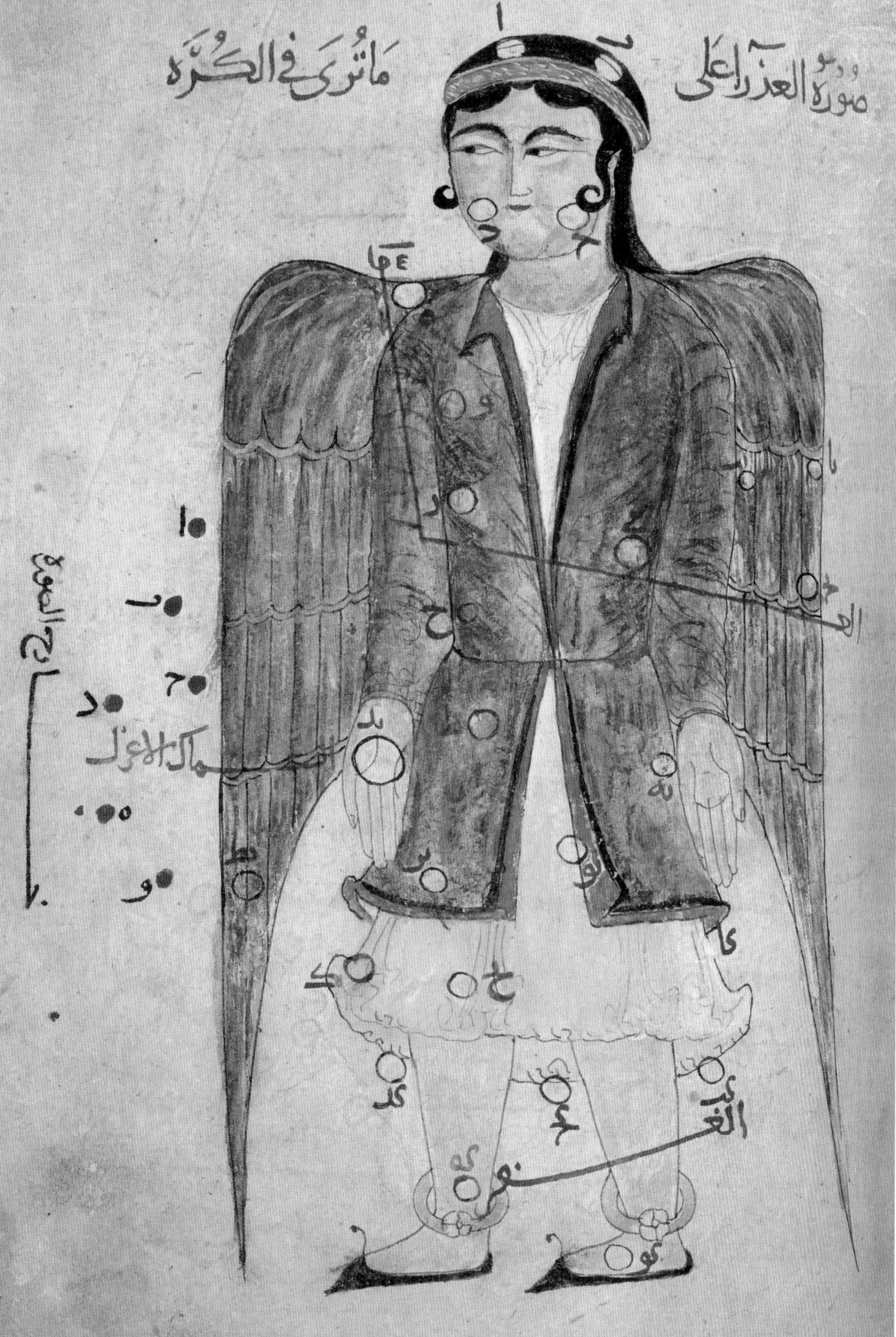

صورة العذراء على ما ترى في الكرة
السماك الاعزل
الغفر

as insular, focused and exclusive – very much the opposite of the notions I had growing up in Malaysia, when we took it for granted that Islam was a world religion that also belonged to countries far from the Arab heartland, adapted to local customs and cultures that sometimes seem at odds with pure Islamic principles. Standing here in a museum of Islamic art looking at a book that represents the flowering of Arab astronomy, I am reminded of the breadth and range of Islam 1,000 years ago, its outward-reaching tendencies. It would reach Malaysia not long after the publication of this manuscript – nearly 900 years before Malaysia would become Malaysia. I feel that the story of my country is, in part, a story of being included, of being absorbed into something bigger. In this way, I feel it is entwined with the story of the book in front of me.

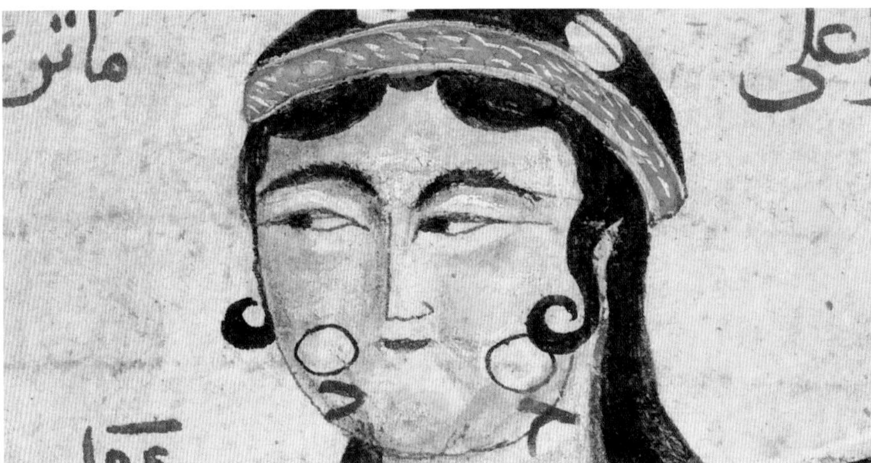

Something else seizes me. The illustrations of the zodiac and constellation in the manuscript are shown in traditional dual fashion: as viewed when standing on earth, the sky a vast dome overhead; and as viewed from the heavens (as God would have viewed them). There is something compelling about the duality of these twin vantage points, the linking of the earthly and the celestial, the practical and the heavenly. It belongs to the same mindset, one thinks, as that which included Greek, Bedouin and Arab sources in the same text – differing points of view are held as parts of a whole rather than opposite strands.

Nowadays we tend to think of globalisation as something that belongs to our age, a phenomenon of our restlessness and search for knowledge, and yet our cross-border movements do not seem to be accompanied by a similar interest in the cultures we come across. Travel has become a right, not a privilege; but the problem with all rights is that they are soon taken for granted, and the accompanying responsibilities – such as the duty to enquire, to learn, to exchange – are lost. We now have the opportunity to take off, at few days' notice, for a boozy weekend in Prague or Tallinn or Barcelona – but in a sense, our destinations have become pointless and indistinguishable. We have never before travelled so much, but our frontiers have never felt so narrow: we travel, it seems, to confirm that home is the best place to be.

Which is why, standing in front of this enigmatic smiling figure, I feel at once shamed and excited – shamed because I, too, have begun to fall into this way of comparing every country to my own points of reference and finding everything lacking; and excited because I am reminded of the possibilities of travelling to another place and engaging in a process of exchange, of including and being included, of absorbing and being absorbed.

Standing in a museum in an arid desert country, I feel connected to the hot rain-soaked landscape of my origins. There is the tangible link in a glass cabinet in front of me, a guide that must have led one ship, then a fleet, then more, to the shores of what would later become Malaysia. It is a story that I would be forced to learn during long soporific afternoons many centuries later. As we scribbled obscenities in our exercise books and made paper aeroplanes, desperate for time to pass quickly (it never did), no one told us that we were, in fact, part of a grand narrative of inclusiveness. We had taken all that for granted, but the truth was that we knew nothing.

I stare one last time at the enigmatic winged figure, trying to fix it in my memory. On the opposite page the calligraphic text unfurls in elegant, concise lines, reminding me of my clumsy schoolboy efforts. My right index finger twitches, almost involuntarily, wanting to trace the shape of almost-forgotten letters, to replicate the form and balanced curves of the letter sin. Later, back in my hotel room, I will try to write out the alphabet with my fountain pen, but my hand is unsteady and will not do what my brain instructs.

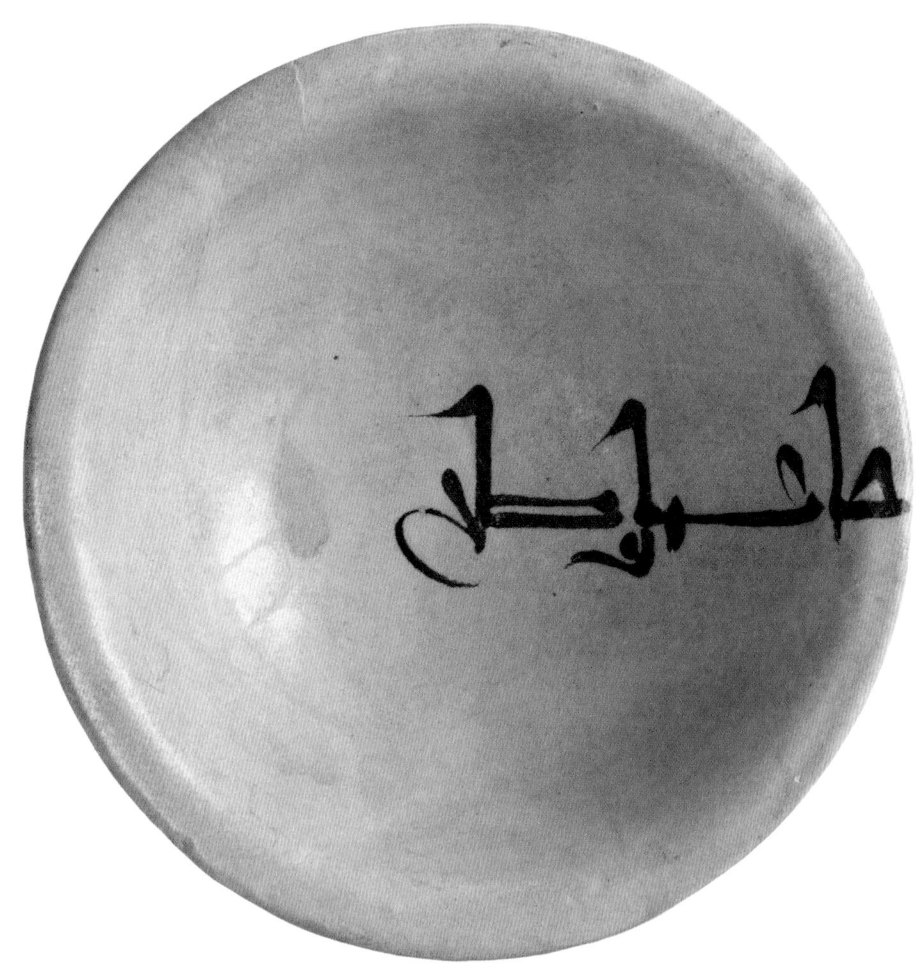

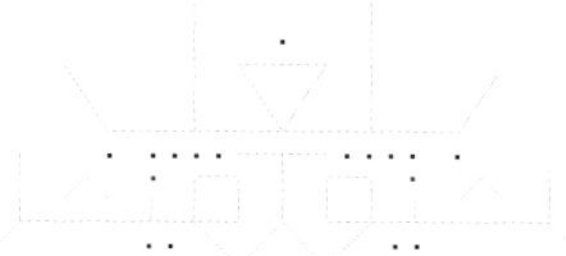

The Potter's Mark

Philip Hensher

Once, long ago, a potter sat at his wheel. The merchants who came to his town had shown him fine work from far away, and he wanted now to match it. It had been too fine for any but the very rich to buy, but, as the first potter in his town, he had been allowed to handle some of the beautiful pieces. He had known immediately that here was work beyond any skill he possessed. But it was also work which had been made by a human hand, and he knew that what one man could do, another could also.

The merchant took back his treasure from the potter, and wrapped it again in the coarse, heavy sackcloth that he used for fragile objects of great value. He placed it in the cupboard where, the potter knew, he kept his finest goods, and made it secure, waiting for the rich man who would come for it. The potter's hands stayed where they were. He could feel the ghost of the bowl, its shape remaining in the air between the rough thick skin of his hands. If he concentrated, he could still feel the unresisting smoothness of the bowl's surface; a grainy smoothness, silky like a soft fine sand falling through the fingers. He wanted to make it himself.

The potter asked questions of the merchant. How had this bowl been made? What was the secret of the white of the surface, pure and deep like clouds on a winter's day? The merchant did not know everything, but he knew some things. The traveller from whom he had bought such things in the past, who had brought these things from the other side of the world, had been intrigued by these objects. The traveller had discovered some things about the surface, about how the purity of the white glaze was attained, and the merchant now passed them on. No doubt there was a chain of knowledge which thinned and lost details, which went wrong and acquired superstitious accretions as the facts were conveyed from merchant to traveller and from traveller to merchant. But still some facts remained, and were preserved. Anybody who unwrapped such an object from its layers of sackcloth would see that the world had not made its like until now. They would be struck by living in an age of wonders, and would want to know how such things were made. The merchant passed on what he knew, and the potter listened.

He knew how to fill the air between his hands with a bowl of just the right shape. He imagined the bowl he would make. When people took it between their hands, the rim falling into place between thumbs and forefingers, they would wonder that hands had been made to hold anything else. But it was the glaze that he meant to master, and over months, he painted small clay tiles with mixtures of earth substances; he experimented with lead, and lime, and salts, and other materials. He worked deep into the night, and looked at the most successful in the bright light of the sun when the day came. And then one day, it seemed to be right. He made a bowl – it came out just as he had imagined it: as though the bowl were making itself. He painted the raw smooth clay with his best mixture, and fired it. It came out perfect. He took a brush, dipped it into blue ink, and with a smooth confident hand drew ten arching lines: 'Made by Salih'; his own name. Now he had done it, and he could do it again whenever he chose.

I want to go back to the beginning of known time. As far as I am concerned, that is the late 1960s, in London. Everything before that is understood, but not truly known. At Christmas, in my country, gifts are brought for children as if overnight, so that they wake on 25 December to discover a pillowcase filled with presents. They believed, and perhaps still believe, that these gifts are brought by Father Christmas, who, travelling in a sled pulled by reindeer, brings presents overnight to every boy and girl in the world. As you went to bed, you left a carrot and a full glass of sherry on the kitchen table; a carrot for the reindeer, the sherry for Father Christmas. In the morning, the glass was empty, with only a slick of sherry in the bottom, the carrot gone, eaten.

One morning, I woke and with my sister went downstairs to find two angular, stuffed white pillowcases – one on that chair for her, one on this one for me. I was so small that I believed without question in Father Christmas, but not so small that I could not read. And halfway down the pillowcase was a small oblong package, which when opened held six pencils. Astonishingly, in gold capitals, on each of them was printed my name: PHILIP HENSHER. I gave myself up with ecstasy to the contemplation of this wonder. But how, I asked, did Father Christmas know my name? My mother was lost in confusion; she did not see the completely different levels of appeal of an object which had been supplied in the night and was just what I wanted, and of an object which had my name written on it. 'It's magic,' she said, probably rather sleepy still.

The magic of an object with a name written on it is overwhelming to us now. The emotion of seeing an object in the world with our name attached to it, for others to see, is a strong one, and not quite the same as the search for fame. In Britain, it is not usual for buildings to bear the names of their architects. The first time I went abroad, to France, one of the most striking touches of strangeness was that quite ordinary buildings – apartment blocks, post offices, even shops – often had, near their doorways, a stone plaque on which was engraved the name of the architect and the date of the building. It seemed strange: but it also seemed the way that things ought to be.

By that time, I had already started to send things out into the world with my name on them. There was also a magic about the small white cotton strips, with our names embroidered in red, that had to be sewn into every item of our school uniform. Wellington boots had to be hand-printed in felt-tip, inside the brim, and were not quite so cherishable. The allure of those white cotton strips was that one's name had been written by some mechanical process in a department store, a process oddly separable from one's own will.

Is it mostly writers who fall for this? Is the primary urge of the writer to attach his name to an object which will then journey through the world, as if propelled by itself? That may be the still wonder of the first moment of publication. When the writing is set in type and published, the power of seeing one's words in print and that of seeing one's name attached to them can be equal. Proust writes, in *À la recherche du temps perdu*, of his narrator seeing an article in *Le Figaro* which was on the same subject as an article he had sent to them; of realising, with indignation, that the article had stolen his expressions, his words, his sentences; and only after some time noticing that the name on the top was his, and it was, after all, his article which the newspaper had printed. No author ever forgets that first moment of transformation.

At ten, I wrote a poem. I thought it a wonderful poem. It was on the subject of gold, and rhymed beautifully. All I can now remember is that it began 'Gold is a flame, flickering and dying/ Gold is a metal which has seen much crying.' I don't believe that I had anything very specific in mind when I wrote 'dying'; I think the need to make a rhyme was uppermost in my thoughts. My form mistress, intent on making us write sincerely, in free verse, was critical. But the local paper, the *Sheffield Star*, had a children's page with a Poetry Corner, and I sent it off. It was printed; it won Poem of the Week; and my name was attached to it.

Since then, whenever a piece of writing of mine made a first step into the world, the thrill has been the same; a review of a life of Joseph Conrad for *The Literary Review*, or a first piece for a national newspaper on the tendencies of first novels. When the bound proof of my first novel arrived at my agent's, I dashed over to hold it in my hands with amazement. Five minutes later, a major Hollywood star, also a client of my agent's, arrived at their offices; their glowing presence had no power to distract me from the astonishing fact of something which looked like a book, with my name on it. In the reception of the agency, the Hollywood star politely attempted to make conversation with me, in spurts, and unsuccessfully.

The power of our name on an object is so strong that we feel it must always have been there, exerting the same power at every time and in every place. Of course the beautiful ninth-century bowl with its cloudy surface like the surface of thought itself must say '*ma 'amala salih*' ('Made by Salih'); Salih the potter must have wanted to put his name on it. It is only strange that the makers of so many other beautiful objects of the time did not, apparently, want to place their mark on them. But in fact, that lovely blue flourish may not say anyone's name at all. It may simply be making a statement about the grace and strength of the bowl. '*Ma 'umila saluha*'.

What was made was made well. It may not think that the name of the maker is of any importance. The phrase is ambiguous. The potter avails himself of the licence given him by the language.

As time goes on, the egotistic fantasy quickly recedes. The desire to see a piece of writing with one's own name at its head fades away as publication becomes familiar and then ordinary. What replaces it is a desire that what one makes should be well made. The two readings of the short inscription on this Iraqi bowl are emblematic of the artist's endeavour. In the one, a desire to impress a name above all on anyone who sees it; in the other, an assertion that the object was worth making, and has been made well. By whom we do not know: by whom does not matter. Sometimes the insistence on the name of an author prevents the object from reaching perfection. Sometimes the object was just made by forces unknown, and the artist should step away from what he has done, and leave it to set and dry; wash his hands and walk out of the room.

I told the story of the bowl's creation at the beginning, as if it were signed. This is its other story, if it is not signed, and in accordance with what it might otherwise say.

Once, in the ninth century in Iraq, a bowl was made. Porcelain had been brought from China, where new processes of firing and glazing had been developed. The miracle was studied. Other bowls were attempted in Iraq, as the processes were investigated. These processes, it turned out, could be reproduced. Bowls of a broad, smooth perfection were made – not like the Chinese bowls but of their own time and place – both of which would for ever more be represented by them. One bowl which survives must have been seen as a success. On it, after its firing, these words were written: 'What was made was made well.'

The beautiful Arabic script looks, to Westerners, like three ducks, strewn with weed, swimming across the surface of a pond. But it is not ducks; it is not a picture of anything. It is a phrase that must be true: a consolation to the artist, perhaps, a warning to the observer who, centuries later, looks at the fathomless depths of its simple grace, and wonders, out of his own egotism, where and how it came to be.

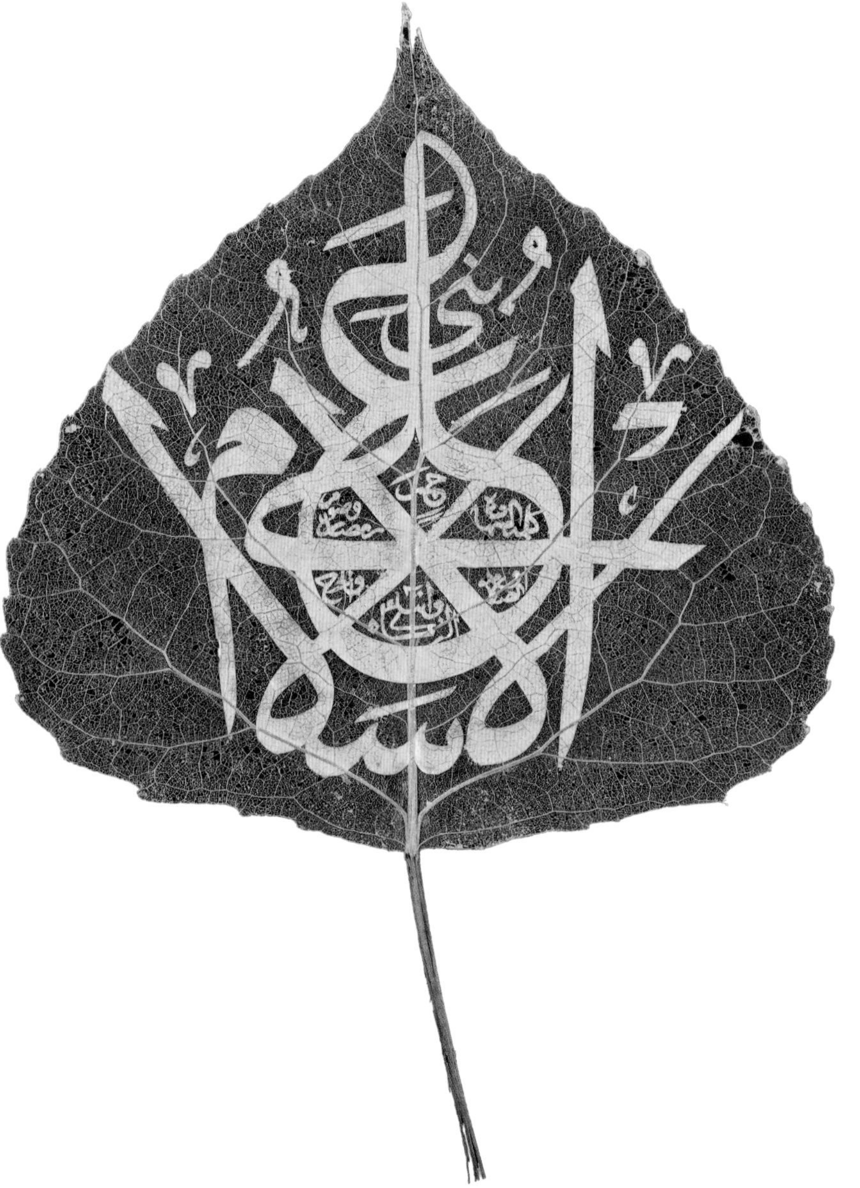

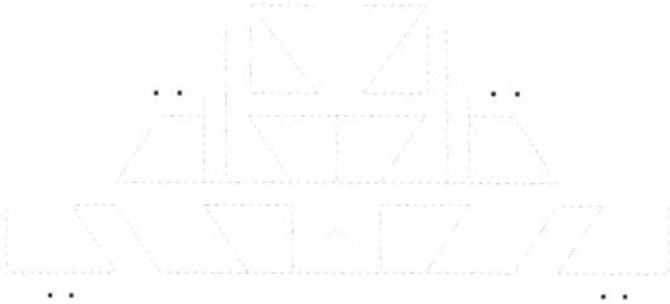

Notes on a Leaf

Kamila Shamsie

I. Commonplace Miracles

One of my earliest memories: I am standing in front of a bookshelf in my grandparents' house and lifting off a seashell. The shell is a tiger cowrie, though I don't learn that until years later. It could be made of porcelain, but I know it isn't. On the shell's underside are lips, pursed as though it's been eating the sour kumquats from my grandparents' garden. Its upper side has dark speckles which give way to an even brownness on which are inscribed white Arabic letters. I know that the words must be from the Qur'an, because why else would they be in Arabic? I hold it to my ears to hear the sound of the ocean, which is only a few miles away. The shell is a double miracle. It has tumbled from the ocean onto the Karachi sands with the very words written on it which, as a three-year-old, I listened to my older sister repeat at her Bismillah ceremony: In the name of Allah, the Beneficent, the Merciful. But the greater miracle to me is the sound of the sea captured in the shell – so that no matter where the shell goes it always carries the song of its home with it. It doesn't strike me as unusual that a shell of double miracles should rest on my grandparents' bookshelves – I am prepared to believe that miracles are commonplace enough to be treated casually.

When my grandmother died, in 2003, twelve years after my grandfather, the only thing I asked for from their home was that Shell of Double Miracles. I thought I wanted it for the sounds of the sea – so I could carry Karachi with me as I wandered the globe. But a day after visiting the Museum of Islamic Art in Doha, when it was the image of calligraphy on leaves that stayed with me more than Sulayman's signature or an illustrated page of the *Hamza-Nameh* from Akbar's library, I had to return to that cowrie shell knowing it held the answer to the question: why is a leaf more arresting than the grandest characters of history and myth?

From this question came the follow-up thought, which had never before occurred to me: if all you wanted was the sound of the sea, why didn't you buy a conch shell which magnifies the roar of the ocean better than the cowrie?

But it wasn't just the sound of the sea, it was also the memory of believing in commonplace miracles that I chose to transport with me when I carried that cowrie shell to London. It was that same memory, I'm sure, which was triggered by the leaves. At another age I would have looked at them and believed that the gold inscriptions, the perfect symmetry of their calligraphy, simply appeared while the leaves were still on a tree.

II. The Mask

'Listen,' said the voice.

The girl looked around the museum. There was no one there. No one except a shining steel mask, with long whiskers and heavy eyebrows, both terrifying and sad.

'Listen,' said the voice again and it echoed as a voice might indeed echo from behind a steel mask.

'In a place which only Believers can find, and that only if they consult the maps of their hearts, there is a grove containing 114 trees.'

'One for every surah of the Qur'an,' said the girl, who had learnt this for an exam.

'On each tree grow the Leaves of the Qur'an. Some trees are little more than saplings, others are vast as a museum. One tree for each surah.'

'And the leaves of the largest tree have Surat al-Baqarah written on them,' said the girl.

'No one likes a show-off in any time period.'

'Sorry.'

'If the wind blows in a certain direction you might hear Ayat al-Kursi in the rustling of the leaves. A drop of dew rolling from a leaf into a thirsty man's mouth would slake his thirst

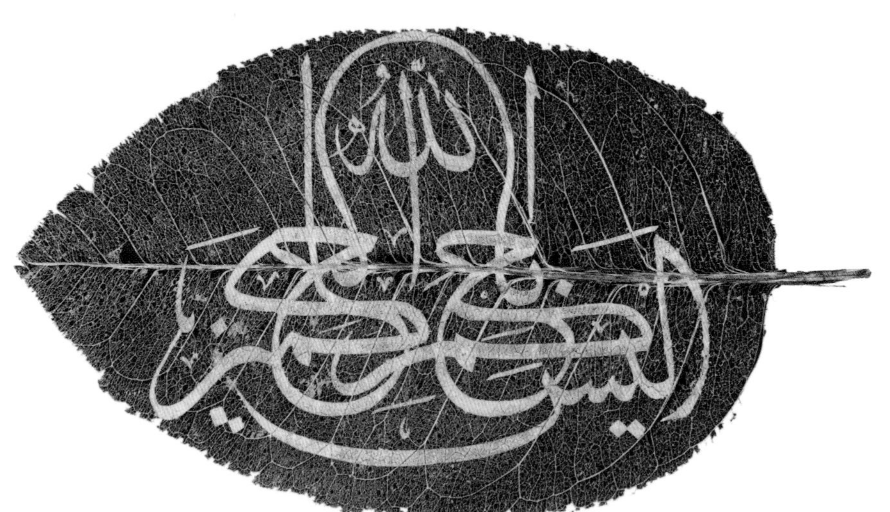

through a hundred days in the desert. The sap of the tree is honey which sweetens not only your mouth but also your heart, and takes away all its poison. The stars are reflections of the words on the leaves, so distant you see each verse as a single blur; but when you're in the grove itself you can see all the surahs reflected in the night sky. Some believe this proves the grove must be in heaven itself.'

The girl was silent for a long time; a time so long that she grew up and became a woman.

'Aren't you even going to ask if I know how to find the grove?'

The woman looked at the breathtaking fragility of the three leaves, their veins beginning to fray and tatter without affecting the solidity of the entwined calligraphy written on them.

'If these are a miracle, well, that's easily enough understood. But if they are the work of human artistry, now that's truly mind-boggling.'

'Ah,' was the final thing the mask said.

III. The Work of Human Artistry

Only the finest leaves were chosen, and at a particular time of year, to ensure they were at their most robust. The tobacco leaf was prized for its sturdiness, the chestnut leaf for the challenge issued by its composition – already it is possible to see a divide in the practitioners of the art. Do you start with the most solid base or the one which has risk and reward built into its very structure? There were other options too: the ivy, the rose, the mulberry, the poplar, the fig. (What about the olive? In the Qur'an, God swears by the fig and the olive, which might be enough to make Believers of some people.) Once chosen, the leaf underwent a conservation treatment that necessitated a gap of a year between its being plucked and its being written upon. The calligraphic composition was sometimes stencilled, sometimes written directly onto the leaf. Here, too, there must have been sharply competing philosophies involved. The ink required a particular concentration of gum arabic to ensure the integrity of the leaf was maintained. And it wasn't time that dissolved the leaf tissue and left behind a leaf skeleton, but an implement with a sharp point which carefully pierced away all that was unwanted.

IV. Language and Ornamentation

There is no question about beauty. It is. They are. The calligraphy is beautiful, the leaves are beautiful. But is beauty meaning in itself? This question, old and oft-discussed, acquires a different resonance when a script becomes ornamentation. Are we who know the script, but not the language, meant to read the overlapping curlicues, understand whether a particular *nuqta* is assigned to this character or that? Or are we to view the mazelike intricacy on one leaf as a metaphor of unity and complexity? On another leaf, if the word 'Allah' is distinct while the other words overlap is it because He is al-Wahid, al-Ahad – the Unity, the Indivisible?

These considerations may have been in the minds of the early twentieth-century calligraphers of Ottoman Turkey who worked with such precision on the leaves. They could not have imagined that in just a few years the script in which they were working would become part of Turkey's past along with the Caliphate itself. When Ataturk Latinised the Turkish script he ensured the words on the leaf could be no more than ornamentation for the generations of Turks to follow.

It is this matter I find myself thinking of, more than the old questions of beauty and meaning, when I look at the calligraphy. The cowrie shell, the leaves, the grain of rice I once saw beneath a magnifying glass with the *kalima* written on it in the finest hand imaginable – these all serve as reminders of the role of the Word in Islam. There is no miracle greater than The Book itself. And if anyone doubts the importance of the word it's necessary to look no further than Jibreel's first word to the Prophet: Read!

On first consideration, this appears uncomplicatedly wonderful. If nothing is more miraculous than the Book, if the first divine instruction was 'Read', then how can anything follow other than the centrality of learning, of education and instruction, of libraries and the printing press? And yet, other things have followed. Those leaves of Ottoman Turkey, regarded in a post-Ataturk world, highlight just one of the issues that arise from the primacy of the Word.

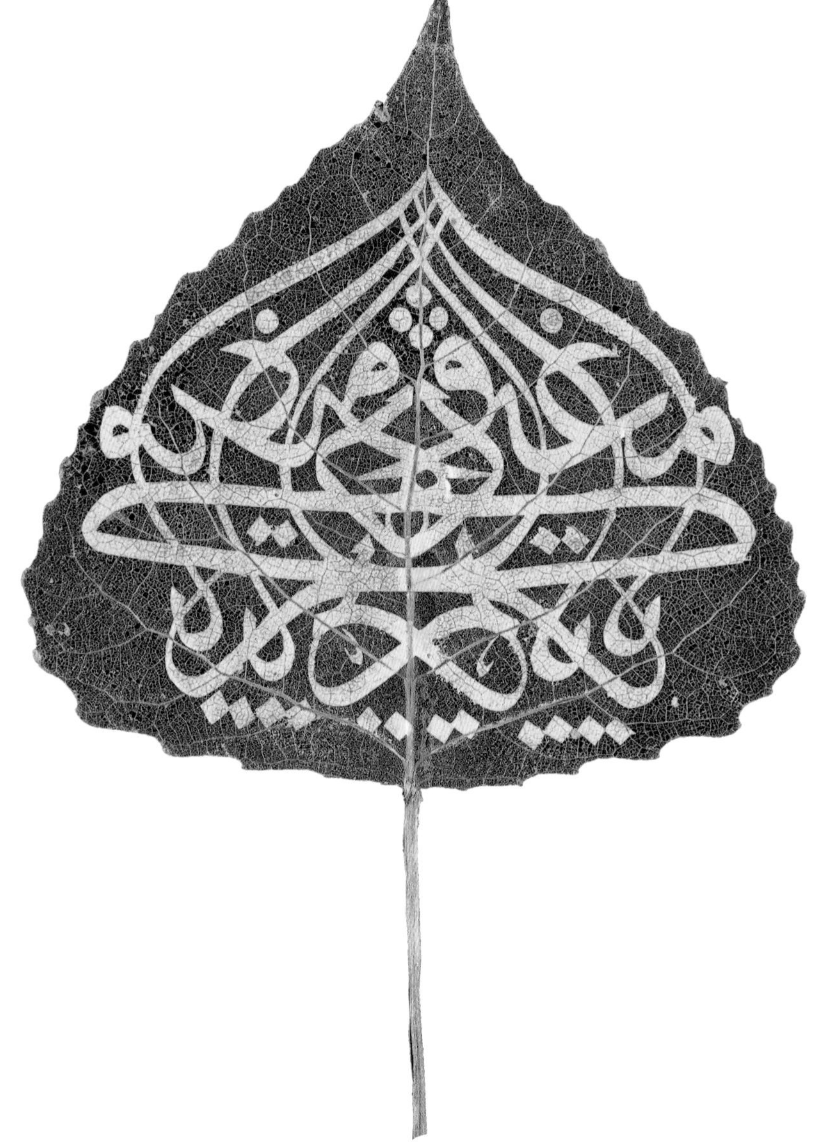

What happens when the Word is in one script and the Believers live in another? What happens when the Believers can read the script of the Word but understand nothing of what it means?

How old was I before I could actually read the words on the cowrie shell? Not old at all. I grew up with Urdu, close enough to Arabic for the latter to require little extra instruction. Before I was ten I had read the Qur'an. Or had I? I had sat beside a *maulvi*, forming my lips into the shape of the words of the Qur'an – not just once, but twice. I thought that meant I'd read it. But I'd merely recited the sounds.

Pakistan is full of people who've recited the Qur'an as a series of sounds. Translations exist, of course, but far higher accord is given to reciting the Qur'an than to reading its imperfect translation. But when language separates from meaning the script becomes only ornamentation. Outward show – accent, rhythm – takes precedence over inner contemplation. Hardly a surprise if this is reflected in other aspects of living...

V. The Shell, the Leaf, the Book

> He knows all that is on land and in the sea;
> Not a leaf falls but He knows it.
> Not a seed in the darkness of earth,
> Not anything, fresh or dried,
> But is inscribed in a Manifest Book.
> (Qur'an 6:59)[1]

Hardly a revelation with a capital 'R', but there's a certain delight in looking up the word 'leaf' in the Qur'an and finding the first verse that the concordance produces also contains both the sea and the Book. The younger me might have taken this confluence of the very objects I've been writing about as yet another commonplace miracle – the older me is content to be pleased with the beautiful symmetry of things, such as can be found in calligraphy, a leaf, or a piece of writing.

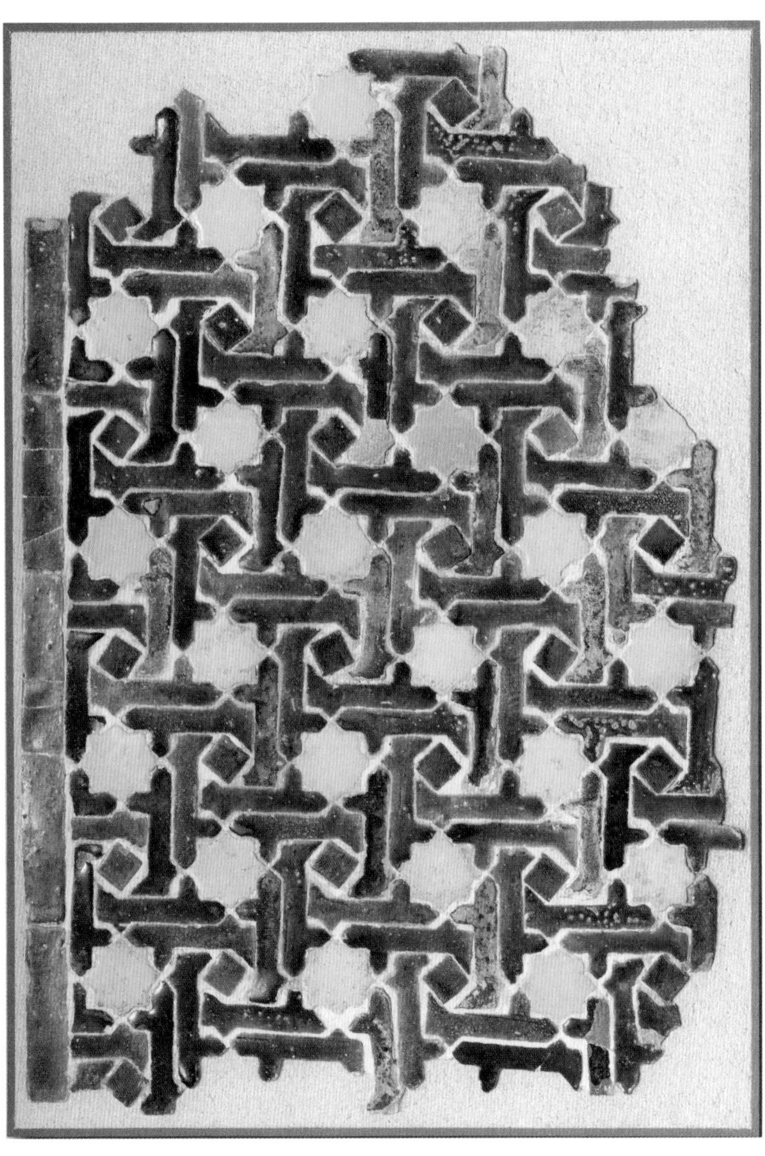

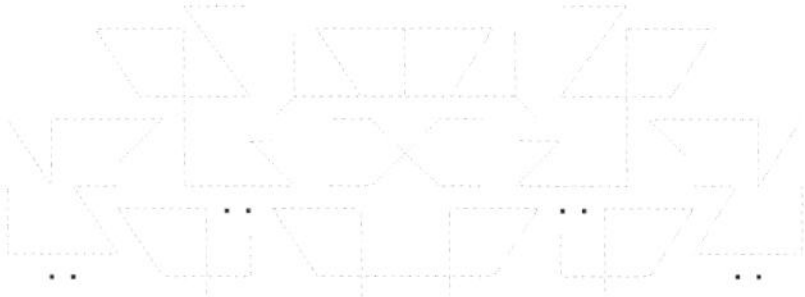

Symmetry: Nature's Language

Marcus du Sautoy

Even before you see the artefacts inside the Museum of Islamic Art in Doha, the very structure of the building prepares you for one of the central themes of this collection: symmetry. I.M. Pei's design for the Museum plays on the Islamic fascination with symmetrical shapes. Octagons, squares, triangles and circles are the building blocks of this extraordinary building that Pei has created; this piece of geometry sitting in the sea.

The internal decoration continues the symmetrical games you see on the outside: the concentric array of eight-pointed stars that enclose the fountain, the lattice of hexagons that cover the windows and doors like a beehive, the circles and squares that adorn the ceilings, the grand circular staircase that draws you to the exhibits which are the heart of this museum.

But it's when you begin to explore the extraordinary array of objects housed in the Museum itself – the Qur'ans, the vases, the textiles, the architectural screens – that you experience the fascination that the artists of the Islamic world have for symmetry. And of all the pieces here it is in the tiles that once adorned the mosques, palaces and buildings of the Islamic world that one sees the artists giving full expression to their love of symmetry.

One of the most beautiful of these designs greets you as you enter the gallery dedicated to pattern. Dating back to the fourteenth century, these tiles originate from southern Spain: al-Andalus. The mosaic of tiles is an intriguing lattice of shapes: each tiny little orange square is surrounded by four strange elongated green tiles whose form almost defies description.

Like the silhouette of an aeroplane, it appears strangely asymmetrical. The other ends of these green tiles mark out the boundary of an eight-pointed star; a shape that pervades not only the architecture of this museum but much Islamic art.

Some have tried to explain the Islamic interest in symmetry as being the result of a religious prohibition against depicting creatures with souls: people or animals. Although the Qur'an itself does not explicitly prohibit pictures of the human or animal form, a hadith is quoted stating that 'he who makes images will suffer the most severe punishment on the Last Day... the angels of mercy do not enter dwellings where there are such images'. While it is true that such images are often avoided in a religious context like mosques or Qur'ans – as the artefacts in the Museum illustrate – outside of a religious setting, artists are very happy to draw images of animals and to tell stories of people through pictures. Many of the tiles originate from palaces or buildings without any specific religious function. So it is an active choice very often to create purely geometric designs in these secular contexts.

This obsession with symmetry has ancient origins. It is deep-rooted, and not just in the Islamic world. Animals and humans seem, through evolution, to be programmed to be sensitive to symmetry. Symmetry denotes something with structure, with meaning; something that needs to be interpreted. In the chaos of the jungle, if you suddenly spot something with symmetry it is likely to be an animal which you could eat. Or it could eat you. Either way those who can spot symmetry survive.

Symmetry is used by Nature like a language to communicate information. For example, the eyesight of a bee is extremely limited. As it flies through the air in search of food, it has to find some way to make sense of the onslaught of images it is bombarded with. Evolution has tuned the bee to recognise shapes full of symmetry because this is where it will find the sustenance that will keep it alive. The flower is equally dependent on the bee for its survival. It has evolved to form a symmetrical shape in the hope of attracting the bee.

Ever since humans have been shaping the environment around them they've been attracted, like the bee, to things with symmetry. Some of the first symmetrical objects carved out by humans relate to our addiction to playing games. In the Ancient Babylonian city of Ur, archaeologists discovered a game dating back to 2,500 BC; it is an early version of backgammon, but rather than cube-shaped dice, players tossed tetrahedrons: the shapes made from four equilateral triangles. Two of the four corners were painted black and the player would count the number of black dots pointing upwards. Symmetry is of course fundamental to creating a fair set of dice; no configuration should be favoured over any other.

At roughly the same time as Babylonians were tossing tetrahedral dice in Ur, stone balls were being carved with symmetrical patterns by Neolithic tribes in northern Scotland. These stone balls have circular patches carved into the sides. The sculptors experimented with the different ways you can arrange these patches around the sphere. For example, mirroring the discovery of the Babylonians, the tetrahedron provides a way to place four circles in a perfectly symmetrical arrangement. But the Neolithic artists discovered a range of other sophisticated configurations. We had to wait till the Ancient Greeks for a systematic mathematical analysis of how many different dice you could build. It was Plato's friend, Theatetus, who first provided a proof that the five solids – the tetrahedron, the cube, the octahedron, the dodecahedron and the icosahedron – are the only ways of piecing symmetrical faces together where each face has the same shape and all the vertices of the shape look the same.

But it is in exploring the symmetry possible on a two-dimensional wall that the artists of the Islamic world excelled. Many artists outside the Islamic world have a rather ambiguous relationship with symmetry, finding it too prescriptive, feeling that it boxed them in. Thomas Mann in *The Magic Mountain* describes a snowflake: 'He shuddered at its perfect precision, found it deathly, the very marrow of death.' But the symmetry that pulses through the artefacts in the MIA in Doha injects life and energy into the pieces it informs.

From simple arrangements of squares (like those that cover most people's bathrooms) to the complex arrangement of tiles found in the piece at the entrance to the pattern gallery, the artists are experimenting with new ways to decorate the walls of their palaces. There is certainly a pattern at the heart of these tiles that once adorned an Andalusian palace or mosque, but is there symmetry? The square and the eight-pointed star individually have symmetry but what about the overall layout of the tiles? The arrangement of these strange green pieces destroys any reflectional symmetry in the design. So is there any symmetry left? What exactly is symmetry? This is a deep and mysterious question that was only answered at the beginning of the nineteenth century when Evariste Galois, a revolutionary young French mathematician, finally unlocked its secrets.

At the heart of Galois' vision is the belief that symmetry is about motion, in contrast to Thomas Mann's view of it as deathly and without life.

For mathematicians, after Galois, the symmetries of an object should be thought of as the actions you can do to an object so that the object looks the same as before you touched it. Symmetry is like a magic trick move. For example, if I take a hexagonal tile, draw an outline around it and get you to close your eyes, then a symmetry is essentially a way to pick up the hexagon then place it back down again inside its outline so that when you open your eyes again you can't tell whether the hexagon has moved.

When you consider the arrangement of these fourteenth-century tiles, symmetry is about the different ways I can pick up the collection of tiles, and move them in some way so that when I place them down collectively they fit back exactly inside their original outline. For example, I can shift all the tiles left or right, up or down. To make this work you must imagine that the tiles extend infinitely in all directions. This idea of capturing the concept of infinity in a finite piece of wall is another reason the artists are drawn to these symmetrical designs. But, in addition to the shifts up and down, left and right, there are some more interesting moves I can make. For example, if I spin all the tiles around a fixed point at the centre of one of the squares or eight-pointed stars, then after a ninety-degree turn the tiles all align again.

There is another symmetrical move that I can make on these tiles which is a little harder to identify. Draw a diagonal line between the centre of one square tile and one of its closest neighbouring tiles. If you fix the point halfway along this line and spin the tiles about this point, then, after a 180-degree turn, magically the tiles all realign.

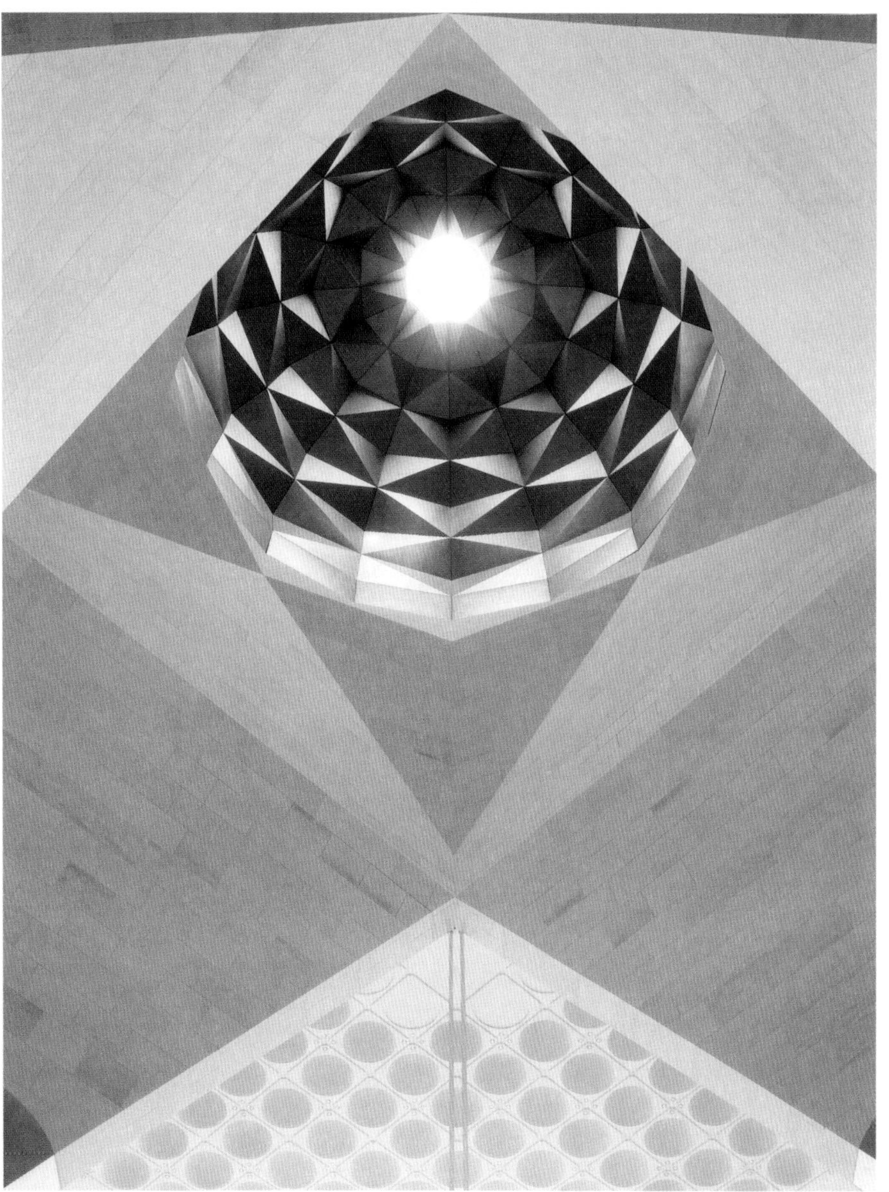

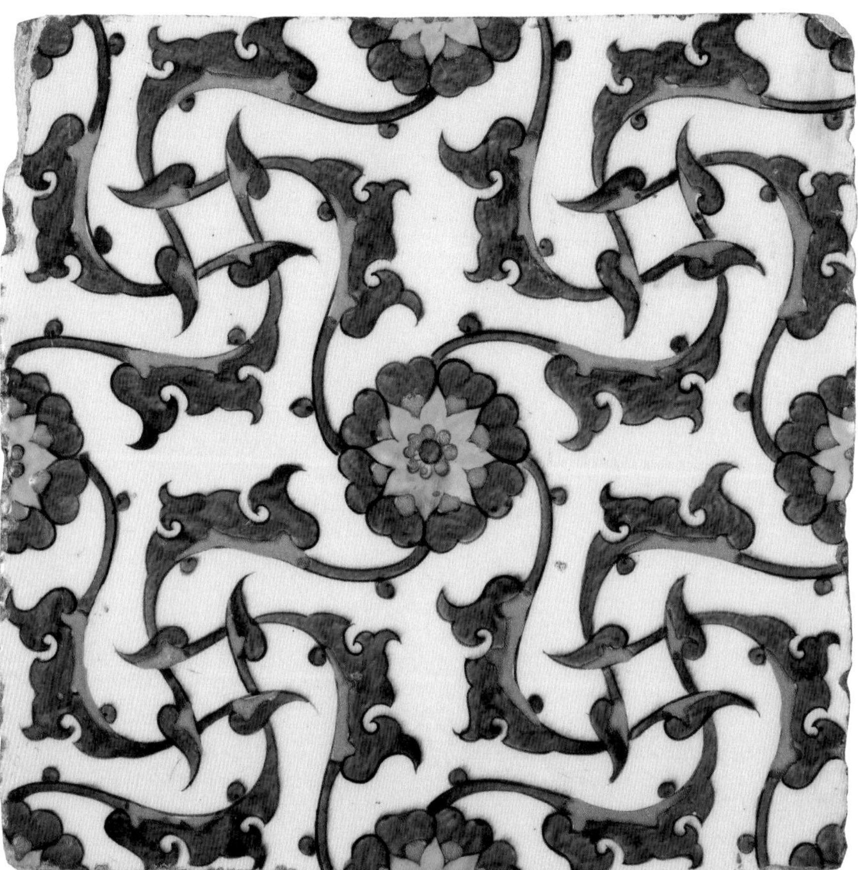

These three symmetrical moves are the building blocks of all the symmetries of this set of tiles. But the real power of Galois' language is that it enables us to articulate when two very different sets of tiles actually have the same underlying group of symmetries. For example, as you explore further into the Museum you come across a square tile from Turkey dating from the sixteenth century. The tile is painted in a blue and orange design with a flower-like image at its centre with vines trailing out. But cover the wall with these tiles and you have an image that although physically very different to the Andalusian tiles, nevertheless is a wall with the same underlying symmetry. Hidden inside these Turkish tiles are exactly the same symmetrical moves that preserve the pattern we found in the Andalusian tiles.

This new perspective allows us to navigate the symmetry in the Museum more widely and identify when two different designs are actually physical realisations of the same group of symmetries. It is almost like discovering the concept of number: I can show you three bottles and three glasses and although they look very different, the threeness is something abstract which is common to both of them. Both the glasses and the bottles are expressions of the concept of the number three. The same thing happens with the idea of symmetry, thanks to Galois' work. Two objects can look very different, but can still be expressions of the same underlying group of symmetries. But are there limits to what is possible on the walls of these Islamic palaces and mosques? You can see throughout the Museum how the artists of the early Islamic world were pushing the boundaries, finding ever more inventive and creative ways to cover walls, floors, fabrics and ceilings with symmetry. It turns out there are limits.

Just as the Ancient Greeks discovered that there are only five symmetrical dice that are possible, there are in fact only seventeen different underlying groups of symmetries that can be depicted on a two-dimensional surface. It took until the end of the nineteenth century to use Galois' language of symmetry to prove this fact. It is an extraordinary discovery. Although you can have infinitely many different physical expressions of these symmetries, nevertheless underlying each one of them is one of these seventeen different groups of symmetries. Any attempts by the medieval artists to conjure up a new group of symmetries were doomed to failure. Whatever games they played, the wall would have symmetry identical to one of the seventeen in the mathematicians' list.

The symmetry that you find throughout the MIA is testament to the incredible creative energy of the artists of this period. Palaces and mosques across the Islamic world contain many examples of each of these seventeen sorts of symmetry. They perfectly demonstrate how mathematics and art go hand in hand, something that has always been appreciated by the Islamic world.

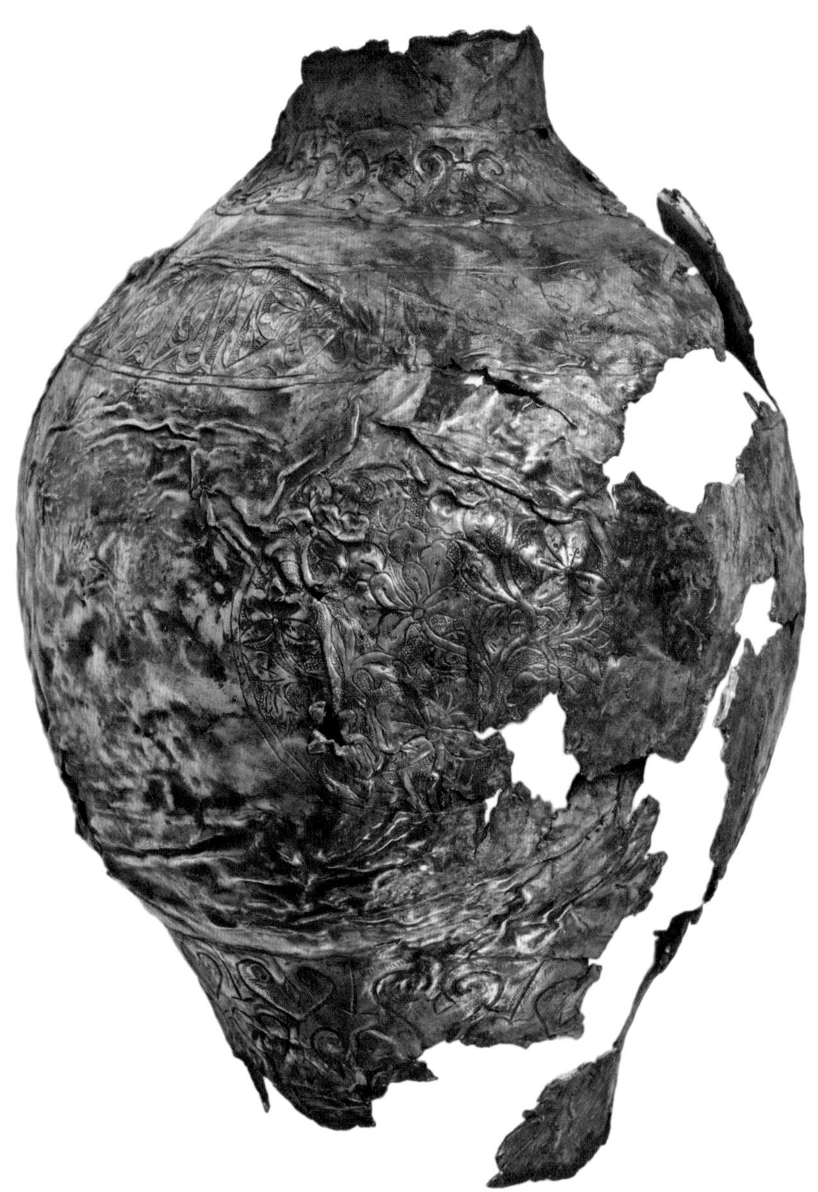

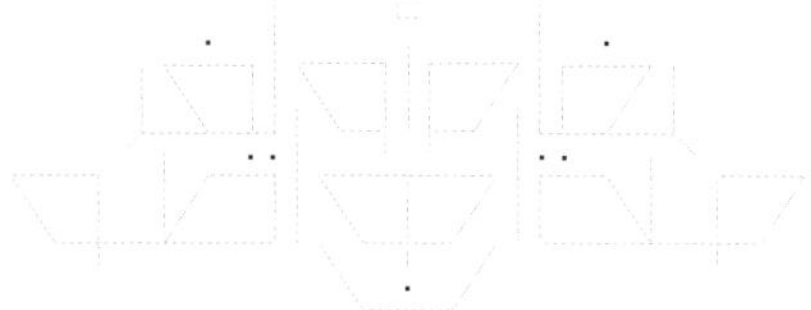

The Silver Vase

Oliver Watson

Sheikh Saud passed me a large book with a black cover. In the centre of the cover was a picture of an enamelled mosque lamp. 'We got this,' he said. Mosque lamps were one of his passions and he acquired every example he could, so I was not surprised. I congratulated him on adding yet another to the Museum of Islamic Art's impressive set. 'Not just the lamp,' he said, 'the whole collection.'

The book was a catalogue of some dozens of works of art, many important and fine things, and others of interest if not of great significance – material for the study collection rather than exhibition. I flipped through it, noting items that would make a difference to our displays, things I thought deserved further study, and some which after accessioning would probably disappear into the stores only to see light again on rare occasions when requested by a visiting curator with a particular specialist interest. Among these latter items were ceramics, tiles and other objects whose lowly status was signalled by the small black-and-white photos.

Some years later, when the Museum had opened and my fellow curators and I were able to relax after the hectic preparatory months of choosing objects, arranging the displays and writing labels, we started to spend some time arranging the stores and reviewing things in the collection which had not initially made it into the displays. There, at the back of a storage cabinet, we found a large black box, like a gigantic jewellery case, and inside it a mass of tissue paper wrapping something surprisingly light in weight for its size. Light and fragile; for it flexed as we started to unwrap it. An initial disappointment: a large contorted metal sheet, dull, fragmented, wrinkled – the wreck of an object. Then a sudden realisation, a jolt of excitement – a wreck maybe, but the wreck of one of the most rare and most interesting types of Islamic objects: a silver vase.

Old things had fascinated me since childhood. This interest was first manifest in my collecting of copper pennies from the change I got when buying sweets with my sixpence or shilling pocket-money in the late 1950s and early 1960s. The growing excitement I felt as I understood that these old worn things were not simply ideas about the past, such as we received in history lessons, or memories like those we heard from our grandparents, but actual bits of the past surviving through the years. The oldest ones were worn smooth, with the outline of the young Queen Victoria just visible, and if you were lucky, the date. The series had started in 1860 when the coinage had been reformed, and was still in circulation a century later. Over a few years I managed to extract from my change, my mother's purse, or the local newspaper-seller's till (always, let it be said, by exchange for later less-interesting coins) a complete run from 1860 to 1901, with only the rarest dates of 1867 and 1869 eluding me (these were reluctantly bought from a dealer years later when I had a salary). I pored over the differences in design – the tiny variations in Britannia's pose and setting, the change of Victoria's head from the earlier 'bun' to the later 'veiled' version, and the differences in wording of the inscriptions claiming her as Queen of Britain, Defender of the Faith and Empress of India. Silver coins were much more difficult to find: impossible to get a series – only the odd sixpence or shilling. I can still remember the thrill I felt when getting a silver two-shilling piece (Edward VII, 1904) in change for a half-crown when buying my four-penny bus ticket – the florin with the standing Britannia!

Looking back, it seems that the importance to me was that these dated objects in some unspecified but direct way authenticated history. They were tangible testimonies to the fact that the years in question had actually happened, that the monarchs depicted had existed. They allowed me to believe in what my history teachers taught. Their worn condition spoke of a continual usage – the innumerable transactions they had enabled, the myriad purses in which they had jostled, the untold numbers of hands through which they'd passed, one at a time. And the goods, and purses and hands all belonged to individuals who experienced not just the recorded moments of history, but the richness of an everyday life; a life now passed and forgotten but for these few material traces. (If an 1860 penny had been used in a transaction every day for a hundred years, it would have enabled the purchasing of a total of £152-worth of goods – the value of a substantial house in 1860, but little more than the cost of a washing machine in 1960). It was this interest in the materiality of old things, a physical presence that spoke of the reality of the past, which led me to study ceramics in the first place, and to work in museums.

Silver is a metal that has been valued for millennia by cultures across the globe: rare enough to be valuable, but plentiful enough to be widely useful; it is easy to work but strong enough for all but the toughest tasks; and beautiful in its finish whether polished or left to develop a natural patina. But these qualities, and particularly its ease of working, have left it with a fragmented history – nowhere more so than in the Islamic world. Silver is not just a material with which to make beautiful objects, but in which to store wealth: easy for the fashion-conscious to send to the silversmith to be reworked in a more up-to-date style and as easy to convert from silver vessels or jewellery into coinage when needed. And converted regularly it was, leaving an older presence in just a few special cases, where historical accident happened to preserve it.

The study of Islamic art, like all studies of the past, is beset with problems. But Islamic religious practice and the political history of the Middle East provide very particular challenges. In Islam, the dead are buried in a simple shroud alone. There is no custom of burying individuals with those things they valued in life or which are deemed to be useful in an afterlife. The absence of grave-goods deprives the Islamic historian of the extraordinary material riches that are found in, for example, the tombs of ancient Egypt, Greece, or China. Also, the mosques of the Islamic world did not systematically collect and protect works of art in the manner of the Christian church with its treasuries full of relics and their precious containers. The political history of the Middle East, with plentiful wars, invasions and the supplanting of one empire by another, led to the wholesale destruction, plunder and dispersal of royal treasuries and libraries. Of the recent past, only the Ottoman Topkapi Palace in Istanbul preserves the remains of an imperial treasury and gives a sense of the extraordinary range and quality of the luxury goods available to the elite of its society. The Persian Safavid treasury has disappeared (but for a handful of things preserved, ironically, in the Topkapi – the treasury of their great rivals) and the Mughal riches of India vanished, with remnants dispersed among the Maharajahs as the Mughals declined and were eventually deposed by the British. For earlier periods we rely almost entirely on archaeological material – things thrown away on rubbish heaps, or buried by earthquakes or military action, lying in the soil for centuries. Libraries alone were institutions devoted to preservation and they provided something of a continuing place of refuge (though destruction and plundering are rife there too) and thanks to this the history of the book is perhaps better preserved than that of other materials.

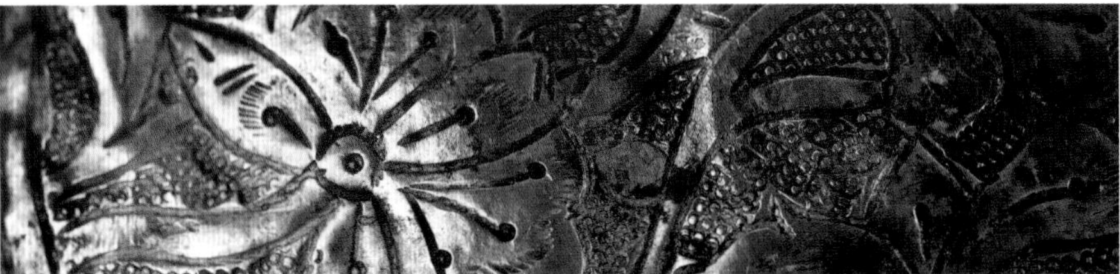

Contemporary texts allow us to picture something of what once existed and what was valued: textiles, for example, provided the predominant luxury of the time and a means of showing off one's wealth and status. And after textiles, gold and silver vessels and jewellery, precious and semi-precious stones, ivory, rare woods and aromatics. And what of all of this survives from the medieval period? Virtually nothing. Fragments of textiles (the better pieces preserved in Christian church treasuries, along with ivory and crystal) give only a hint of the riches that once were. Here and there a chance survival, but these few remnants a vanishingly small fraction of what once was. What does survive? Well, a certain amount of metalwork and glass but, in particular, ceramics. Ceramics, made from the commonest of materials, alone of the things of modest luxury and comfort of the past, have no intrinsic value. They cannot be recycled, as can all metals and glass (re-smelted and reworked into new things), wood (repurposed, even if only as firewood), and textiles (eventually pulped for paper). They break but do not rot, rust or decay; indeed pottery is one of the most robust of man-made artefacts. Broken, it loses its value and is thrown away. In the rubbish dumps, the broken fragments survive, often in perfect condition, until archaeologists and collectors, with care and excitement, find and recombine and proudly present them in our museums. Look carefully, and you will see that virtually all pre-modern pieces of Islamic pottery on display in the world's museums are broken and restored, with missing areas cunningly recreated in plaster. The impression as one enters any of the world's galleries of Islamic art is that Islamic culture valued ceramics highly and specifically; yet this is misleading – an artificial bias caused by the accidents of survival. Pottery was a widespread but minor luxury for the middling classes – a chance for them to enjoy in a cheaper material those luxuries they could not in reality afford. And this substitution is reflected, as one might expect, in the shapes and decoration of the pots. Say what they like about 'true ceramic form' and 'the natural expression of clay', the early modernists were simply wrong about most pottery. Clay, such an enormously versatile material, overwhelmingly seeks its shapes and patterns in other materials. And in fine ceramics, which material particularly? Why, silver of course.

We can trace a history of silver in the pottery skeuomorphs that faithfully reflect the development of the more expensive material over the centuries, adding perhaps just colour alone as a true ceramic contribution. This is history done in the mirror, by reflection, in the absence of the actual thing.

This wreck of a silver vase, then, is a vindication of this approach – confirmation that our ideas are not just a figment of our imagination, but are rooted somewhere in a reality. The shape of the piece, still clear in spite of the crushed and wrinkled form; the patterns of flowers in cartouches, the bold inscription frieze, the interlocking hearts at the base, all these are paralleled on contemporary ceramics which do survive in numbers. The vase, sad and worn though it is, conjures up a true luxurious scene of the time and one not available in our museum galleries. Our vase was made in Iran or Central Asia, probably as a commission for the court of one of the numerous princedoms that sprang up as the great Mongol Ilkhanid empire that collapsed in the mid-fourteenth century. It doubtless was one of a number that formed part of the usual furnishings of a grand reception room – a room where the ruler enjoyed private parties and nobles dressed in fine silks reclined on soft silk cushions and carpets and were entertained by dancers, musicians and poets. It may have contained the wine (forbidden but frequently present) to be drunk from crystal goblets, or held magnificent sprays of flowers which scented the air and delighted the eye. And probably hardly a ceramic in sight.

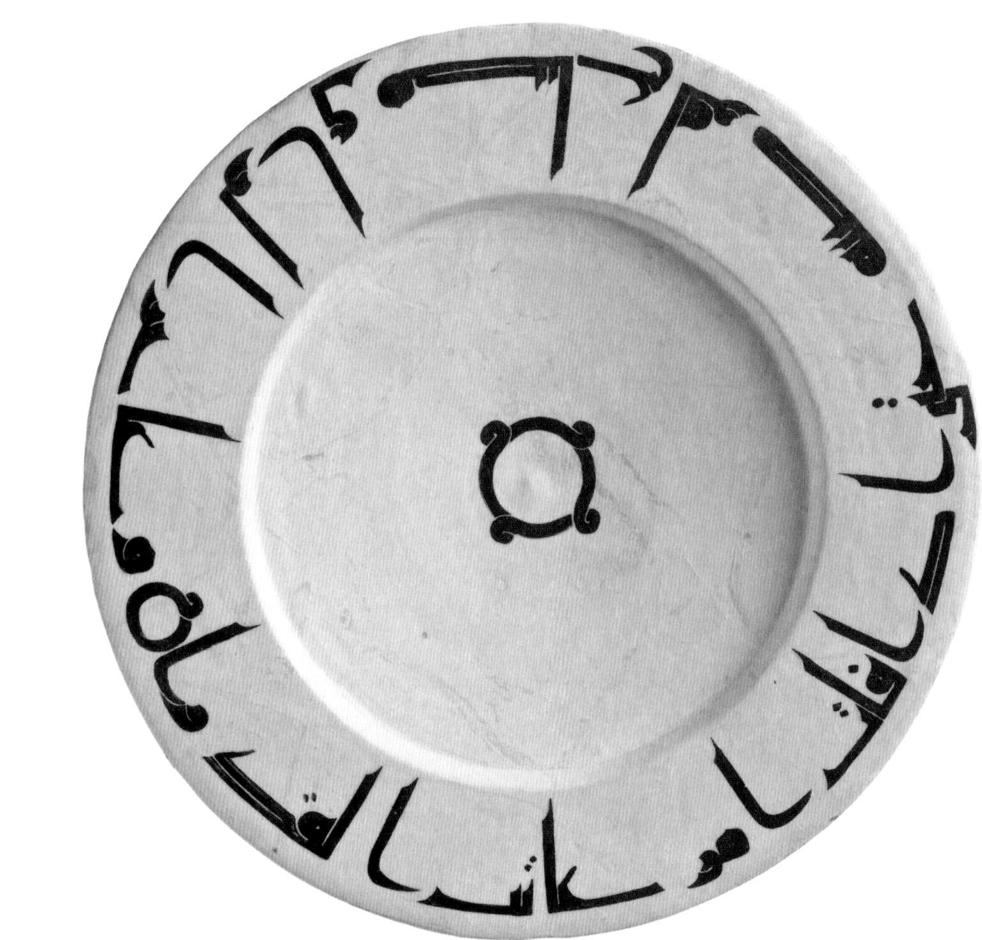

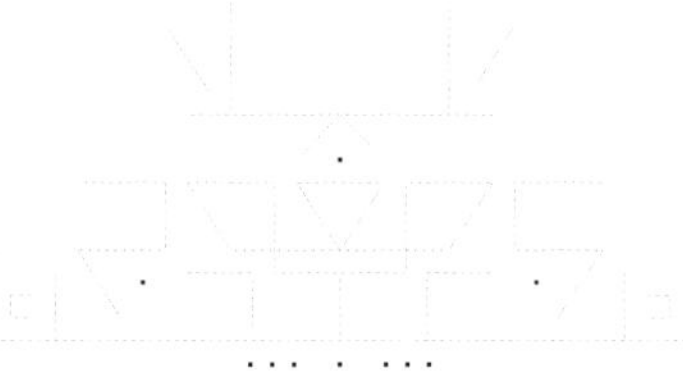

Choosing our Fate

Slavoj Zizek

Item number PO.24 in the Museum of Islamic Art is a simple tenth-century earthenware circular dish from Nishapur or Samarkand; its diameter is forty-three centimetres, and it is decorated with a (Farsi) proverb attributed to Yahya ibn Ziyad, written in black on a white background: 'Foolish is the person who misses his chance and afterwards reproaches fate.' Such dishes were meant to solicit an appropriate conversation among the learned eaters during and after the meal; an old forgotten art whose last great practitioner was maybe Immanuel Kant. Such a practice is foreign to our fast-food times when we know only business meals not thinking meals.

This is the integration of the dish as art into its environs: the meal represents a general feature of Muslim art, in clear contrast to the standard European practice of isolating the object of art into the sacred space of its exposition, exempting it from daily practices. I.M. Pei, the architect of the MIA, understood this feature: when he struggled with the basic principles of his architectural design, he realised that, instead of treating the play of sun and shadow as a disturbing element, he should integrate it into his project; the line that separates dazzling sun rays from those parts which remain in shadow is an integral aspect of the building. And the same goes for our dish: in order to fully grasp it as a work of art, we should locate it into the process of eating.

The way people eating from such dishes related to their messages followed a specific temporal rhythm: the inscription is gradually revealed as the food on the dish disappears. With this dish, however, a more complex twist is at work: when the meal is served and the dish is full of food, one can still read the proverb written on its edge; but there is also a rectangular drawing in the centre – obviously the symbol of the circularity of life – and this, of course, is what is gradually revealed. But is this 'great circle of life' the ultimate message of the dish? What if the central drawing is rather a kind of empty symbol pretending to deliver a profound truth, but effectively providing only the kind of platitude which characterises pseudo-wisdom?

That is to say, is the circular drawing in the centre not at the level of the deep tautologies (such as 'life is life', 'everything that is born has to die', etc.), which merely mask as profound wisdom our simple perplexity? We use such phrases when we do not know what to say but want nonetheless to say something and to sound wise. A proof of the vacuity of wisdoms is that no matter how you turn them around, negate them, etc., the result will always sound wise. 'Do not get caught in the vanity of earthly life and its pleasures, think about eternity as the only true life!' sounds deep, but so does 'Do not try to grasp the rainbow of eternity, enjoy our terrestrial life, it is the only life we have!' But what about 'A wise man does not oppose eternity to a passing terrestrial life, he is able to see the ray of eternity shining in our ordinary life!'? Or, again, 'A wise man accepts the gap that separates our terrestrial life from eternity, he knows that we, mortals, cannot bring the two dimensions together – only God can do it!'? Wisdoms, wisdoms...

However, the proverb on the edge of the dish attributed to Yahya ibn Ziyad is precisely not such a wisdom. 'Foolish is the person who misses his opportunity and afterwards reproaches fate.' Let us turn it around: 'Foolish is a man who, after he misses his opportunity, does not see that his failure was the work of fate.' This 'wisdom' is simply a commonplace which tells us that there are really no opportunities, no chances; that everything is controlled by an inscrutable fate. But the proverb on the dish, read closely, does not say the opposite of this commonplace: its message is not simply: 'There is no fate, everything is a chance.' Let us return to the temporal dimension of using the dish: when, at the beginning of the meal, eaters first perceive the inscription on the edges of the full dish, they dismiss it as a lesson in chance and the opportunistic ability to seize it, waiting for the true message beneath the pile of food. However, once the dish is empty, they see that the hidden message is a platitude, and they realise they missed the (chance to see) truth in the first message, so they return to it, read it again, and *then* it strikes them that it is not about chance or opportunity versus fate, but about something much more complex and interesting: how it is in their power to *choose their fate*.

This message has something to do with the very core of the Muslim experience overlooked by Western Christians who often mistake 'Islam', a specific surrender to God, with *istislam*, a general surrender. But a close reading of Yahya ibn Ziyad's proverb (which, as we can see now, is ultimately not a proverb at all, but a crucial philosophical insight) quickly dispels this cliché: we put the blame on fate when we miss an opportunity – which opportunity? The opportunity not simply to act freely and use given possibilities, but the opportunity to change what we perceive as our fate, to choose a different fate. This insight is of special importance today, when the crises humanity is facing cannot but appear as part of an inexorable fate pushing us closer and closer to an apocalyptic point: ecological breakdown, biogenetic reduction of humans to manipulable machines, total digital control over our lives... At all these levels, things are approaching a zero-point, 'the end of time is near'. Here is Ed Ayres's description: 'We are being confronted by something so completely outside our collective experience that we don't really see it, even when the evidence is overwhelming... that "something" is a blitz of enormous biological and physical alterations in the world that has been sustaining us.'[1] At the geological and biological level, Ayres enumerates four 'spikes' (accelerated developments) asymptotically approaching a zero-point at which the quantitative expansion will reach its point of exhaustion and will have to change into a different quality: (1) population growth, (2) consumption of resources, (3) carbon gas emissions, (4) the mass extinction of species. In order to cope with this threat, our collective ideology is mobilising mechanisms of dissimulation and self-deception amounting to a direct will to ignorance: 'a general pattern of behaviour among threatened human societies is to become more blinkered, rather than more focused on the crisis, as they fail'.

What, then, can we do in such a predicament? Recall the Arab story about the appointment in Samarra: a servant on an errand in the busy market of Baghdad meets Death there. Terrified by Death's gaze, he runs home to his master and asks for a horse he can ride to Samarra where Death will not find him. The good master not only provides the servant with a horse, but goes himself to the market, looks for Death and reproaches him for scaring his servant.

Death replies: 'But I didn't want to scare your servant. I was just surprised that he was here when I have an appointment with him in Samarra tonight...' What if the message of this story is not that a man's demise is impossible to avoid, that trying to twist free of it will only tighten its grip, but rather its exact opposite: that if one accepts fate as inevitable one can break its grasp? Imagine that upon encountering Death in the market the servant had said: 'What's your problem? If you have something to do with me, do it, otherwise beat it!' Perplexed, Death would have mumbled something like: 'But... we were supposed to meet in Samarra, I cannot kill you here!'

If we are effectively to counteract the drift towards catastrophe, it is not enough just to submit to a critical analysis the standard notion of historical progress; one should also deploy the limitation of the ordinary 'historical' notion of time: at each moment of time, there are multiple possibilities waiting to be realised; once one of them actualises itself, others are cancelled. We need to break out of the 'historical' notion of temporality, which runs from the past to the future, and to introduce a new mode of time, the 'time of a project' (Jean-Pierre Dupuy), of a closed circuit between the past and the future: the future is causally produced by our acts in the past, while the way we act is determined by our anticipation of the future and our reaction to this anticipation. This, then, is how Dupuy proposes to confront the catastrophe: we should first perceive it as our fate, as unavoidable, and then, projecting ourselves into it, adopting its standpoint, we should retroactively insert into its past (the past of the future) counterfactual possibilities ('If we had done that and that, the catastrophe we are in now would not have occurred!') upon which we then act today. Therein resides Dupuy's paradoxical formula: we have to accept that, at the level of possibilities, our future is doomed, the catastrophe will take place, it is our fate – and, then, on the background of this acceptance, we should mobilise ourselves to perform the act which will change fate itself. Instead of saying 'the future is still open, we still have the time to act and prevent the worst', one should accept the catastrophe as inevitable, and then act to retroactively undo what is already 'written in the stars' as our fate.[2]

In the suburbs of many Gulf cities, there are camps for immigrant workers. They only have time to visit the city centre on Fridays; however, on Fridays, entry into the shopping malls is prohibited to single men – officially, to maintain the family spirit in the malls. Let us then step down from the archaeological and art-historical heights into today's ordinary life, let us imagine a group of poor immigrant workers resting on the grass south of the central market on Friday, eating a modest meal of hummus and bread on our dish, PO.24, gradually emptying it, facing the words of Yahya ibn Ziyad and engaging in a conversation. One of them says: 'But what if this applies also to us? What if it is not our fate to live here as outcasts? What if, instead of bemoaning our fate, we should seize the chance and change this fate?'

The question here is: does Islam effectively contain this radical-emancipatory dimension?

In order to grasp the unique character of Islam, we have to focus on a feature which distinguishes it from Judaism and from Christianity, the other two religions of the Book. In contrast to both Judaism and Christianity, Islam excludes God from the domain of the paternal logic: Allah is not a father, not even a symbolic one – God is One, He is neither begotten nor a begetter. *There is no place for a Holy Family in Islam.* This is why Islam emphasises so much the fact that the prophet, Muhammad, himself was an orphan; this is why, in Islam, God intervenes precisely at the moments of the suspension, withdrawal, failure, 'black-out', of the paternal function. What this means is that God remains thoroughly in the domain of impossible-Real: he is the impossible-Real outside father, so that there is a 'genealogical desert between man and God'.[3] This was the problem with Islam for Freud, since his entire theory of religion is based on the parallel of 'God' with 'father'. More importantly even, this inscribes politics into the very heart of Islam, since the 'genealogical desert' renders it impossible to ground a community in the structures of parenthood or other blood-links – thence Islam's actuality. This issue is at the very heart of the *ummah*, the Muslim 'community of believers'; it accounts for the overlapping of the religious and the political (the community should be grounded directly in God's word), as well as for the fact that Islam is 'at its best' when it grounds the formation of a community 'out of nowhere', in the genealogical desert, as the egalitarian revolutionary fraternity – no wonder Islam succeeds when young men find themselves deprived of traditional family safety networks. And, perhaps, it is this 'orphanic' character of Islam which accounts for its lack of inherent institutionalisation. And it is precisely because Islam lacks an inherent principle of institutionalisation that it has been so vulnerable to being co-opted by state power which did the work of institutionalisation for it.

Therein resides the choice that confronts Islam: direct 'politicisation' is inscribed into its very nature, and this overlapping of the religious and the political can either be achieved in the guise of the statist co-option, or in the form of *anti-statist* collectives.

This radical-emancipator potential of Islam can be detected in an unexpected place: in the Haitian Revolution, 'a truly defining moment in world history'.[4] Haiti was exceptional from the very beginning, from its revolutionary fight against slavery which ended in independence in January 1804: 'Only in Haiti was the declaration of human freedom universally consistent. Only in Haiti was this declaration sustained at all costs, in direct opposition to the social order and economic logic of the day.' For this reason, 'there is no single event in the whole of modern history whose implications were more threatening to the dominant global order of things'. It is little known that one of the organisers of the Haiti rebellion was a black slave preacher known as 'John Bookman', a name designating him as literate, and – surprise – the 'book' referred to was not the Bible but the Qur'an. This brings to mind the great tradition of millenarian 'Communist' rebellions in Islam, especially the 'Qarmatian Republic' and the Zanj Revolt.

The Qarmatians were a millenarian Ismaili group from today's Bahrain, where they established a utopian republic in 899 (285 AH). During the 930 (317 AH) *Hajj* season, they seized the Black Stone from Makkah – an act signalling that the age of Love had arrived, so one no longer had to obey the Law. The Qarmatians' goal was to build a society based on reason and equality. The state was governed by a council of six with a chief who was a first among equals. All property within the community was distributed evenly among all initiates.

The Qarmatians' rise had been instigated by the slave rebellion in Basra which disrupted the power of Baghdad. This 'Zanj Revolt', which took place over a period of nearly fifteen years, 869-83 (255-69 AH), involved over 500,000 slaves who were imported to this region from across the Muslim empire. Their leader Ali ibn Muhammad was a black slave. Shocked by the suffering of the slaves working in the Basra marshes, he preached the radically egalitarian doctrine according to which the most qualified man should reign, 'though he be an Abyssinian slave'.[5]

And why should we not take a step further – back to the immigrant workers resting, eating – imagine a woman (also an immigrant worker, say) who serves them food on our plate? The fact that it is a woman who brings them food, not only to eat but to think and to engage, is of a special significance with regard to the role of women in Islam. Muhammad, in the shock of his first experience of revelation, turns to whom? To the one who saves him from an unbearable uncertainty, the first believer in his message, the first Muslim: Khadija, his wife. In this scene, she is the Lacanian 'big Other', the guarantee of Truth of the subject's enunciation, and it is through this circular support, through someone who believes in him, that the Prophet can believe in his own message and serve as a Messenger of Truth to believers. A woman thus possesses a knowledge about the truth which precedes even the Prophet's knowledge.

This brings us back to the topic with which we began: can fate be changed? We can see how, although Islam receives recently bad press in the West, there are quite different potentials in it beneath the apparent patriarchal surface.

This, then, is the message of the item numbered PO.24 in the MIA: insofar as we tend to oppose East and West as fate and freedom, Islam stands for a third position which undermines this binary opposition – neither subordination to blind fate nor freedom to do what one wants, both of which presuppose an abstract external opposition between the two terms, but a deeper freedom: to alter or to choose our fate.

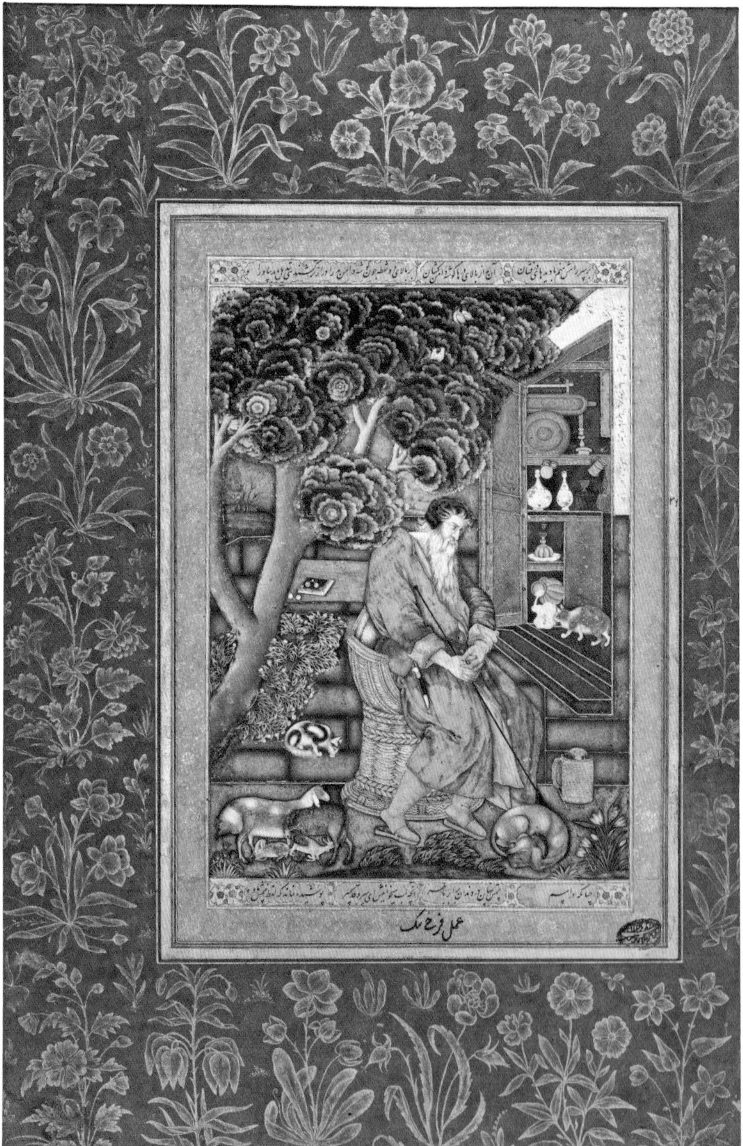

'St Jerome' as the Representation of Melancholy

Jabbour al-Douaihy

The meeting with St Jerome in Doha was unforeseen. For who'd have thought that I, a Christian Maronite from a town in Mount Lebanon whose churches and homes are replete with gilded icons and painted statues of the Virgin Mary, would find suddenly, in Qatar's unique Museum of Islamic Art – a place I'd have wagered would be free from any predilection for iconophilia – a friend from my childhood days; hanging there, in a softly lit corner, between the exceptional Indian 'Hyderabad Carpet' and an array of brass astrolabes of Andalusian and Persian craft.

This elderly gentleman who holds his writing plume in his right hand and gestures with his left towards a human skull placed without the slightest ceremony on his desk, had kept me company (nay, troubled some of my childhood) in my bedroom for a number of years; I'd stare – whenever my mind drifted into a daydream or when I woke during the night – at his manner of sitting, the details informing his labours, the brush of sadness which lay across his features.

A picture we inherited in all likelihood from my maternal grandmother, who in her turn had bought it from one of the itinerant merchants trading in the narrow streets, tempting housewives with linens and blue 'Nile' stones, which would lend their laundry lustre and sweet fragrance. The barter over prices would end with the merchant – later my grandmother would discover that he was a Syrian Muslim – producing a selection of pictures of the saints from his bag and offering them as a bonus 'on the house' – or as compensation for a price that might have been thought a bit high. In fact I did not get to know the saint's real name until many years later, because my mother at that time had bestowed upon him the name 'Antonius the Elder', the hermit of the Egyptian desert. This was because popular pictures of the hermit showed him, like St Jerome, surrounded by dogs and donkeys and giraffes, and so my mother confused the two when she saw a majestic and lazy lion languishing beside the man I later discovered (because of a curiosity that impelled me to trace his origins) to be St Jerome, immersed in the bellies of books.

The same man who followed the supposed geographical path of Christ had returned to us; to the neighbourhood of his previous home in Syria, where he had spent five years of his life in the desert in prayer and penance. He reappeared at a time when the popularity of colour printing was encouraging some Lebanese painters, such as Daoud al-Qurm or Habib Srour, who had studied in Italy at the end of the nineteenth and the beginning of the twentieth century, to follow the tradition of the European Renaissance in depicting the saints, and to use them to adorn the churches and homes of the Maronites. But the journey of St Jerome from Bethlehem to Europe and back to Mount Lebanon was not fraught with peril or loneliness compared with the journey, which took him, in the year 347 CE, from his birthplace – somewhere west of present-day Hungary, in places which have now lost their Roman geographical names, such as Stridonium, Dalmatia or Pannonia – to the Museum of Islamic Art, magnificent in its architecture and structure, in Qatar at the beginning of the twenty-first century. This man, who passed away in the year 420 CE having built himself a tomb close to the cave where it is said Christ was buried before his triumph over death, had a personal history laden with superstition and details borrowed from other saints. In its final form his history appears as a perfect example of the history of the saints of the second epoch of Christianity, those who lived lives full of patience, the martyrs of tears who lived after the rule of the Christian emperor Constantine was established and the church moved from glorifying the first martyrs (who gave their lives for their faith) to extolling the 'ideal' qualities of dedication, learning and suffering of the second.

All these qualities were present in Jerome, the deep, the sober, of whom the great European ecclesiastical and Renaissance artists took their fill of painting, from the Sicilian Antonello da Messina and the Flemish Jan van Eyck of the fifteenth century – who portrayed him hard at work behind a desk in full regalia, or even smiling in the warmth of his study ornate with detail and geometrical shapes, joyful in colour – to the Venetians Titian and Paolo Veronese and later to Baroque artists such as the Flemish Anthony van Dyck and the French classicists Georges de la Tour and Philippe de Champaigne in the seventeenth century, who portrayed him more turbulently in terms of line and colour, expressing the condition of the half-naked penitent facing the barren wilderness. Paintings in which he is almost always accompanied by the Holy Book, which he spent his lifetime translating into Latin, a language he was fluent in, as he was in Hebrew and Greek, and to an extent in Syriac, Aramaic and Arabic (despite which his work did not satisfy St Augustine who objected to the translation from the Hebrew as opposed to the Greek, which was agreed upon in the West). These painters twinned him with a lion, which he had tamed one day after tending its wound, transforming it into a faithful servant and the guardian of the monks in his monastery. The saints favoured animals in general during that period and each one had a favourite; such as the beloved St John of the Bible, who bred partridges, and St Patrick, who was befriended by a doe and her little one, and St Benno (Benoît), who fed the ravens, or St Roch and his dog.

The dog, with its customary loyalty, is often present in docile positions in paintings of St Jerome, whom the German Albrecht Dürer in turn also depicted. Dürer, who was born in Nuremberg in 1471 (875 AH), and whose paintings and woodcuts portray the secular and the sacred, was known to have travelled to Italy, from where he returned, perhaps, with the techniques of perspective, an awareness of the relationship between painting and the sciences, and a familiarity with his subject: St Jerome, who was also depicted by Dürer's famous countryman Lucas Cranach the Elder. The portrayal of the learned saint or the saint suffering in the wilderness marked the arrival of Italian Renaissance art in the German regions. After Italy, Dürer, who was so enamoured of mathematics that he asserted, in *The Art of Measurement*, that no art could be sound unless built on technical knowledge, and that no artist could be complete while he remained ignorant of geometry, transformed the woodcuts, perfected early in his career, into exercises in three dimensions, their lines proud and defined as though showing off what was then an amazing and relatively recent discovery. Not content with portraying St Jerome in all his usual settings, Dürer also set him in a wider context of meaning and symbolism by placing him in a trinity of engravings, which includes the *Knight, Death and the Devil*, an engraving similiar in size to his *Angel of Sorrow* (usually known as *Melencolia*). He gave his St Jerome a profound, meditative expression, as well as an hourglass, to indicate the passage of time.

Perhaps it was because of this that St Jerome arrived in India carrying the name 'the Symbol of Sorrow', which remained with him on his journey from Dürer's printed woodcuts to Farrukh Beg's miniature in watercolours, ink and gold on paper. A whole century of time during which Portuguese colonisers rushed to India, preceded by the discovery, in 1488 (893 AH), of the naval passage at the Cape of Good Hope by Vasco da Gama and Bartholomew Diaz and, under their leadership, mercenaries and outlaws promised the enjoyment of kidnapped women and the trade of gemstones for cheap and flashy goods. This until their influence was established in the first half of the sixteenth century in the coastal district of Goa in the south-west of India, where, at the orders of the Portuguese Admiral, Alfonso de Albuquerque, more than fifty churches were erected and a similar number of palaces. In 1526 (932 AH), the Mughal Turk, Zahir ud-din Muhammad Babur, descendant of Timur Lang (Tamerlane), declared himself Padi Shah of Hindustan and proceeded to found one of the greatest and most important dynasties, which through seventeen sultans would rule well into the eighteenth century. Some years later, in 1542 (948 AH), a Spanish Jesuit by the name of François Xavier, later elevated to sainthood, landed in Goa carrying copies of the Holy Book and the Book of Psalms, which St Jerome had also had a hand in translating, as well as some works of art... and soon he was joined by about fifty more Jesuits, who would continue the missionary invasion for two centuries.

The arrival of followers of Ignatius de Loyola in India coincided with the death of Humayun, son of Babur, and the transfer of power to his grandson, Akbar. It's likely that the first images and Western 'Christian' woodcuts and engravings began reaching the court of Sultan Akbar in the last quarter of the sixteenth century, having been brought first by a mission to Goa, which was followed by a steady stream of Jesuit missions until the end of the century. And later it became known that the Sultan was an admirer of Western works of art and that he commissioned the artists in his court to copy them. This Mughal sultan was known for his openness to the Christian religion, and he is credited with an initiative to bring together different faiths and promote harmony between them. One contemporary miniature shows what appears to be a religious conference in the 'House of Devotions', a kind of interfaith meeting: each party brings their holy book to the Sultan Akbar; to his right stand two men wearing black, the colour identified with the Jesuits' monastery; an Italian and a Portuguese bring him a European work par excellence, the famous *Biblia Polyglotta* (in its four languages, Hebrew,

Latin, Greek and Aramaic) published a few years before by the French Christophe Plantin at the request and commission of Philip II of Spain; this is decorated with paintings by Dutch artists and engravers, the most prominent of whom was Pieter van der Heyden, who engraved *The Blind Leading The Blind*.

Nur ud-din Salim Jahangir, who followed in the footsteps of Sultan Akbar, was also enamoured of this kind of debate between Muslim scholars and Christian monks, and was known to have played the devil's advocate in a kind of game where he assumed the role of referee, at times defending Christianity then suddenly asking the monks to convince him of the personification of God in the body of Christ so that he might adopt their faith, having himself tried the position of a man on a crucifix so that he could gauge what Jesus of Nazareth suffered on the cross. He also explored Zoroastrianism, built a sacred fire, and tried to devise a new religion that would satisfy all his subjects. And if the faiths did not meet and each man stuck to his own, and if the aristocratic Italian Jesuit, Rodolfo Acquaviva, gave up hope of converting Akbar or any of his sons to Christianity as he had hoped, and focused on preaching among the Hindus until they killed him at the age of thirty-three, the admiration of the Mughal sultans for Christian art continued to propel the meeting of figurative art in its Western, Persian and Indian forms, combining oil painting, European engraving and gilded Persian miniatures, and allowing a European influence in the great architectural projects which distinguished the rule of Shah Jahan, the builder of the Taj Mahal, whom Farrukh Beg favoured – while still a young man – with an album in which he included St Jerome. The court painters of Jahangir, including Farrukh Beg, were inspired by, for example, decorative styles in the painting of 'The Virgin: Our Lady of Piety and the Queen of the World' in the *Biblia Polyglotta* and other paintings, to paint Sultan Jahangir in his full splendour.

Jahangir took particular interest in the woodcuts of Dürer and personally supervised the copying of faces, flora and fauna from them, until came the turn of St Jerome, whose picture Jahangir commissioned from Farrukh Beg, the Persian, who had worked in Khorosan for the ruler of Mashad, Ibrahim Mirza, before working as a craftsman for Sultan Akbar, for fifteen years, until 1600. During that time he was classified among the top artists of the day by Abu al-Fadl, Akbar's first minister and the author of the *Akbar-nameh*, the distinguished biography of the Sultan, the battles and chapters of which were illustrated by the artists of the court. But Farrukh Beg lost favour after that and moved to the Indian district of Deccan before returning to the court of Jahangir, where he leaned towards painting plants and nature and earned the title 'Rarity of the Age'.

It is clear that Farrukh Beg took Dürer's engraving of St Jerome as his model, but did not pay much heed to the Christian symbolism, which generally accompanied the saint, or to the esoteric hints in Dürer's work. Jerome, as we may now call him, did not appear from the brush of Farrukh Beg engaged in study or in repentance, his two most common aspects in Western Christian iconography. There is no trace in the Mughal miniatures of the books which usually accompanied this man who deservedly became the intercessor of booksellers and translators; nothing but a neglected booklet thrown down in the background of the picture. Absent also is the human skull, the reminder of the mortality of humans and all living beings, and we search in vain for the famous lion, who has no other tamer in the history of Christian saints but St Jerome – known in the East as Hieronymus of Stridonium. Farrukh Beg seated our friend under an ornamental tree in many shades of brown in the tradition of Persian Indian miniature painting, in an atmosphere of peace and harmony, underlined by the vivid green of the saint's robe and his backdrop and the calm attitudes of the small pets, dogs and cats, curled up as though copied exactly from Dürer's woodcut. We note the many 'unnecessary' objects inspired by Dürer, but stripped of their link to the concept of Melancholia: a group of Eastern-style bottles in what looks like a shelved display cabinet. An important aspect of all this is Farrukh Beg's attempt to include perspective, successful on the right-hand side where he shows the table in three dimensions as in Dürer's engraving.

The old Jerome appears – and old age is his lot in every representation, as though he were born old, as opposed to St George's perennial youth, for example – calm, here and in all his paintings, despite what is told of his fierce impatience and his willingness to fight for his beliefs. In his head with its slight inclination, his flowing white beard and his calm expression there is that which brings him close to Farrukh Beg's idea of a Muslim cleric in meditation, as seen in another miniature.

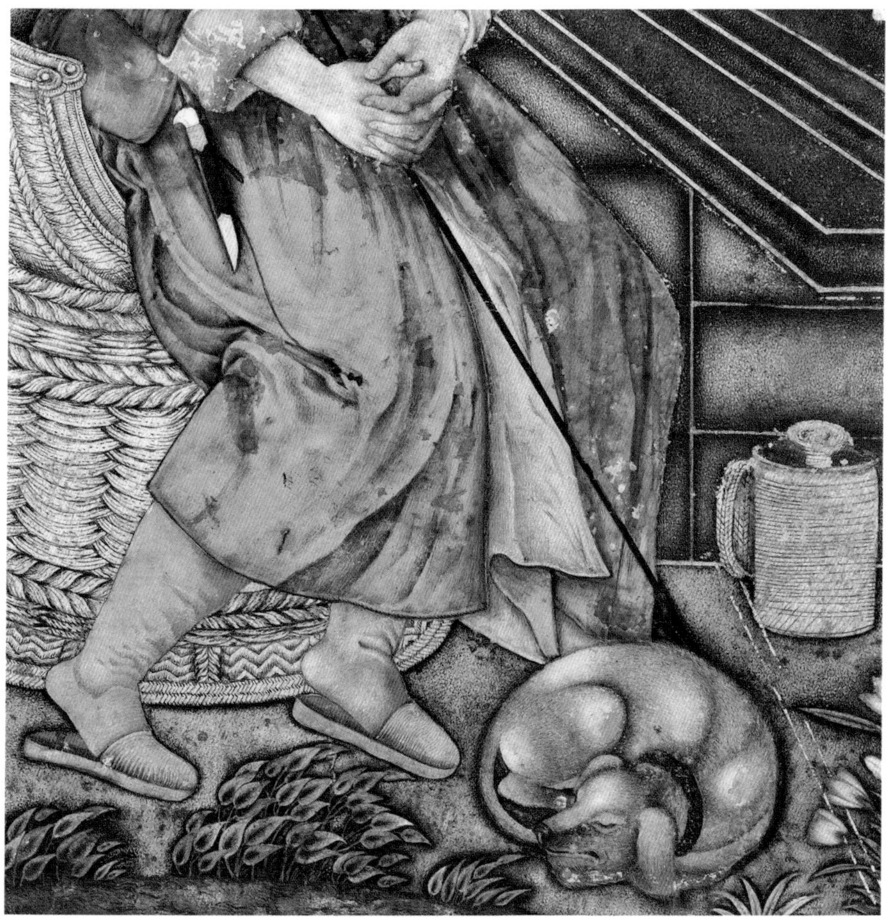

The Mughal Jerome, who looks as though he is resting after a job completed to his satisfaction, is very different from the saint with the frowning face, companion to the lion and the skull, who shared my childhood bedroom. I needed to travel to India and the Mughal sultans, via Qatar's Museum of Islamic Art, so that at last the worrying image I carried with me of St Jerome might be washed over with gentleness and harmony.

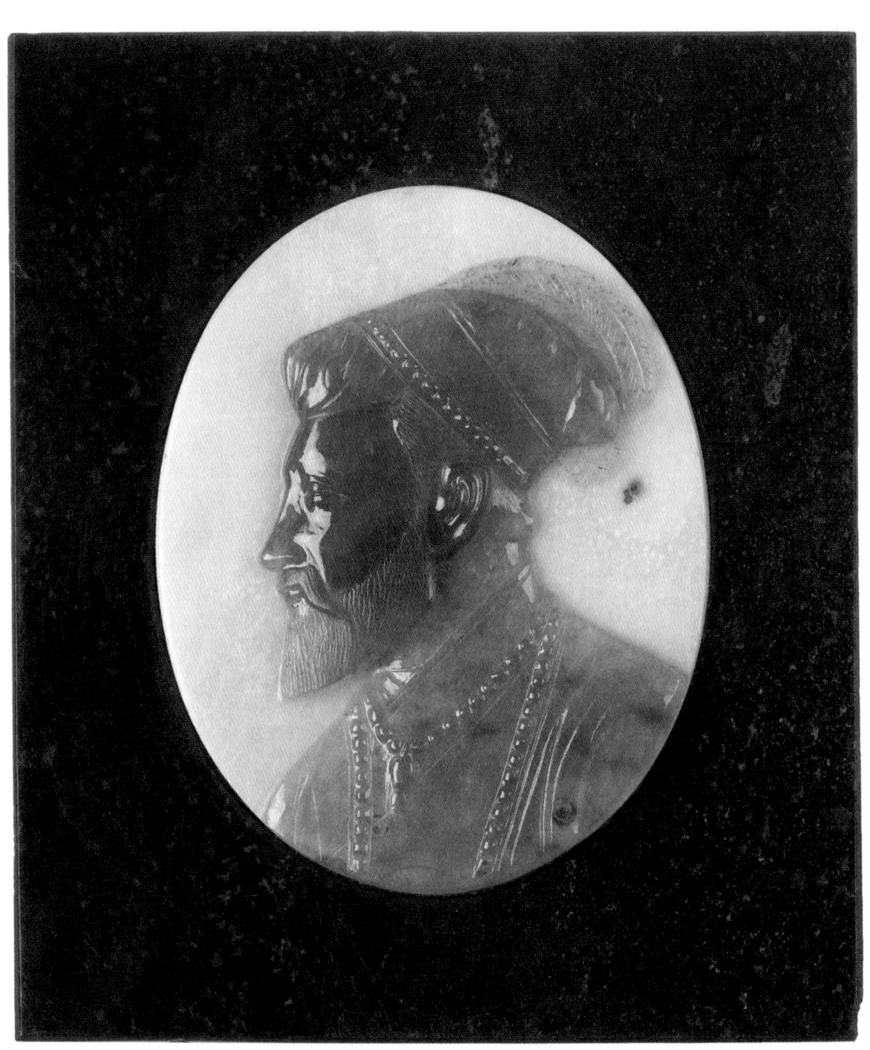

Reflections on a Mughal portrait

Eric Hobsbawm

On 10 January 1401 (by the Western calendar) an event occurred at which I would dearly like to have been present. It was the first meeting between the Mongol world conqueror, Timur of Samarkand (Tamerlane), and the greatest social and historical mind of the medieval world, Ibn Khaldun, who had reluctantly interrupted his studies to return to be an adviser to governments. I can see the old scholar – he was almost seventy – being lowered by ropes from the walls of Damascus, which Timur was then besieging and about to take, and with less consideration than he gave to diplomats and eminent intellectuals. (The Damascenes were massacred.) We know some of the things they talked about. Since he wanted to conquer it also, Timur needed information about North Africa, on which Ibn Khaldun was the leading expert. He received the required memorandum, but Ibn Khaldun was sufficiently worried to produce an equivalent memorandum on the Eastern conqueror for the Sultan of Morocco. It was never needed. Both Timur and his interlocutor died within a few years.

I shall get back to Ibn Khaldun later. As for Timur, he became the ancestor of other central Asian conquerors, notably the Mughal conquerors of India (who, as their name suggests, also saw themselves as descendants of the Mongol Genghis Khan): and of the garden-loving fighter and autobiographer Babur, the great Akbar, and the emperor whose portrait I have chosen from the remarkable Museum of Islamic Art in Doha. Among many other titles, he also called himself 'king of the world' out of Timurid pride.

The piece I have chosen is a small, glowing cameo; a likeness, head and shoulders, of Shah Jahan (1627-58/1036-68 AH). As an emperor he was much, some would say excessively, portrayed by sycophants, mostly in the miniatures that are the glory of Mughal painting. But the two-dimensional view does not bring him as close to us as reliefs like this one and the superb alabaster work in the Amsterdam Rijksmuseum. The portraits of absolute rulers, then and now, are rarely intended to provide photographic accuracy – a miniature of Shah Jahan elsewhere in the MIA makes the point – but here I have the impression that this tiny relief, incised into precious stone, is closer to what the Shahenshah looked like, because it was too small to contain most of the iconographic appurtenances of imperial presentation. We see the right profile of a straight-nosed gentleman in a turban, with high cheekbones, a well-trimmed beard and a gently curving long moustache.

Does he look like a warrior, as any Mughal emperor had to be? Not obviously at first sight. If this were a twentieth- and not a seventeenth-century piece, it might be the likeness of a self-confident actor-manager, used to public appearance. He certainly does not look like a man who would be overthrown by his son Aurangzeb, to live out his life under house arrest in the wonderful White Fort in Agra, his window facing what is probably the only great Islamic building identifiable by most Britons, if only as the name of Indian restaurants, the Taj Mahal. It was his most heartfelt creation, the funeral monument to his beloved wife. Is it the head of an aesthete? The greatest patron of the arts in the golden age of the Islamic arts? One couldn't tell. Yet that is what he was.

The greatest glories of the golden age of Islamic art are far beyond the size that can be displayed in museums, or effectively reproduced on paper. They must be seen and experienced, as strangers discover who come to Agra for the first time, and recognise how little they knew what the Taj Mahal looks like until they are in its presence. They are the great mosques like the Pearl Mosque in Lahore, urban spaces like Agra or Old Delhi, the interplay of light and shade in dry and sun-drenched lands, which inspires the exterior of I.M. Pei's superb building for the MIA, and not least the wonderful gardens designed to create small oases of paradise in such climates. Architecturally I do not think there is anything, not even Rome as reconstructed by Papal absolutism, that can bear comparison with the imagination and civilised elegance of the great creations by Islamic rulers in the sixteenth and seventeenth centuries in the Ottoman, Safavid and Mughal empires. Perhaps their only equivalent is the construction of St Petersburg in the eighteenth century, also at short notice by equally free-spending autocrats with aesthetic ambitions and equally careless of the lives of their labouring subjects.

Shah Jahan's prodigality as builder and patron may have been exceptional, since he ruled what was by far the wealthiest and most populous of the Islamic empires. None but a ruler who wished to demonstrate the unlimited resources (which so impressed the rare visiting European), would have commissioned that most luxurious exhibit in the Doha museum: the golden falcon covered in diamonds and jewels, which inevitably diverts my thoughts from Islamic culture to the greatest monument to the hard-boiled private-eye, Dashiell Hammett's and Humphrey Bogart's *The Maltese Falcon*. In Shah Jahan's day, it would have been a reminder not only of wealth beyond the dream of avarice, but of the founders of empires, tough fighting chieftains from the outback hunting with falcons on their wrist. For the Mughal empire shared a basic characteristic with the other great empires of the golden age of the Islamic arts: they were sedentary and advanced societies that absorbed the hard-living and hard-riding warrior clans from highland, desert and steppe who had invaded and conquered them.

At this point we return from the descendants of Tamerlane to the great Ibn Khaldun, or rather to the remarkable Prolegomena to his universal history: *Kitab al-'Ibar*, where this is analysed as the basic pattern of historic development of the old world's civilisations during the millennium when it was dominated by waves of barbarian invasion. Pastoralist warrior tribes, sometimes under a puritan ideology suited to poor raiding nomads, periodically irrupted into and conquered the great sedentary empires, both attracted to their riches and contemptuous of their luxurious decadence, and then were absorbed by them. Islamic monotheism, egalitarian, spare and ritually simple proved to be the most successful of these ideologies among the peoples of the Arabian and North African deserts and the Turkish tribes of Central Asia, but empires could only be overthrown, not governed by jihadist campaigns. They were only too likely to destroy wholesale what made no sense to nomadic herdsmen, notably the economies of the old empires. Where they could not use an established imperial structure, as in China,

Genghis Khan's Mongol realm, the greatest land mass ever under single rule, soon broke into pieces. Insofar as fragments of it survived, it was because they learned from the former empires how to govern cities and a settled society.

Proud as they were of their conquering tribal ancestors, the rulers of the great empires of the golden age of Islamic art were no longer tempted by the austerities that shaped the lives of hungry and puritan pastoralist raiders, nor could they afford them as rulers. In a sense that had been so since the earliest days of Islam, when it was decided to prevent the Bedouin raiders from damaging agricultural society and to cooperate with the chiefs and notables of the newly conquered populations. The impact of the nomadic conquerors from Inner Asia from the tenth century on, made it even more urgent to integrate them into settled society and to come to terms with the multiple peoples and beliefs (including Muslim beliefs) that by necessity co-existed in large empires. Nowhere was this more obvious than in Mughal India, where the great majority of the inhabitants actually remained non-Muslims and their rulers showed little interest in converting them.

Imperial Islam was therefore inevitably a confluence and symbiosis of cultures, as its centre moved away from Arabia to the invaders from Central Asia and the region steeped in the traditions and language of the Persian empire. Inevitably this shaped its arts and lifestyles. Islamic empires were autocratic but tolerant – certainly more so than Christian kingdoms. Emperors, however pious, saw to it that they were not fettered by hardline interpretations of *Shari'a*. Although Islam, like the Jewish religion, was in general hostile to figurative art, none of the exhibits in this museum devoted to showing the greatness of Ottoman, Safavid and Mughal emperors shows the slightest sign of iconophobia, except in works directly relevant to religious worship and holy texts. On the contrary, they display a profusion of essentially secular images and illustrations of the world as recreated to be seen by its ruler and to glorify his power and authority.

In a sense the miniatures and other artefacts like the Shah Jahan cameo, too small for public show, express both its ambitions and its limits. They are designed to be seen essentially by one individual and shown to others. Only in this case that individual was the 'king of the world'. They are world domination reduced to private enjoyment.

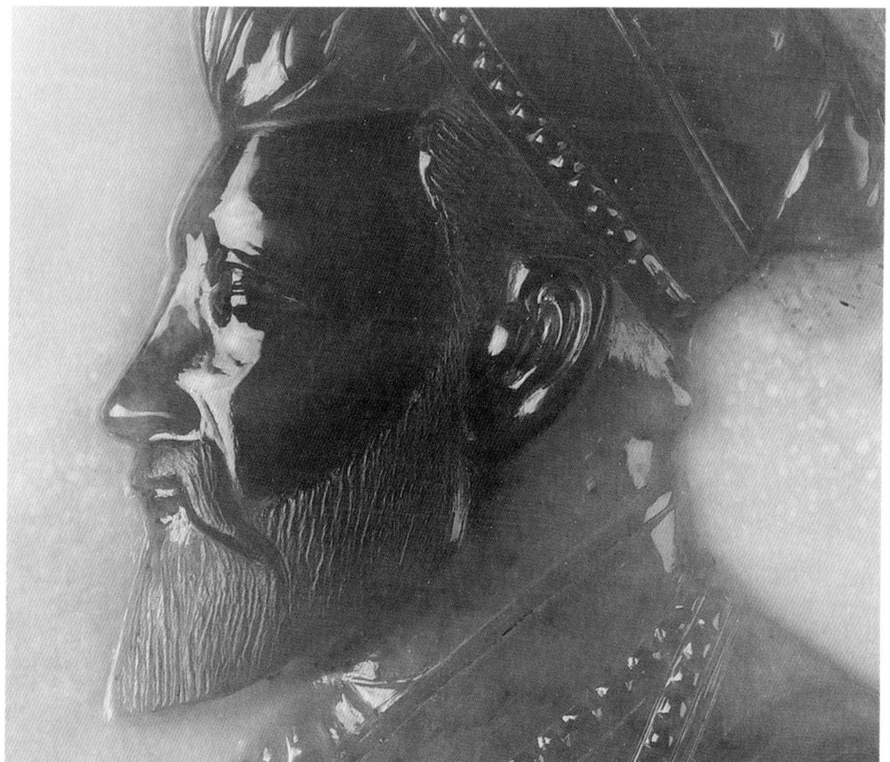

I look at the cameo of Shah Jahan again. This also is essentially a private portrait. It is the likeness not of the greatest of imperial builders (how many labourers died constructing his masterpieces?) but of the man who built the Taj Mahal as a memorial to a private love and, as it turned out, as his own grave. Here is the art that wanted to translate Baudelaire's *ordre et beauté, luxe, calme et volupté* into marble, sky and watered garden for ever, even if it strained the almost limitless resources of the Mughal empire. As indeed he did and it did. Here is the triumph of art over, indeed at the cost of, a reality beyond the horizon of palace and court, one might even say while Mughal magnificence waited, unprepared, for the next wave of conquerors full of greed and self-confidence, this time not from Afghanistan but from the western seas.

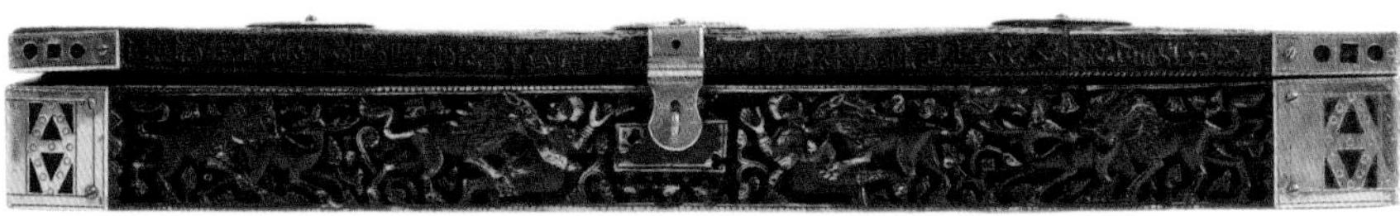

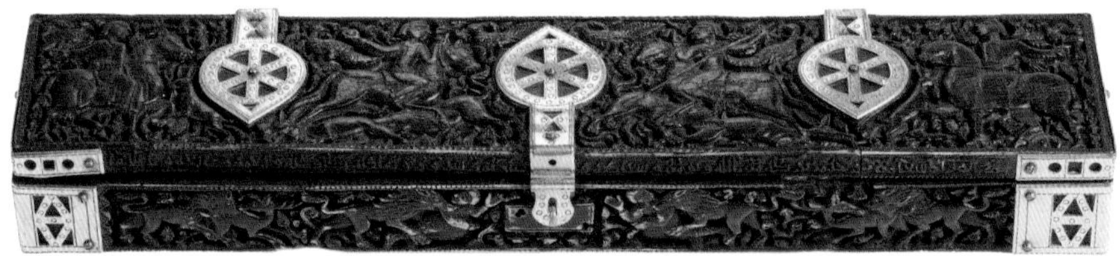

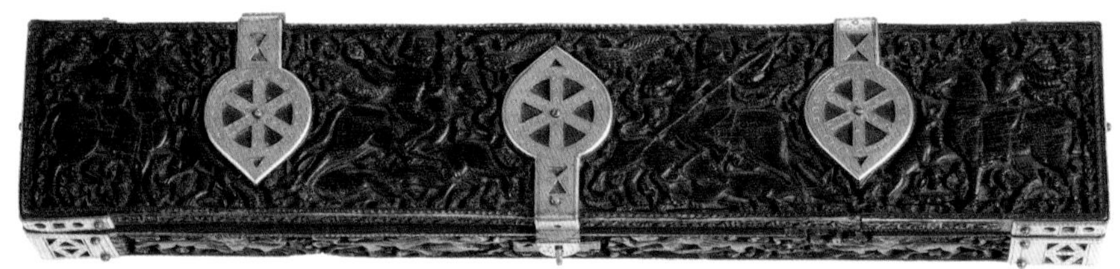

An Andalusian Penbox

Radwa Ashour

I saw it and took a long look.

Then went off to acquaint myself with others. But I came back.

A little under a year later I got the call about the project for this book. I said: I know what I'm going to write about. But, just in case, I decided to join my fellow writers and revisit the Museum; perhaps another piece will catch hold of me.

In the Museum again, I move between the second- and third-floor galleries. I stand in front of a manuscript here and another there. A delicate illumination. A wooden door. A penbox in silver and copper. A carpet spread out as though it were a country. A ceramic piece that throws a strange question at me: did Joan Miró see this and learn from the boldness of its blue and yellow part of his craft?

I consider.

But I go back and stand transfixed in front of the penbox, which caught my attention on that first visit.

I

A penbox which bears the date of its making at the end of a phrase engraved in Kufic script at the edge of its cover: Rabi' al-Awwal 394 (equivalent to December 1003 or January 1004), resting on a raised stand inside a glass box to the right of the entrance, in the south gallery on the second floor.

An Andalusian penbox.

How did it manage to carry on with its story while cities around it were falling, their inhabitants fleeing or being forced to leave, dwellings transformed from homes into ruins to become the stuff of poetry, and time, as usual, a law unto itself, turning like an ox blindfolded at the water wheel?

How was it spared? By chance? Or a blessing left by the fingers of its anonymous maker, or the care of an owner who carried it with his children from a burning city to a city not burning yet? It was made in Córdoba, most probably. Its body carries the memory of the tusk of an African elephant; an elephant who died more than 1,200 years ago – this is what science says on the basis of carbon analysis. Perhaps it was made of that ivory which historians tell us reached the ruler of Córdoba in 991 (380 AH) as part of a precious gift from North Africa; a gift of camels and racehorses and ostrich feathers and spears and bows of beech and other rarities. And among all this, 8,000 pounds of ivory.

And for one reason or another, it was painted – at some stage in its long history – with black paint. Some think the paint was added in the stage before its last, in England, maybe. But the black is no longer just an external coat because the ivory, being old when it was painted, had cracked and the paint flowed into the cracks, and the black, made in Europe, mixed with the white, which came from Africa. An exchange of roles in a curious game between the two colours so burdened with significance.

Let's start with the cover: the scene is balanced like a line of verse: two halves complement and mirror each other. And each half in turn consists of two parallel units. In the scene are four knights; two knights here faced by two knights there, on each side of the brass ornament of the lock, exactly in the middle. And in the far right there's another knight, and in the far left too. A horse here, a similar horse there. Each horse stands with two legs straight and two legs bent. The horse is not running yet, although it's about to be. The knight to the right carries a falcon on his left wrist, the one to the left carries a falcon on his right wrist; that falcon which is sometimes the emblem of the Umayyads. Their Caliphate will collapse in Córdoba and strife will take root there and start that lengthy collapse so reminiscent of Imru' al-Qais's rock, hurled by the torrent from on high.

Has this penbox seen part of this fall? All of this fall? Was it in Córdoba when it finally fell to the Frank monarchs in 1236 (633 AH)?

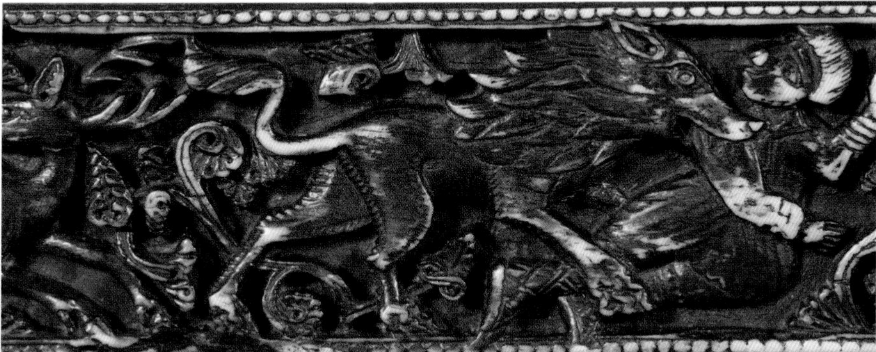

Back to the engraving: a sense of danger exists; a sense of potential rebellion, I think. A dog (or perhaps a wolf) rears up on its hind legs, confronting a knight, devouring plants and fruit. The two knights at the edge of the case are like two crescent moons, or like quotation marks enclosing the two other knights separated by the brass ornament that divides the case in the middle, dividing the engraving into its two sections. Each of the knights rides a horse, but the horses are different, their legs are stretched as far as they will go: a galloping movement that endorses the state of engagement. Behind the shoulder of a knight a peacock, and a similar peacock behind the shoulder of the knight who faces him. The right-hand knight thrusts his spear into a wild boar attacking a deer (the knight protects the weak, then, and attacks the unjust, this is his image and his example) and the knight on the opposite side almost stamps with his horse's hoofs on another boar pursuing a deer. Surrounding the knights plant engravings indicate bounty and fruitfulness.

The frame around the cover is dedicated to text; a sentence in Kufic script: 'In the name of God the Compassionate and the Merciful, the blessings of God and yumin [sic] and happiness, joy and gladness, sufficient health and all-encombassing [sic] grace, a lofty han [probably 'hand'] and continuous grace for its owner. Made in the month of Rib'a [Rabi'] al-Awwal in the year four and ninety and th[ree hundred].'

Around the sides of the rectangular case scenes of the hunt and the chase. Lions and griffins and falcons and deer and rabbits and a hunter aiming his long spear, all interwoven with dense engravings of plants. And a particular engraving repeated in the background once on the right and once on the left: a large falcon on the back of a hare or perhaps a wolf. The falcon is in complete control, possessing the hare and bending its head slightly to catch its prey's tail with its beak.

The two hinges of the penbox and its lock have brass casings that are probably a late addition; for we know that ivory boxes made in Córdoba were ornamented with silver not with brass. We can imagine the original with its intermingling of two whites: the secretive ivory haunted by an unspoken yellow, and the gossipy silver flaunting its affair with grey and blue. But the ivory has turned black and its silver has been exchanged for brass. And in some station of its long journey the penbox was lined with a red baize material and supplied with two compartments, each big enough for an inkpot. The red baize carries us to different eras and atmospheres; eighteenth-century France, perhaps, or nineteenth-century England.

II

When I stood rooted in front of this piece on my first visit to the Museum, I took a small notebook out of my pocket and started to draw the case and record its dimensions, I did not catch up with the questions and fragments that crowded into my mind because they were hidden, I think, behind the presence of the case; the actual, material presence of an object that pulls your attention to its detail. You suppose, when you read the small label that informs you that this is an Andalusian penbox from the early eleventh century, that it is of Córdoban ivory, and the word 'Córdoba' comes to you, as usual, with a clamour that overwhelms the memory and the senses.

And now that I sit down to write I try to recall some of these questions and fragments. We do not know who owned the penbox or the circumstances of its manufacture. We don't know who commissioned whom to make a gift for whom. Was it originally a penbox, or was it a precious box in which a lover intended to place a message, a line of verse, perhaps, or a bracelet, ear-rings or a necklace or prayer-beads? Or was it, like other boxes of the period, just an expensive 'envelope' for amber or musk? But amber and musk boxes were cylindrical, and bigger. Did the lover have it made like this so that his messenger, or he himself, could smuggle it to his beloved without arousing suspicion? Or perhaps the lover was not charmed by a woman at all but by the spell of language and wanted the case for his pens. Was he a poet? Or was the case a professional accessory because he was the Prince's scribe writing down what his master dictated: letters to his favourites, his peers and his enemies?

I say: perhaps this penbox dropped out of the silk merchant's scene in *Don Quixote*. Why then did Cervantes forget it and remember everything else? In the scene, the narrator tells us how he met a boy carrying Arabic manuscripts in the alleys of Toledo. The boy was trying to sell the manuscripts to the silk merchant. The narrator takes one of the manuscripts to an Arab to read for him and discovers that the story he's looking for is recorded in this manuscript with the title: 'The History of Don Quixote de la Mancha as written by Sidi Hamed al-Benenjali, the Arab historian.' The narrator rushes off to the silk merchant and buys from him all the manuscripts the boy has sold him. Then he hurries back to the Arab translator and takes him to a monastery where he offers to pay him any money he wants if he will translate everything that's in the papers about Don Quixote.

Did Cervantes forget to mention the penbox used by the Arab? Or was the Arab in Cervantes's story a man of modest means who did spoken translations and did not own an ivory penbox because he was not a writer?

The imagination leaps four centuries back, from Don Quixote to twelfth-century Toledo, where the translation industry is thriving and the city has become a library for the best books and manuscripts in Europe. The Arab translator reads an Arabic manuscript and speaks the translation in the spoken language to an intermediary who speaks it in Latin to a scribe who writes it down. Or, starting in the thirteenth century, it would be written in the language spoken in Castile (later known as Spanish). Did the penbox belong to one of these scribes? Which one? The one writing in Latin in twelfth-century Toledo, or the thirteenth-century scribe writing in the spoken language and so contributing to its transformation into a language for written literature?

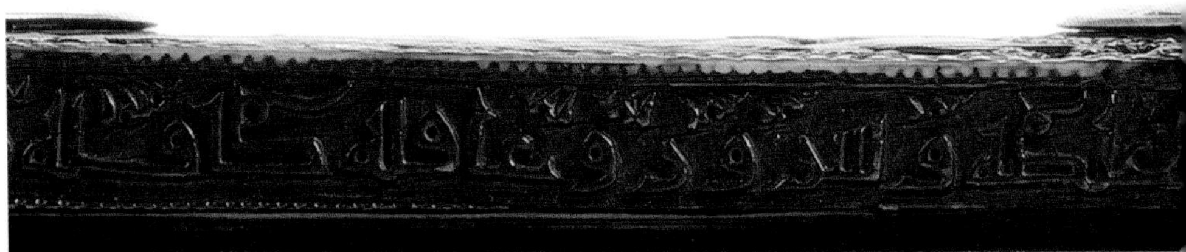

But why push the penbox towards estrangement? Perhaps it never went to Toledo, was never owned by a writer of Latin or Castilian, but stayed home in one of the villages close to Córdoba. And then its owner, or one of his grandchildren, or the grandchild of someone who'd bought it later, carried it as he carried his children at the fall of Córdoba, and took it across the Straits of Morocco to North Africa, where he settled in Fez or Qairuwan. And maybe he went further East and found people in Alexandria who, like him, had their roots in Andalusia and so settled near the Mosque of el-Shatbi or el-Mursi Abu el-Abbas, breathing the fresh sea breeze each morning and opening his penbox to take out his pen, naming God's name as he dipped it in ink and resumed writing.

And then it became estranged? Perhaps so, when an officer of the occupying French army in the nineteenth century carried it from North Africa to France when he went home. He showed it off proudly to his acquaintances, part of the booty he had brought back from the East. Or perhaps he didn't, but shyly presented it to a woman he loved. And perhaps the penbox didn't live in France because it never went there. It never left Andalusia.

It remained among the trophies the Frankish knights deposited in the churches and monasteries. For how long and in which church and when did it get to England? All we know is its contemporary history. The Museum bought it at auction in London, in Sotheby's in 1998. Oliver Watson, who has studied the piece, says that an uncle of the owner had bought it in 1947, when the contents of Earl Halifax's home were sold upon his death.

The penbox was sold – in an assorted lot which also contained two chess sets – for nine pounds,

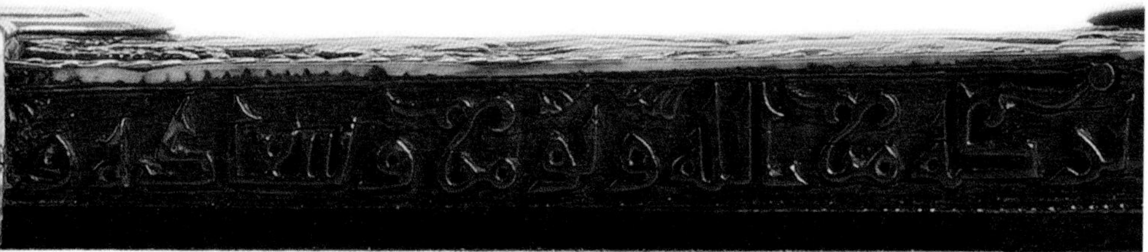

nineteen shillings and nine pence. When did the penbox arrive in that noble British home? No one knows.

And perhaps the penbox didn't go anywhere because its owners hid it with what they hid of Arabic manuscripts in fear of the Inquisition, and so it stayed in its homeland, holding pens used by Moriscos in eastern Andalusia to write in Aljamiado, that strange cryptic language that inscribes a spoken Romance language in Arabic characters so that it's obscured to non-Arabs, and so that the writer may be comforted by the Arabic character and a few phrases connected to his forbidden religion. Perhaps this penbox stayed in a deserted Arab house, hidden with books and manuscripts in a wall or under a floor, until someone found it and sold it to an English tourist fond of Oriental souvenirs who went home and showed it to his friends with some pride since the Orient, with its souvenirs and its arts, was fashionable in an age which exploited it and denigrated its inhabitants.

A penbox 1,000 years old. Tactile as the engravings etched into its ivory. Specific. Carrying the date of its birth in written characters and engraved in the style of ivory etchings in Córdoba between 1150 and 1250 (544 and 647 AH). We know where it started and we know where it ends.

And between those two moments are 1,000 years, mysterious as history. We know nothing of it except the big headlines: a moment, a flash of light. As for what this history saw, or what was seen within it, that remains closed and evasive. All we can do is use our imagination, use 'maybe' and 'perhaps' for these disconnected fragments and unending questions.

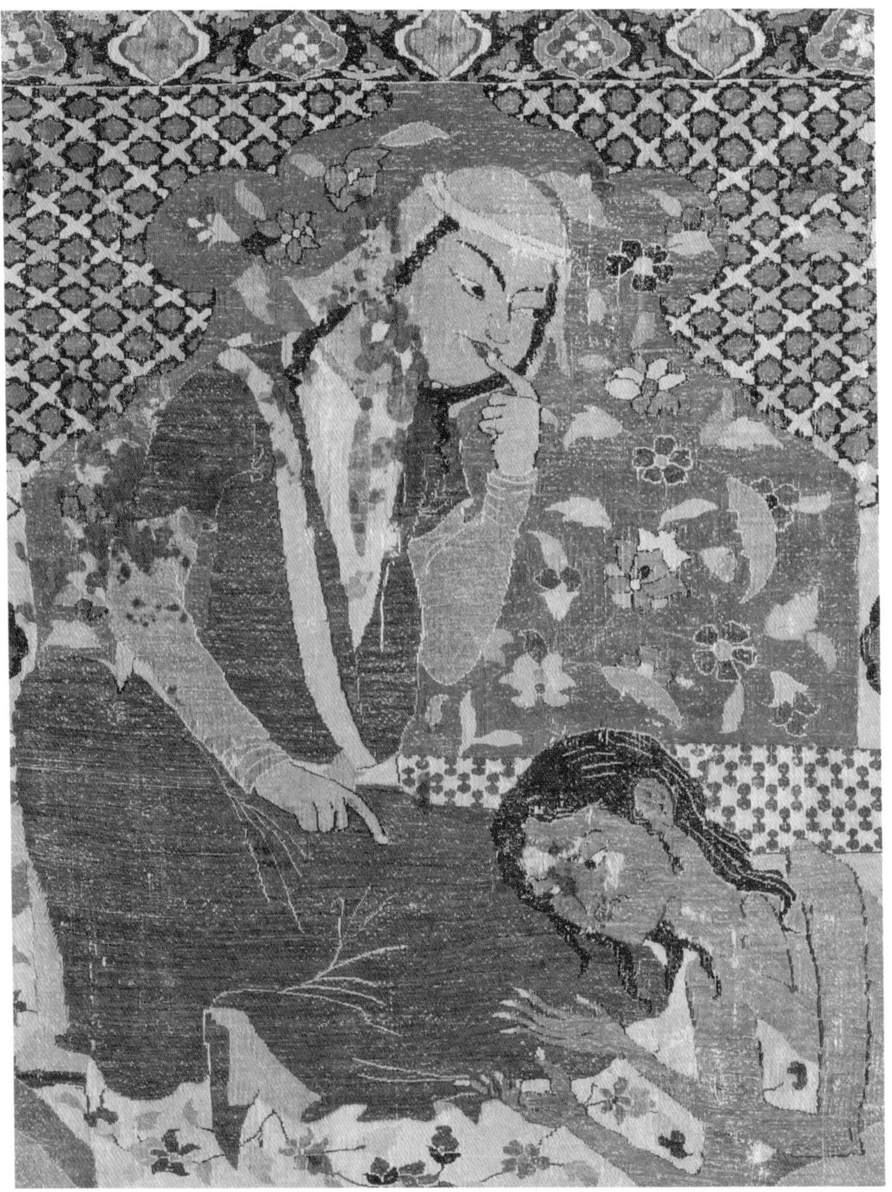

Laila and the Majnoun

Ghassan Zaqtan

A severe block, ascetic and cautious, floating on the water in a chosen isolation. There is no chatter in the body leaning to whiteness. Faded inscriptions break the whiteness of the stone in parallel lines as though they were the wish to speak – not speech itself.

This, somehow, is my first impression as I pass quickly in front of the Museum of Islamic Art the evening I arrive in Doha. Later, this impression will be consolidated. It seemed as though the place was a search for the opposite of the eloquent ornamentation that denotes – as an agreed and summary definition – Islamic art. This is where the ordinary non-specialist viewer will begin – as I did.

The broad avenue that leads to the entrance and the lines of palm trees that divide it into four paths – all of them rising in unison towards the entrance – are an early celebration of what is to come. The power bestowed by this long ascent – an ascent that makes necessary a slight stoop of the body and a straightening of the step, while on the other side the solid stone block also ascends as though rising out of the water, or like a white tree propelling its own growth, or a temple transmitting its energy to those labouring up the slope – is what gives the place the mysterious authority that enfolds it.

In the distance the skyline of the modern city spreads out: the dominant grey or black towers; a variation on the scene, and among all this you can make out a conical minaret rising lit out of the dark; a layered metaphor for a variety of times and places.

Did I.M. Pei think of all this when he first saw the place or imagined it? I would like it if he did.

The severity and reserve suggested by colour – the colour of the ascetic spaces of the desert – give the place the feel of a mysterious temple, which is what will vanish completely when you pass through the entrance and find yourself in front of a dense network of decorations and staircases and wide passages encircling the open interior of the Museum: a chaotic celebration that quietly reveals its order, giving you the sense of crossing a threshold into a world moving towards a coalition of worlds, or into a harmonious agreement between infinite diversities, there, where time intersects with the staircases, the open spaces, the ceiling decorations and the collection. The conservative lighting is enough to bring each piece to life, while the visitors remain ghosts in the shadowy corridors that lead into each other, moving and criss-crossing as though from story to story, or as though they were entering 'the story' itself, the Eastern story with its flowing narrative, its diversions and rhetorical flourishes and sidestreets leading to new heroes and new times and places which introduce themselves assiduously and silently: there, where a small golden pin shines with the same strength that informs the 'Hyderabad' rug stretching itself out like a creature made of silk, or the bowed head of St Jerome in the album of an Indian Mughal prince echoes Carvour's Egyptian Vase and Feridoun storming Zahhak's castle in the *Shahnameh* not far from 'Al-Majnoun in the Wilderness' derived from Nizami's *Laila and al-Majnoun*, and inscribed, as it is stated, by 'Abd al-Jabbar' in Isfahan in dark watercolours and ink on paper in Isfahan. 'Al-Majnoun' appears half-naked, with a thin, dark body, and with the same long black hair that he shows in the 'Laila and al-Majnoun' tapestry. He is surrounded by rocky ground and by wild animals that have grown used to his presence. Plants bend as though they were listening or clearing a line of vision, and the simple human form appears an extension of this wildlife as well as an idealistic continuation of the philosophy of the Arab Sa'aleek poets who exchanged the company of their societies and their habits and traditions for the company of the creatures of the wild. This is the theme of the epic which Nizami fashioned at the commission of Shirwan Shah in the twelfth century and which he delivered in 4,700 lines.

The absence of certainty is what led me to this tapestry, the hesitation informing all its components, and which begins with the note describing its provenance with evident hesitation: 'Iran. Possibly Kashan', and continues into the risky attempt to convey the place through colours not too distant from dust, and to the dark complexion – the complexion of a stranger – of the Majnoun who looks like a victimised god.

Hesitation is the theme of the narrative, and the space which the artist both builds on and draws inspiration from, the ghostliness of the hero and the high definition of the others, the fantastic ability of the weavers to isolate al-Majnoun in that dark shade of brown that makes his thinness something integral to him rather than a passing state. There are no clear reasons for his profound compliance in the face of love; his position emanates from within himself and not from his standing in the presence of the beloved. And while he demonstrates an extreme of fragility, confidence accumulates in the figure of the 'Messenger' who has brought al-Majnoun and Laila together. Doubt oscillates in the scene: in the distance that separates al-Majnoun from Laila, the clever positioning of the Messenger to one side, his prohibitory gesture and the double movement of Laila's two index fingers, one raised in warning in the face of al-Majnoun, as though she were guarding the distance between them, and the other, perplexed, held up to her lip. An oscillation that resembles the narrative itself and its journey across four centuries from Najd in the Arab desert to Ganja in Azerbaijan.

You cannot stand neutral in the face of what's happening here, in this tapestry. You go beyond contemplating the frozen scene, you go directly to the narrative itself with all its confusions. Taken with his fragility you find yourself standing parallel to the Majnoun; the point of view, the angle at which the artist has chosen to enter the scene, puts you there, where he is the closest to you, as though it were an invitation, extended through the centuries to support his stooped body, to stroke his thin knees and cover his bare feet and the boyish frame that contains him – while he is unaware, completely, of all these urges.

There is cruelty somewhere in this scene; the cruelty of the text and of the artists. I don't know if this is the same Abd al-Jabbar mentioned in 'Al-Majnoun in the Wilderness' (for the structure of Majnoun's body and the colours are similar) or if Abd al-Jabbar was just the copyist and the artist was someone else, unknown to us. But it is a profound cruelty, dispersed in the fabric itself, pressing from the text and the silk on the bent frame which seems at peace with all that

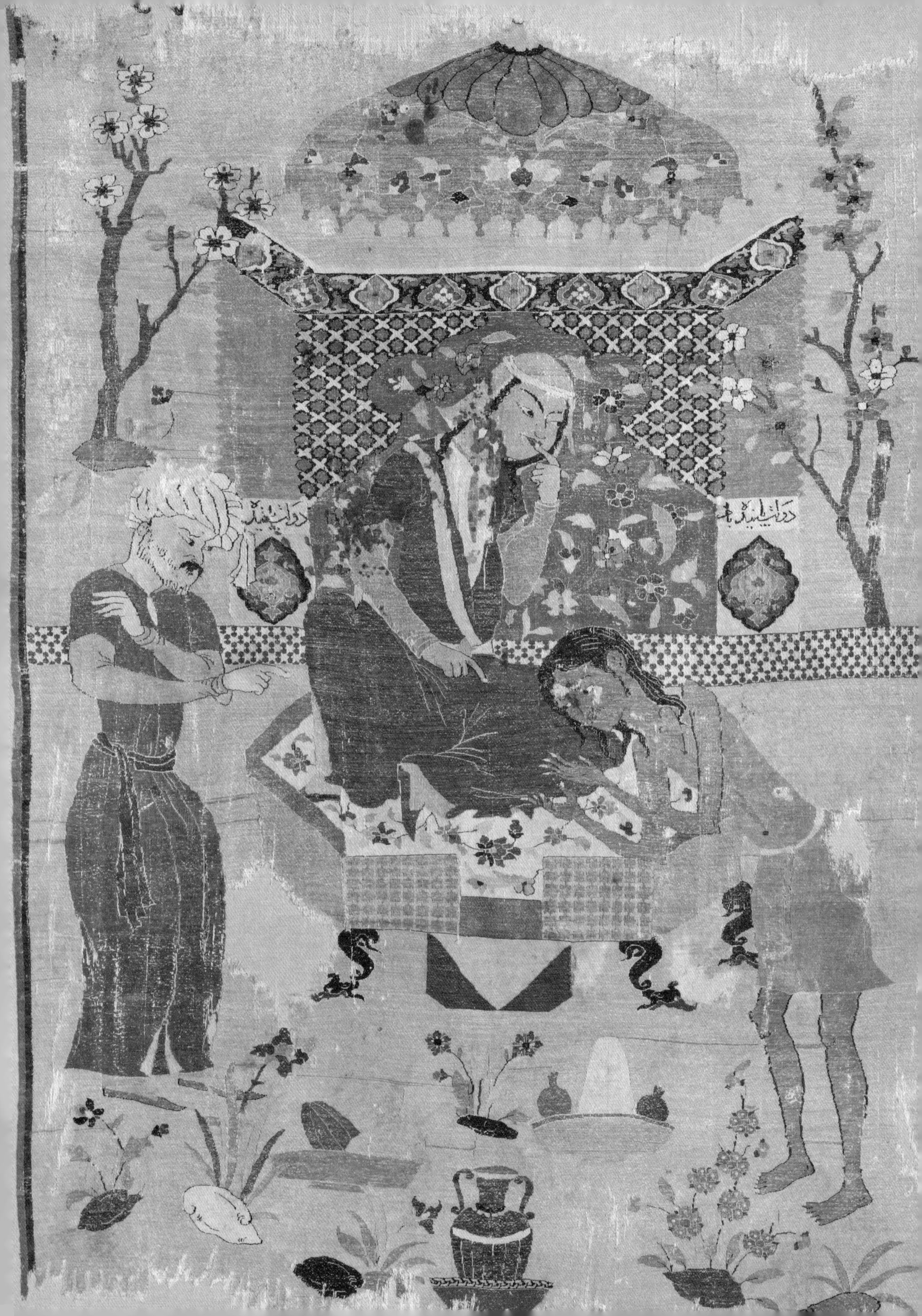

is happening: that bowed head, the eyes that have gone further than joy at meeting the beloved towards something we do not see, something outside the tapestry, while the thin-fingered hands are spread out like a mirror or a fount of prayer.

There is contentment here, an interplay between despair and obstinacy, and a compliance so profound it becomes gratitude. The power of the scene is in this absolute compliance. There is no protesting Fate's decree, as we so often find in Greek mythology, no confronting the gods or demurring at their decisions, or exploiting their alliances, their impulsiveness, their appetites or their boredom. This confrontation, this protest, is what furnishes heroism and bestows on the hero his halo and his destiny. Here, heroism is in compliance, in the attenuation of the slender body and its fragility. Compliance transforms the long road of suffering into an illuminated path towards Oneness; towards sealing the cracks and closing the gaps and cancelling the duality of the two bodies.

And it is the same fragile strength supported by loneliness and distance, that sees poetry, the shortest path to the heart and the soul, as the only instrument with which to address the world. It is the same strength that gifted al-Majnoun with the ability to make that total choice in all its degrees and exchanges: the home for the wilderness, people and family for the creatures of the wild, language for silence, confession for poetry and longing for Oneness. The journey which al-Majnoun started as a young man tending his flocks in Jabal al-Tawbad, as in the Arabic original of the tale, or as a prince and the son of the king, as Nizami – in the furthest reaches of Muslim Asia – desired, is a journey that moves with all its burden towards the self and not to any other place whatever the narrative might suggest.

The power of the work, which is also its cruelty, springs from its accuracy and from its objectifying the pathways of the story, and its open end, outside and beyond death, and its identification with the written narrative and with the transformations of the place and the creatures that inhabit it; so that the universe – propelled by the patience of the lover, his devotion and his absolute faith in his destiny – arrives at that point where all things are equal, so that the tree and the gazelle will speak, as Nizami's text says, and the narrative will continue its upward path until the moment when all dualities dissolve and merge into the amazing chemistry of Oneness.

Perhaps I have burdened this tapestry with more than it can bear, and taken it further than I intended; this too is proof of its power, the power that gives silk its authority, the power of the craftsman who carries on living and breathing in the weave and the embroidery many centuries after the work is done. This is the journey of the wall-hanging of 'Laila and the Majnoun' and the miniatures that spring out of every angle in it like whispering plants that grow and propagate themselves. This is what happened every time I stood in front of the scene, imagining the journey of the tapestry, and its stations, and those who had gazed at its characters and its details, and those who had touched its silk and gone, before it arrived here. It survived with a mastered balance; its blue with its shades like a staircase rising from the base of the work to infiltrate its space in consecutives that endorse the weight of the centre while lightly touching the flowers and the pot in front of al-Majnoun, then the base of the seat upon which Laila sits, then her two sleeves and her head-dress, rising towards that empathetic dome. Meanwhile the Messenger and the Majnoun stand in accurate extension of the two flowering branches that encircle Laila's bower so that together they form an inner frame for the scene.

When I went back to Nizami's poem in an attempt to follow the storyline that led to this scene, it was like looking for what the craftsman had hidden from the weave while maintaining its presence and its influence in the work. I was looking for what it was that had saved this scene from simply being 'skilled embroidery' on silk of a scene separated from its context, what had imbued it with the weight of the text and the destinies of its characters. In the story that Nizami worked from there are three pivotal meetings between the lovers.

The first is when al-Majnoun, with his friends, breaches Laila's private apartments at the beginning of their love. Nizami: 'When he pushed aside the curtain to the private apartment he found Laila, with her hair flowing sweetly over her shoulders, and the Majnoun stood like a loyal slave with bent head in front of her, while she held out to him a glass of wine from which the scent rose like musk.'

The second meeting is arranged by the Old Man/the Messenger who – at Laila's insistence – carries their first letters after Laila's marriage to ibn Salam and is given, according to Nizami, her ear-rings as a reward. In this meeting al-Majnoun stands, maintaining a distance between himself and Laila, and recites 'between her hands' his poetry of love and longing for her. Their third and last meeting is after ibn Salam dies and Laila's return home and her declared admission of her love for the Majnoun. This is the meeting arranged by their common friend, Zaid, and is crowned by silence and contemplation. In it the Majnoun reaches his most transcendent moment and achieves Oneness with Laila before rushing back to his wilderness, made whole by love.

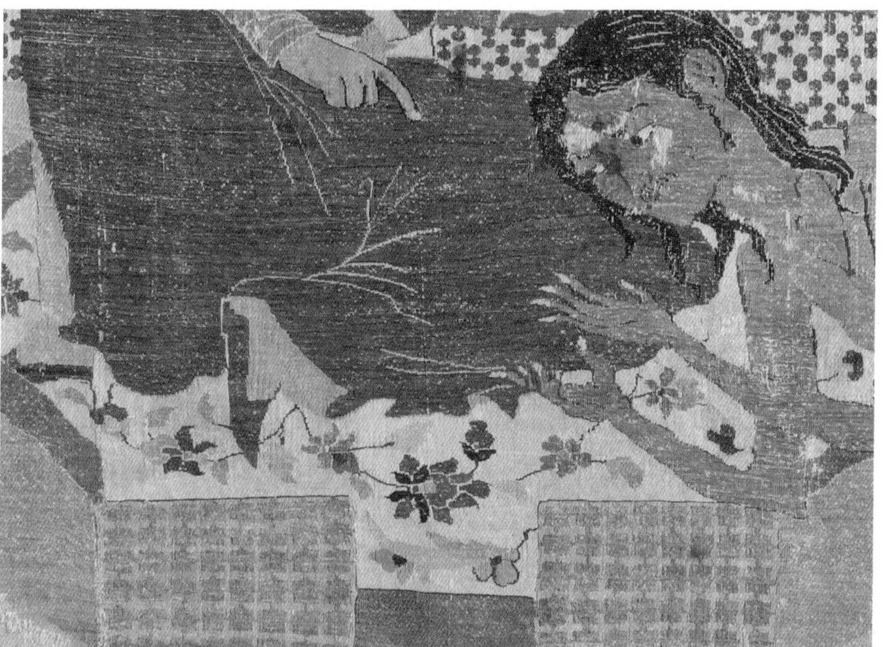

This tapestry that carries the name of the complete work, 'Laila and al-Majnoun', probably depicts the second meeting. What leads me to this conclusion is the white hair that the craftsman gave to the Messenger, for Zaid – who was present at the third meeting – was, presumably of the same age as the two lovers who are his friends. But more than that it is the nature of the meeting that posits a distance of separation between the lovers, a distance that stems from the rights of the absent husband and his invisible presence in their destinies.

In its choice of this moment the tapestry chooses the 'climax' of the work where all the components of the story meet in a scene which will soon fall apart. Every detail of the scene is of significance: the distance between the two lovers is the energy and influence of the forbidden; the husband and the father and tradition and the 'maleness' of the narration, it is also the compliance of the two lovers with that energy and that influence. Laila's elevated position, her isolation in her bower with its deliberate and luxurious ornamentation that limits her presence and her movement and guards them, as though she were on a stage or a small island, her body slightly full, curved and moving, speaking of indecision and hesitation more than it speaks of contentment or patience. Her stance reflects her ambiguous choice in accepting marriage while preserving her virginity and in seeking to meet the Majnoun but maintaining the distance between them. She has exchanged one residence for another, and a father for a husband, but remained essentially within the same space – whereas near her the space surrounding the Majnoun is poorer and more bare, the ornamentation fades to allow flowers and bushes to appear, real things and a calm nature appear at his feet in the lower position he occupies, underlined by his stoop and his emaciation. This is the power of his decisive choice and its outward signs. There is no indecision or ambiguity here: he has moved beyond the story itself and its events now have to race after him. He is no longer part of events: he is outside the story, as he is outside all norms and outside the enforcing meaning of obedience. He alone augments himself with that which he loves, and finds his place as an extension of the world surrounding him. He no longer needs to measure the distance or gaze upon the beloved or faint with longing: he has summoned everything to himself and achieved Oneness while the story rushes after his transformations in vain.

This profound, calm rebellion which has accumulated itself through a vague love story was one of my reasons for standing in front of this tapestry, for contemplating it through three days, searching for the Majnoun in me, for my transformations in my long arguments with him. Those things that I thought of as his faults and have long held against him: his impulsiveness, his fragility – and all that seems now – in the light of this stand of his – distant and marginal. Perhaps the energy of the story is located here, exactly, in the power emanating from the fragility of the lover and his aloneness/Oneness. Perhaps this is what has given the story its influence and its ability to carry on breathing so clearly in our lives, even though it was born in the perilous form of poetry and returned after a long journey in the even more perilous form of drawing or image-making.

It seems that this influence lies, also, in its position among the forbidden, in its transformations, its gaps and the missing bits of its history since its first mysterious appearance in Najd in the Arabian peninsula; an exposed story, developing with its narrators and assuming their varied forms, open to interpretation, not possessing that with which to affirm or deny itself, as it moves around aurally, with few possessions and incomplete documents: the names only, the names of the characters and of the wilderness. Poetry gave it protection and moved with it like a communal dream rebelling against silence and stealth and insisting that 'purity' lay not in concealment but in revelation and a willingness to be put to the test.

Perhaps I've found a kind of answer to my indecision regarding this Arab poet, and found it with the help of the imagination of a great Persian poet and copyists and weavers from Kashan. Or perhaps I've found a vindication of Laila; I had always thought of Laila as cruel and passive and that obedience had ruined her and destroyed the soul of the lover within her. I could not understand her silence and her barricading herself with such obdurate peace of mind behind the barrier of absolute surrender to obedience. But it, the tapestry, somehow, passed to me something of forgiveness, perhaps because of that confusion that seems to overwhelm Laila with her twisted body and her two extended forefingers. And it, the tapestry, loaded me with its questions and the mysteriousness of its journey and the hesitancy of its characters whom I left there, on the wall of the gallery, picked out by the light.

Outside the gallery, at the entrance, there were visitors walking up towards the Museum, women and men and youths pushed by the curiosity or desire aroused by the attractiveness of the building and its mystery. Families and girls and boys appeared from the rising paths and paused in front of the revealed building as though a nod of introduction took place there. This was a cause for joy. And I remembered what the Majnoun said, in one of the narratives, when he was asked about Laila and answered – summarising everything: 'I am Laila.'

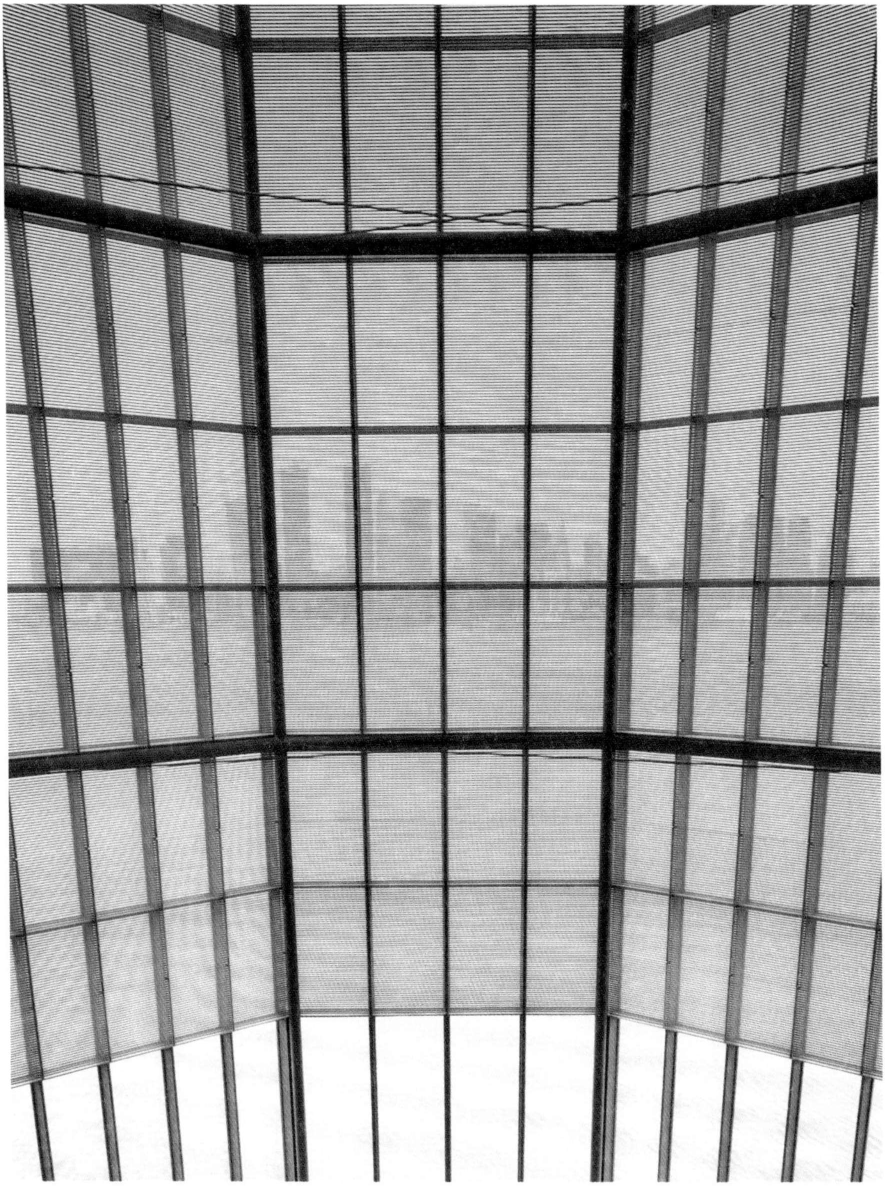

Aniconism, Huntresses and Men's Jewellery

Suad Amiry

Day One. Manhattan

The light was certainly different that day.

It was a warm autumn in 2010.

I have lived in New York City, in Manhattan, long enough to realise that this was not exactly one of the city's plays of light: it was not Manhattan's shades nor its shadows.

I have often walked across the Brooklyn Bridge, eyes mesmerised by Manhattan's high-rise wonders.

But Manhattan today looked different, very different, as I watched it from the glass curtain-wall of the five-storey atrium of the beautiful stone building where I stood.

I squinted as I stared at the reflections coming from the newly constructed metal and glass buildings to the north.

Like Manhattan, when watched from a far distance, the newly constructed city seemed like an architectural model.

The colour of the Hudson River also looked different; not dirty grey but a lovely light blue or azure.

Colours that reminded me of Zanzibar beaches and the Indian Ocean; light turquoise colours that also reminded me of the splendid fifteenth-century Iznik ceramics and tiles that I had just seen here, in the Museum of Islamic Art in Doha.

Al-Basra

I look out of the same huge glass bay window and to the left of Manhattan I see the splendour of the traditional wooden dhow boats in the West Bay area whose name, al-Khor, I learned the day after.

Someone next to me said: 'It is so *much like al-Basra*.'

From his accent I could tell he was Iraqi.

But unfortunately, unlike with Manhattan, I could not verify what he'd said.

Born in Damascus, raised in Amman; lived in Beirut; lived in Cairo.

Have been here... have been there.

Have been to Venice tens of times

But...

I have never been to Baghdad or to al-Basra, once known as the 'Venice of the Middle East'.

I looked out of the window and I started recalling my geography class – or was it my history teacher? '*Dhow sail boats carried the famous al-Basra dates and went to India where they exchanged their delicious dates for fine Indian tea and tiles. And when they went to Africa, they exchanged al-Basra dates for mangrove poles to build their houses and spices for the delicious al-Basra style meals.*'

I thought of New York and I thought of al-Basra.

I feared that next time I came to this beautiful building there would be more of Manhattan and much less of al-Basra, if anything at all.

It takes a Chinese genius like architect I.M. Pei to have a bay window tell us so much about the future of the world in which we live today.

But who knows better than the Chinese who once ruled the world. And they are on their way to do it again. And the Silk Routes of Old China are today's routes of Gucci, Armani, Versace, Lacoste, to mention only a few.

And when I went back to my hotel room I Googled al-Basra to get to know it better but all I got were more and more photos of American soldiers.

I fell asleep that night thinking of Manhattan and of al-Basra.

And I cried.

Day Two. Animals Have the Lion's Share

I walked once, I walked twice, I walked a third time.
I went on a first round; I went on a second round and on a third.

There were animals here, animals there, and animals everywhere. On an exquisite tapestry called Franchetti: a phoenix, a deer, birds of paradise and imaginary and weird creatures; on breathtaking silk textiles, on a huge Persian carpet, in the world's greatest paintings of the *Shahnameh* of Ferdowsi and on the sixteenth-century Persian Ardabil carpet.

More animals on art works: a dotted yellow goat on a glazed Iznik tile, four dogs on a green ceramic tile, a brass candle-holder with three exotic animals as its base, a bird on a beautiful brown and white metallic glaze bowl from tenth-century Iraq, a rare horse design on a ninth-century Abbasid blown glass. I learned that birds, rabbits and lions were quite common, but a horse was rather rare. A camel on another light brown flask, an animal farm on wood with whole scenes of hunting, a dagger with a beautiful white jade horse. Ducks carved on an eleventh-century Sicilian ivory hunting horn, another stunning hunting horn with a tiger on one end and a number of animals attacking one another on the other end. Flocks of deer drawn on splendid sixteenth-century Iranian lacquered wood, two happy donkeys – one black, another white – on a page in *The Usefulness of Animals* by Ibn Bakhtishu from fourteenth-century Iran, a charming little turquoise ceramic statue of a monkey with two round holes for eyes and a very sad brass owl. An Indian powder flask with two ends: a dragon and a goose. And an absolutely adorable little cast statue of a green cow and her baby calf from thirteenth-century Syria. A ceramic flask in the form of a cat, and, finally, armour mounted on a full-size metal horse.

Then, there were human figures here, human figures there, and depictions of human scenes everywhere.

A seventeenth-century 'Laila and Majnoun' tapestry from Kashan, a portrait of the nineteenth-century Fateh Ali Shah by the artist Mir Shah. That was fun and interesting, as I had not realised that portraits were such an essential feature of Islamic art.

And soon after I passed by a happily smiling head of a male statue in stucco. I leaned forward and read: 'a rare example of human representation of Medieval Islamic Saljuq period known for their use of figurative representation'. At that exact moment I stopped and pondered: with so many figurative representations was Islam truly aniconic?

Aniconism

And if you're wondering what 'aniconism' means I can tell you that yes, an icon came to mean a religious (Orthodox and Catholic) art work; an oil painting that depicted a religious theme; but an icon could simply mean an image, a picture or a representation, and hence an-iconism is anti-icons, anti-image, anti-picture and anti-representations.

But with the exception of the calligraphy and pages from the Qur'an, the majority of objects in this collection (or for that matter in any other Islamic collection) illustrate that aniconism in Islam has been overemphasised, as has the 'importance' and 'high regard' for Arabic calligraphy (sometimes wrongly referred to as Islamic).

There is no doubt that calligraphy was a unifying art form in a vast and culturally varied Muslim world that included most of the world's ancient cultures and languages. Hence calligraphy was seen as a shared common Islamic heritage. Perhaps calligraphy should be seen in the same light as Arabic as a language: both the Arabic language and calligraphy were perceived as important means of spreading Islam, hence their role and importance have perhaps been overstated.

Day Three. Women Hunters and Men's Jewellery

One thing that never ceases to amaze me is how much one can learn from an art object: whether it's a ceramic plate, a painting, a glass vase, a miniature, or, in this case, superb seventeenth-century Safavid silk panels. But also how essential it is to have a profound knowledge of history to understand and fully appreciate and enjoy the object. I may be stating the obvious but how much one needs to be reminded of the obvious. History might very well be the only factor that separates a Roman column from one made yesterday, assuming that both were of high quality and superb craftsmanship.

Realising that the MIA had invited a number of writers, rather than experts and scholars of Islamic art, made me less anxious about writing or 'reflecting' on one of its artworks. So, relaxed I wondered around the impressive architectural spaces of the Museum. And with as much fascination I experienced the dazzling Exhibition Halls designed by the French architect and interior designer Jean-Michel Wilmotte.

As I wandered around the many fascinating objects on the two floors (one organised by periods and countries: early Islamic art, Iran and Asia twelfth-fourteenth century, etc; and one by themes: figurative art, writing in art and calligraphy) many objects engaged me emotionally, aesthetically, and intellectually.

I first contemplated writing about a beautifully illustrated seven-metre-long *Hajj* certificate (MS.267), which mentioned Jerusalem as one of the *Hajj* stations, one of the cities that Muslims had to visit so as to complete their religious duty and be given a proof of pilgrimage. It truly saddened me to see how the majority of Muslims cannot make it to Jerusalem today and can never receive such a beautifully decorated certificate. I also contemplated writing about the thirteenth-century Seljuk head: the one and only statue in the collection (SW.74). I was attracted to write about it not only because of its rarity but because of the warm smile with which it received me. Something about his smile made me recall the *Mona Lisa*. He was much older than her; he was born in Iran around 1200 (596 AH), while she was born in Italy 300 years later.

Being an architect I could have written about the splendid architecture of the Museum or one of its many fascinating architectural elements and details, or for that matter on one of the many architectural elements in the MIA's splendid collection, such as the tenth-century Umayyad columns' capitals that came from the ruins of al-Zahra city in Andalusia, or the intricate geometric and floral details of the ninth-century stucco panels from al-Samra' in Iraq.

At the end of my three-day visit to the museum, two objects remained with me (I wish): the seventeenth-century Safavid silk velvet panel (TE.204), and the breathtaking Shah Jahan white jade pendant: the haldili (JE.85) (1631-2/1040 AH).

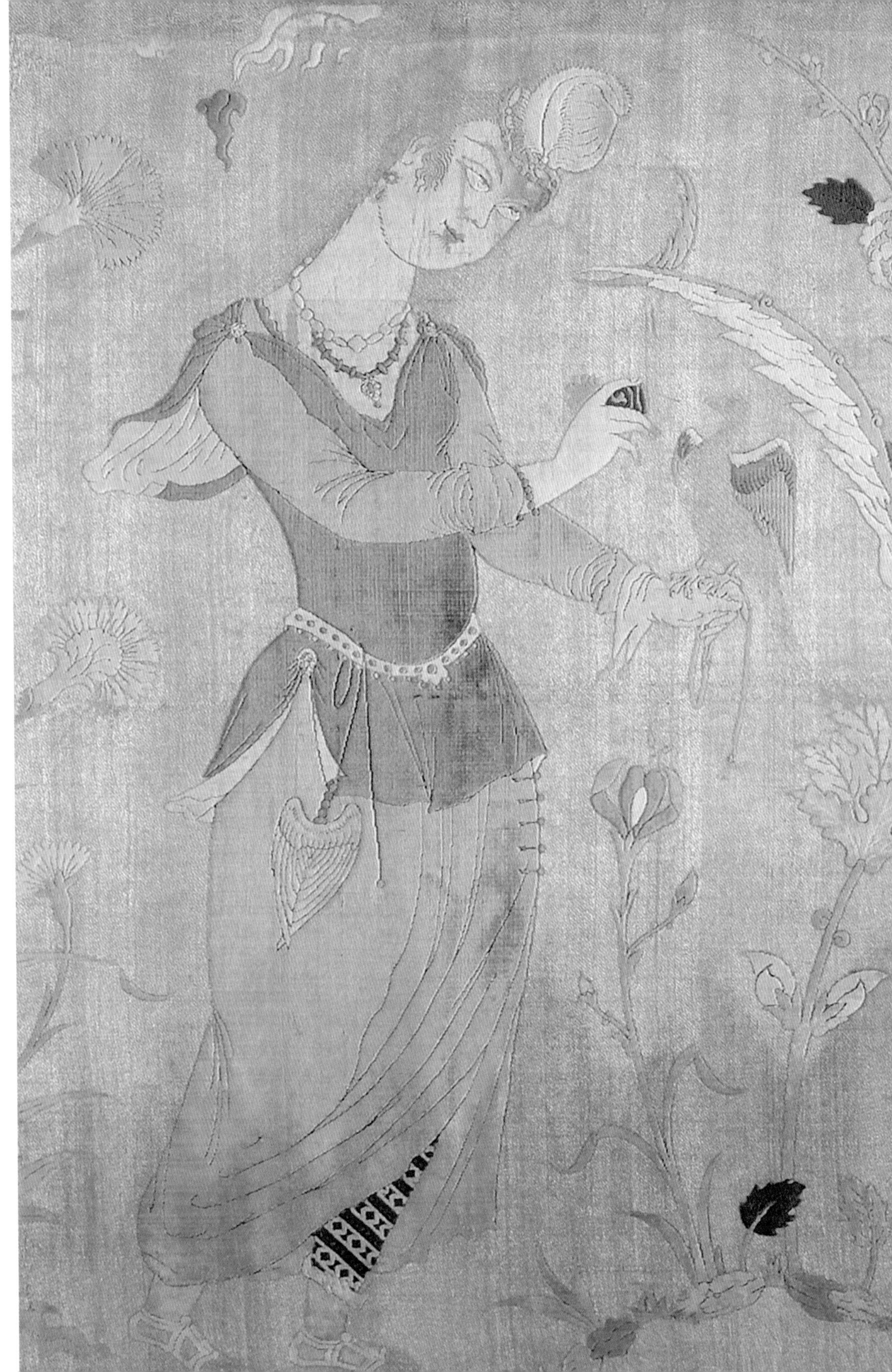

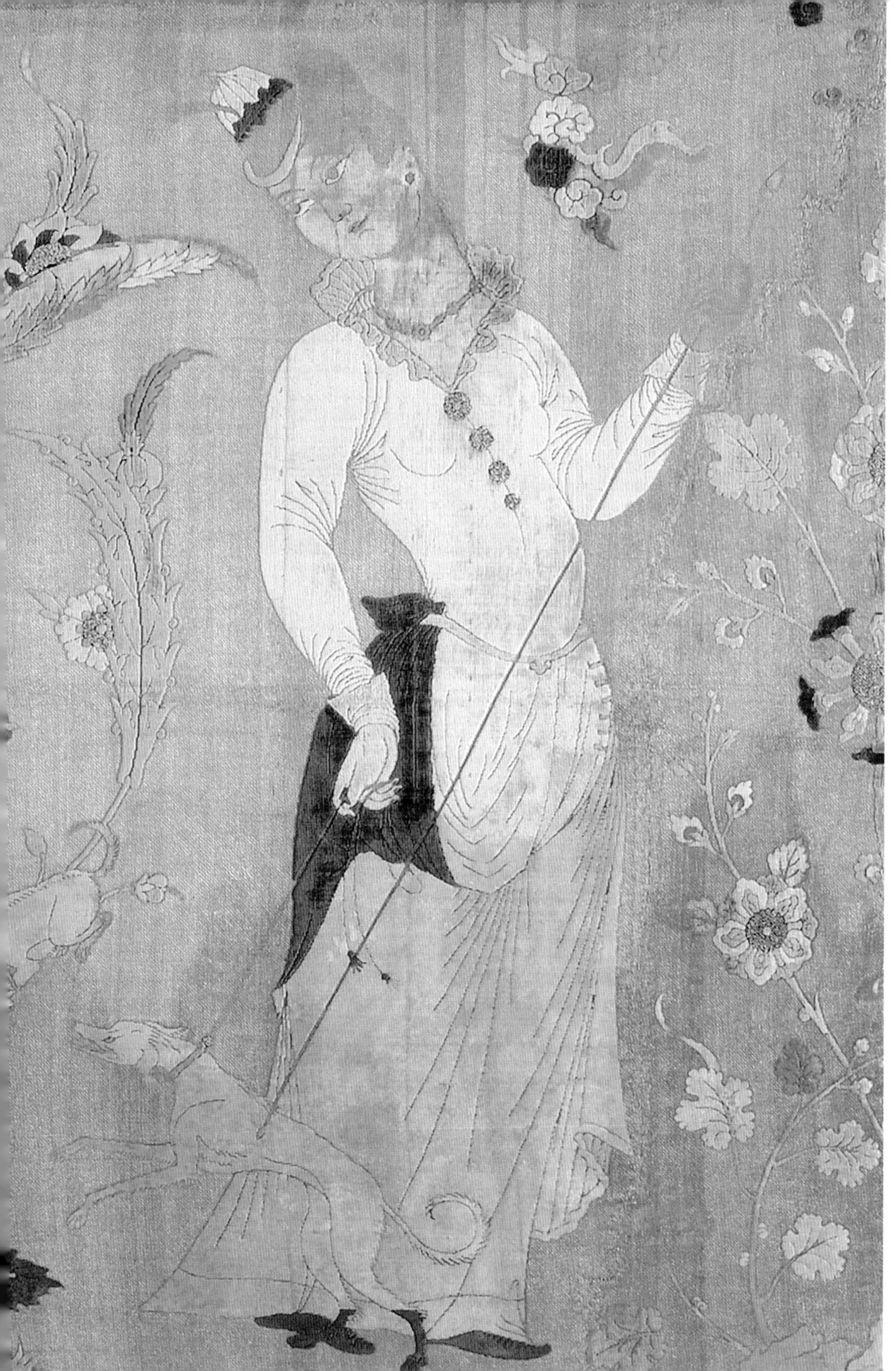

In addition to their superb qualities and beauty, it was their motifs – women hunters and men's jewellery – that fascinated me. It is believed that Shah Jahan wore this jade pendant so as to ease his heart and reduce his grief while building Taj Mahal to the memory of his beloved wife Mumtaz. Finally I opted for *the one*; one of the world's masterpieces of silk velvet panels.

Lady Falconers: Guilty or Innocent?

I must admit that the starting point was one of the two dogs, who looked exactly like my little dog, Nammoura. But soon my eyes were captured by the hat of the elegant aristocratic woman on the right, then her ruby necklace and ear-rings, the drapes of her white silk dress, and its dark and deep burgundy lining, which matched the pointed velvety shoes. Her peaceful and totally relaxed expression was in sharp contrast to the fighting mood of her little dog, which she held on a tight leash.

The facial expressions and features, as well as the less formal clothing, still as exuberant in style and colours, made me believe that the woman standing opposite her in this exquisite composition must have been her daughter. The small yellow hat, the drapes of her orange gold dress and the velvet brown sleeveless blouse perfectly matched the striped trousers under her dress. But the one detail that caught my eye was the movements of her two hands. It took me a bit of time to figure out that a fine bird was actually perched on her left fist. A close look at the silk velvet made me realise that the white, orange and light green patches were actually the wings of a bird. The light beige or gold of the falcon made it difficult to see at first. A closer look at her right hand and I realised that the small red object she was carrying was indeed a falcon hood. So, after all, these two aristocratic women in front of me were actually hunters, and that was rather intriguing. This made me look into the history of women hunters and falconers. It also threw me into an ocean of information on the most venerated Greek goddess, Artemis, the Roman goddess of the hunt, Diana, and Kochiku, who is believed to have been the first Japanese falconer, and her only daughter, who was also a falconer.

So are we looking at a Persian version of Kochiku and her daughter? Were these women real falconers? It seems that from the ninth century on, falconry, and perhaps also women's falconry, was common in the Middle East. Or are the two ladies simply an allegory of the hunt similar to

Artemis and Diana? Being totally against hunting as a hobby (as opposed to survival hunting) I was hoping it would be the second. The more I looked into this matter the more difficult it became to give a fair verdict as more and more possibilities appeared: 'Safavid fascination with falconry... was not only seen as a popular pastime but also a symbol of sophistication and wealth,'[1] or, 'it is known that falcons were given as presents to Chinese princes as early as 2200 BC, but these may have been for pets and not for hunting,' writes Lydia Ash in her website, 'The Modern Apprentice; Falconry, Ecology, Education.'[2]

But also throughout history, hunting as a motif has been very popular, not only for textile and carpet weavers, but also in other art forms. The collection of this museum is proof of that. Actually hunting scenes were so popular that they gave rise to a particular type of carpets called, appropriately, 'hunting carpets'.

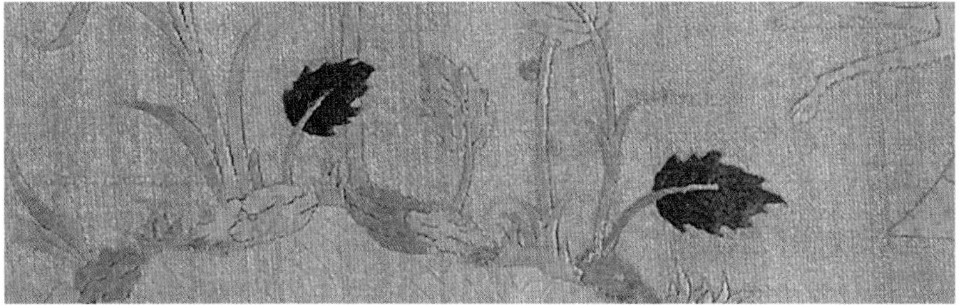

My obsession to figure out whether these women were guilty or innocent made me forget to look into another issue: was the elongated form and the movement of the flowering irises and carnations, which filled the central part of the panel, more Chinese, European, or Pompeian in influence? Realising the strong ties between Safavid Iran and Europe, particularly during the reign of Shah Abbas II (1624-60/1033-70 AH), makes me believe it was the second.

Wanting to end my article with a verdict that these two beautiful Safavid women were completely innocent and were only trying to impress the West, I am simply amazed by how much one can learn from an exquisite silk velvet panel like this one. Or for that matter from the tens of absolutely splendid other items in this fine collection.

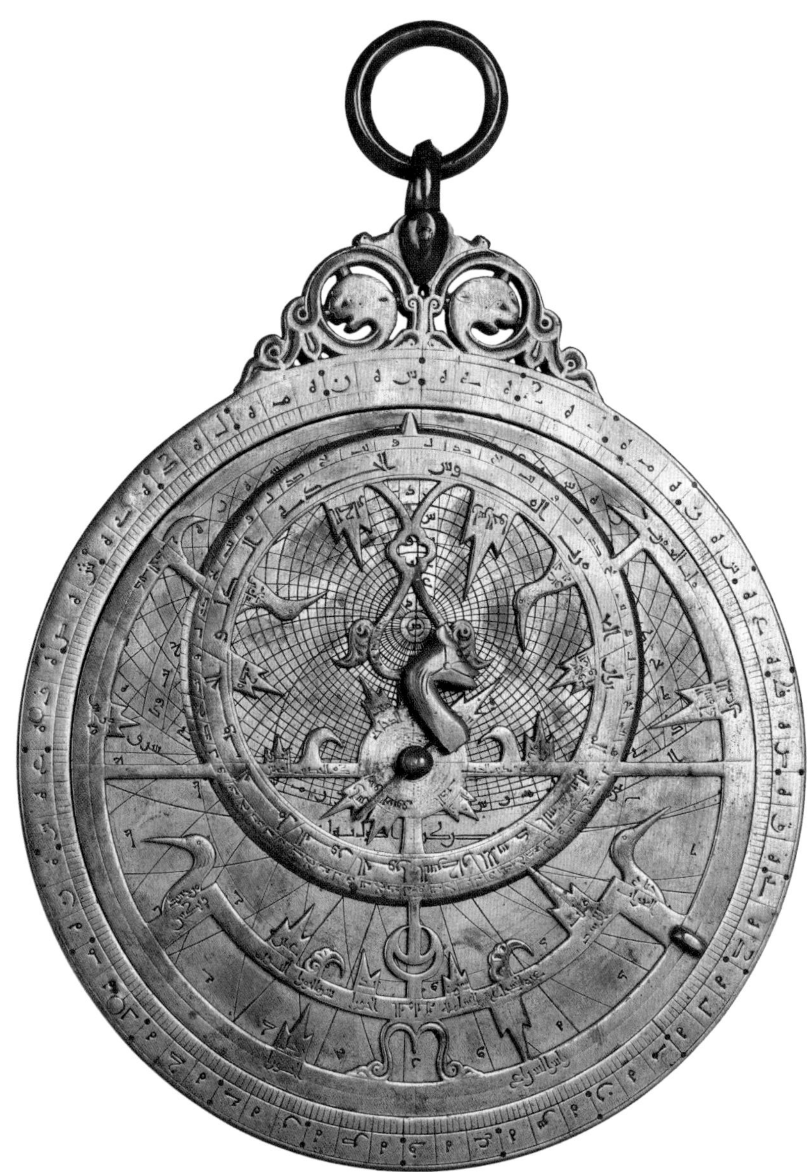

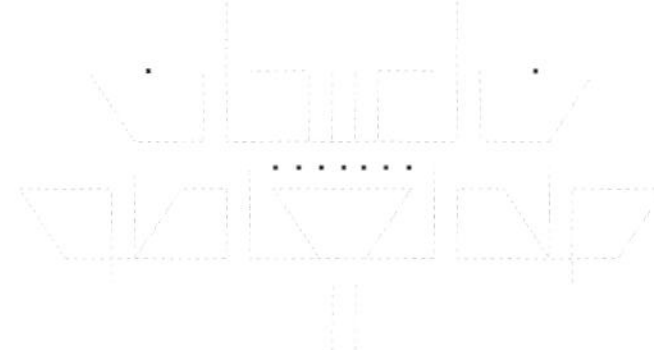

Infinity's Watchman

Bejan Matur

I.

Whispered to me
through letters and signs;
in this tenth century a place,
a peak.
Waiting at the stop near him is one
who seeks a base for the cosmos.
And the base that appears on the seventh sign
Is the mercy of God.

I.

Harfler ve işaretler boyunca fısıldanan
Söylendi bana.
Onuncu yüzyılda bir yer
Bir zirve.
Allaha yakın o durakta beklemekte biri.
Bir kaide aramakta kainat için.
Ve yedinci levhada beliren kaide
Tanrının şefkatidir.

II.

Here's what I heard!
My curiosity didn't kill me.
As maps of the world
were still in embryonic blue and unclear
I asked the cosmos my question.
And I heard the sound.
The colliding of distant galaxies
whispered to me like music
and gates opened.
What was clear in the sky's six levels

II.

Duydum işte!
Merakım öldürmedi beni.
Yeryüzünün haritaları
Henüz cenin maviliğinde ve belirsizken
Kainata sordum sorumu.
Ve duydum sesi.
Uzak galaksilerin çakışması
Bir müzik olarak fısıldandı bana.
Böylece kapılar açıldı.
Göğün altı katında beliren

found meaning in seven
and appeared to me.
I saw what would be.
My gaze reached him.

III.
Undoubtedly there's a beginning that reaches
from a lake shore right to the desert.
A conversation never heard before
in the blue-tiled city of sounds.
Winged by carnations and pomegranates
Colours mingle with desire.
In the same lake reflections begin,
stars descend to the waters.
So the cosmos
fits into a lake.

IV.
More whispers to me.
The pain of pomegranate and narcissus flowers.
Beauty,
This melancholy sense of the fullness of being.
What comfort in closeness can it find?
How often?
Here I was,
Being long ago whispered in my ear
I was asked for a measurement
A decision was expected,
And it's now in my palm.
What began in Iznik and travelled to Baghdad
And as far as Andalusia.

Ve yedide mana bulan
Göründü bana.
Olacağı gördüm.
Bakışım ulaştı Allaha.

III.
Kuşkusuz bir başlangıç var
Bir göl kıyısından, çöle ulaşan.
Mavi çini seslerinin şehrinde
Hiç duyulmamış bir konuşma.
Narların ve karanfillerin kanatlandırdığı renkler
Karışır isteğe .
Aynı gölde yansıma başlar
Sulara iner yıldızlar.
Böylece kainat
Bir göle sığar.

IV.
Daha fazlası bana fısıldanan.
Narların ve nergislerin bildiği acı.
Bir güzellik,
Varlıkla dolu olmaktan duyulan bu hüzün.
Hangi yakınlıkla teselli bulacak?
Hangi aralıkla?
İşte buraydım
Kulağıma çoktan fısıldandı varlık
Benden istenen bir ölçü
Bir karar benden beklenen,
Ve avucumda artık.
İznik'te başlayıp Bağdat'a giden
Endülüs'e uzanan

Is not only wonder
It's love.

V.
So the cosmos turns to the tongue of tigers;
mingled with the stripes of tigers
are the prophet's sharpened swords...
While the feuds of his sons continue
the stars assess the spilling of blood,
the harmony and justice
of night.
What takes places in the heart is mourning.
The desert where a sister
Talked in her sleep.
Signs throughout mourning.
Pain brings us closer to him in the heart.

VI.
For signs and numbers
Hide in the tiger's stripes.
Latitudes meet in the stripes of tigers
And perhaps in the tiger's mind
That's how we hang from the cosmos.

Questions began in the desert.
The sky magnified by the Ascension in Iran
Called me.
On the brink of the soul, near the heart
The eye longing for light
Saw the flight.

Merak değildir sadece.
Aşktır.

V.
Böylece kaplanların diline döner kainat.
Kaplanların çizgilerinde karışır
Bilenmiş peygamber kılıçları...
Ve oğulların hesabı sürerken
Yıldızlar kanı saymaya başlar.
Ahengi gecenin
Ve adaleti.
Kalpte yer eden yastır.
Bir kız kardeşin
Sayıkladığı çöl.
Taşınan yas boyunca işaretler.
Acıdır kalpte Allaha yaklaştırır.

VI.
Çünkü sayılar ve işaretler
Kaplanların çizgilerinde saklanır.
Kaplanların çizgilerinde buluşur enlemler.
Belki de oradan asılıyız kainata.
Kaplanın düşüncesinde.

Bir çölde başladı sorular.
Harran'da miracın büyüttüğü gök
Çağırdı beni.
Kalbe yakın, ruhun kıyısında
Işığı sayıklayan göz
Gördü gidişi.

As I walked barefoot the distance I felt
Was just the beginning.
The angel asked,
'Mother, what's God?'
'It's infinity, child,
And it has no end...'

VII.

Stardust and truth.
The heart's knowledge is tied in knots.
I want to hear the sky.
I'm in search of a hilltop
where I can stop and count the latitudes.
The sky-dome is growing warm in my palm
bringing distance near.
In my hands are the stars
I brought them down,
Included them in the heart.
I aligned the cosmos with the heart.
All the stars that sailors watch
have foreign names, unfamiliar.
'*Wega, alfata, miraç,*
Aiferaz, rigil, alta hir,'
All, all point north of the desert
Giving direction to travellers.
Arabic letters that unite sky and land.
Belief that makes a home of the sky.

VIII.

To those on the ocean sky is a desert.
The only salvation for sailors

Yalın ayak yürürken duyduğum uzaklık
Başlangıçtı.
Böylece melek sordu,
Anne tanrı nedir?
Sonsuzluktur yavrum,
Ama sonu yok onun da...

VII.

Yıldız tozu ve hakikat.
Kalbin bildiği düğümlendi.
Bir tepe arıyorum gökyüzünü duyacağım.
Enlemleri sayacağım bir durak.
Gökkubbenin avucumda ısınmasıdır
Uzağı yakın eden.
Ellerimde çünkü yıldızlar.
İndirdim onları, kalbe ekledim.
Kalbin hizasına koydum
Kainatı.
Denizcilerin baktığı bütün yıldızlar
Başka dilde ve yaban.
Wega, alfata, miraç,
Aiferaz, rigil, altahir,
Hepsi ama hepsi
Çölden kuzeye gitmekte.
Ve yol göstermekte yolculara.
Kıtaları, gökyüzünü birleştiren Arap harfleri.
Gökyüzünü ev yapan inanç.

VIII.

Okyanusta gökyüzü bir çöldür.
Sadece denizcilerin bildiği kurtuluş

Comes from the land.
He who turns our hearts inside out
In the end is the One
The One who envelops our hearts.

IX.
A touch of God's hands
Tests me.
While earth's darkness dreams of him
And cosmic darkness wonders.
Now we move on the same latitude
Bedazzled and blinded by the same light.
My heart teaches me a language
The language of distance,
In my pocket the words of infinity.
Passing over all eras I travel to the lands
Of Andalusia, Greece,
In the loneliness of far-off islands
I greet the poets.
Children who gaze at the sky in wonder.
My thin fingers blinded with feeling.
The footstep I leave on earth
Is heavy as a horse's hoofs
But I stretch the neck of a racing-horse
To the stars.
Long ago the music of the cosmos
Included the language of birds and plants,
Bird-beaks and scribbles of marginal décor.
I look once more
On earth his breath is near me.
He takes me

Karadan esirgenen.
Çünkü kalbimizi evirip çeviren
Odur nihayetinde.
Odur kalbimizi sarmalayan.

IX.
Tanrının elleriyle başlayan bir dokunuş
Yokluyor beni.
Karanlığı yeryüzünün Allahı sayıklarken
Karanlığı kainatın merakken.
Şimdi aynı enlemde ilerliyoruz.
Aynı duyuş ve kamaşma.
Kalbim bana bir dil öğretiyor.
Uzaklığın dilini
Sonsuzluğun kelimeleri cebimde
Bütün çağları aşarak gidiyorum kıtalara
Endülüste, Yunanda,
Uzak adaların yalnızlığında
Şairleri selamlıyorum.
Merak içinde gökyüzüne bakan çocukları.
İncecik parmaklarım kamaşmış histen.
Bir atın toynakları kadar ağır
Yeryüzünde bıraktığım adım.
Bir atın boynunu uzatıyorum
Yıldızlara.
Kuşların ve bitkilerin dili çoktan katıldı
Müziğine kainatın.
Kuşların gagası yıldızların kenar süsü çoktan.
Ve bir kez daha bakıyorum
Yeryüzünde Allahın soluğu bana yaklaşıyor.
Alıyor benliğimi

I'm his.
He gives me wonder.
He turns my heart's darkness into poetry
For in his darkness a jewel is hidden.
The glow that appears to us as a star
Is a sacred sign.

X.
I'm a pilgrim,
barefoot from the hills of Rey
on the way to Baghdad,
a farmer on his earth
scratching the earth to find a star
saluting the water-wells with joy.

XI.
In the farthest realms,
The collision of cosmic planets
the sadness of Pluto, the anger of Mars,
and a generous beauty, consoling as Venus,
embedded in my soul.
On the plains of my soul
infinity's riders are running.
I gaze at distant lands,
the world intersected by latitudes.
The equator piercing my heart.
It grows old.

XII.
I draw the stuff of the world to my soul
dragging its atlas behind me

Onunum.
Merakımı yapan o.
Karanlığı kalbimde şiire dönüştüren o.
Çünkü onun karanlığında mücevher gizlidir.
Bize yıldız gibi görünen o parıltı
Bir ayettir.

X.
Reyy'in tepelerinden yalın ayak
Bağdat'a giden
Bir yolcuyum
Allahın toprağında bir çiftçi.
Bir yıldız bulmak için toprağı eşeleyen
Kuyuların gözlerinden öpen.

XI.
En uzağında
Kainatın gezegenlerin çakışması.
Plütonun hüznü, marsın öfkesi.
Ve Venüs kadar teselli verici bir güzellik.
Hepsi ruhumda yerleşmiş
Ruhumun düzlüğünde
Sonsuzluğun atlıları koşturmakta.
Bakıyorum uzak kıtalara.
Enlemelerin ve paralellerin kestiği bu dünya.
Kalbimden geçen bu ekvator.
Eskiyor.

XII.
Atlasını geçirerek ruhuma çektim
Peşimden kumaşını dünyanın.

Earth's cities behind me
Are dreaming of him.
Each longs to become a star.
In the house of truth
I immerse bird-beaks in the planets.
They bring me stardust,
light from the atoms of a star.
I yearn for closeness to give me comfort.
I could find meaning if I could touch it.
My heart full of worry but never of doubt
I walked the hilltops
barefoot.
I went on alone.
In that solitude he
was waiting in a hollowed-out tank.
He looked at me with a long, expectant gaze.
'Go,' he said,
'make your family from my earth.'

Peşimden gelen yeryüzü şehirleri
Sayıklamakta Allahı.
Yıldız olmayı dilemekte her biri.
O hakikat evinde
Kuşların gagalarını daldırıyorum gezegenlere.
Bana yıldız tozu taşıyorlar.
Yıldız zerrelerinden ışık.
Beni teselli edecek bir yakınlık arzusundayım.
Dokunsam bulacağım anlamı.
Kalbim kaygılı evet ama kuşkulu değil hiç.
Yürüdüm tepeleri
Yalınayak.
Yalnızlık içinde ilerledim.
O yalnızlıkta Allah
İçi oyulmuş bir haznede bekliyordu.
Çook beklemiş bir bakışla baktı bana.
Ve gidin dedi
Soyunuzu çekin toprağımdan.

XIII.
The language that comes to us in solitude
is poetry.
Wonder crowned with the language of stars.

XIII.
Bize yalnızlıkta gelen dil
Şiirdir.
Yıldızların diliyle taçlanan merak...

XIV.
Now is the start and finish of all seasons.
This rusty metal sheet I hold in my palm
is a star-seeker.
What I look at is a rusty cluster of stars,
a rusty galaxy in the soul.

XIV.
Şimdi bütün mevsimlerin başlangıcı ve sonu.
Avucumda tuttuğum bu paslanmış levha
Bir yıldız arayıcısıdır.
Pas tutmuş bir yıldız kümesidir baktığım.
Pas tutmuş bir galaksi ruhta.

XV.	XV.
What era's darkness is falling on me,	Hangi çağın karanlığı bu üzerime gelen.
the weight of what star?	hangi yıldızın ağırlığı?
I've dreamed of distant planets,	Uzak gezegenleri hayal ederdim
On clear nights.	Berrak gecelerde.
The sadness of stars	Kendine bile uzak
Far even from themselves.	Yıldızların hüznünü.
My slender fingers searched	İnce parmaklarım kutup çizgisi boyunca
For a scale on the Polar line,	Bir ölçüyü aradı,
For what the heart feels.	kalpte duyulanı...
There must be a further dimension.	Ötesi olmalı.
Yes, darkness,	Karanlık evet
But long ago the soul's origin was tied to light.	Ama ruhun kuşağı çoktan bağlandı ışığa
The map that carried us is tired.	Ve bizi taşıyan harita yorgun.
My fingers trace the sky sunk in a dome.	Parmaklarım bir kubbeye dalmış göğü izliyor.
They wish for a closeness the sky denies.	Göğün esirgediği yakınlığı istiyor.
To understand distance...	uzağı bilmek...
But there's the soul,	Ama ruh var
before all questions, the soul.	Bütün sorulardan önce ruh var.
The tropical zone	Tende bir yara gibi derinleşen
Deepening like a physical wound	Bu tropik kuşak
Calls all the stars.	Bütün yıldızları çağırdı.
XVI.	XVI.
I'm alone	Yalnızım işte.
On the brink of discovery.	Bir keşif durağındayım.
I was sick with an illness from afar	uzak hastalığına tutuldum.
an illness sensitive to starlight.	yıldız ışığını duyma hastalığına.
Now all the learned who speak of stardust	Şimdi yıldız tozundan söz eden bütün alimler
Live in the Zodiac's house of poetry.	Şiir burcundalar.
Now the souls touched with starlight	şimdi yıldız tozuna bulanan ruhlar

Are building a cosmos.	Bir kainat kuruyorlar.
Galaxies stir within me	içimde kımıldayan galaksiler
each one a garland.	her biri bir çiçek demeti.
Within me a heart cold and lonely as Pluto...	İçimde Plüto kadar yalnız ve soğuk bir kalp...
but still aware.	ama duyuyor yine de.
Of existence...	Olanı...
Under this dark dome	Bu karanlık kubbenin altında
It is the heart I try to sense.	Duymaya çalıştığım yürektir.
What I strive to know are the causes.	Sebeplerdir bilmeye çalıştığım.
An image overflowing all the seas	Bütün denizleri aşan bir hayal
and sadness in the heart.	ve hüzün yürekte.
We must begin from the first event	ilk olandan başlamalı
from the birth of darkness.	Karanlığın doğumundan.
XVII.	XVII.
Named by Allah and the sky together	Göğün ve Allahın aynı anda
A map of 'humanity'	'İnsan' dediği bir harita
Opens before me.	Açılıyor önümde.
On the metal sheet	Kalbe yakın tutulmaktan incelmiş
Worn thin by the clasp to the heart	O levhada
There's the question of truth wherever I turn.	Nereye dönsem hakikat sorusu.
It must begin from the uttermost dark.	En karanlık olandan başlamalı.
Space opened	Atların toynakları yer yüzüne vurduğunda
When horses' hoofs struck the earth.	Açılan mekan.
The manes of horses and stars in one quadrant	Bir kadranda yıldızların ve atların yelesi
Stars and manes endlessly mingled,	Yıldızlar ve yeleler karışmış sonsuzda
And throughout space the piercing gaze	Ve uzay boyunca deliren bakış
The unending sky...	Bitmez gökyüzü...

XVIII.
We know the angel's reply.
In the tenth century with the eyes
of all mankind a man looked at the sky,
extending the beaks of birds
To the cluster of stars.
All stars begin in the heart
then are joined to infinity.
Sadness never lets them sleep.
Darkness never lets them sleep.
Curiosity, rider of the heart
drives us on.
It adds space to time.
It is love.

XVIII.
Meleğin cevabı biliniyor
Onuncu yüzyılda bütün insanlığın gözleriyle
gökyüzüne bakan bir adam.
kuşların gagalarını
Yıldız kümelerine uzatan.
Bütün yıldızlar kalpte başlar
Sonra eklenir sonsuzluğa.
Bu hüzün onu uyutmaz
Uyutmaz onu karanlık.
Merak yüreğin atlısıdır
Peşinden koşturur insanı.
Ve zamana mekanı ekler.
Bu aşktır.

XIX.
At the astrolabe's base
Is a horse with a fiery mane.
It waits for an abode.
And counts the heart.

XIX.
Usturlabımın kaidesinde
Yeleleri ateşten bir at.
Mekanı beklemekte.
Ve saymakta yüreği...

XX.
When the magnetic needles
Of heart and infinity agree,
That is God.
The vast realm of infinity lies in our palm.

Am I to make known
An unknown birth of the cosmos?
This astrolabe
Worn thin by the clasp to the heart.

XX.
Kalp ibresi
Sonsuzluğun ibresiyle kesiştiğinde
İşte tanrı.
Sonsuzluk avucumuzda büyük bir ülke.

Ben miyim
Bilinmeyen bir doğuda kainatı bilinir kılan.
Kalbe yakın tutulmaktan incelmiş
Bu usturlab

My fingers from wonder become a soul.	Meraktan ruh olmuş parmaklarım.
Everywhere a vein that he knows	Ve Allahın evirip çevirdiği her yerde
Through and through.	Bir damar.
Ah, I am weary of darkness.	Yorgunum ah karanlığı duymaktan.
I am weary of stars	Yorgunum nabız gibi bana göz kırpan
That blink at me like a pulse.	Yıldızlardan.
XXI.	XXI.
The cosmos of thousands of years.	Bin yılların kainatı
Its waiting	Ve bekleyişi
Is pain.	Acıdır.
For the origin of feeling is darkness.	Çünkü karanlıktır duyguların başlangıcı.
The heart of man is wonder.	Merak insanın kalbidir
He sees immensities with the heart,	Yürekle görür uzakları.
His eyes deep as the stars.	Yıldızlar kadar derin gözler.
The gaze of a thousand years	Bin yıl öncesinin bakışı
Poured into this day.	Bu güne akmış.
The music of wonder	Hayret makamı
Of children	Çocukların
Of poets	Şairlerin
Of scholars	Ve alimlerin
Transports the soul like love.	Aşk gibi uzağa götüren ruhu.
I've waited so long	Öyle çok bekledim ki
that an Ascension passed above me	Bir miraç geçti üzerimden
Galaxies passed.	Geçti üzerimden galaksiler.
Whispered to the prophet on the Ascension,	O miraçta peygambere fısıldanan
'Put your foot on the other'	'Ayağını diğer ayağının üzerine koy'
Your foot on the other...	Ayağını diğer ayağının üzerine...
Just then	Tam o anda
A colliding star	Bir yıldız çakışması
Just then	Kalbin ibresinin doğrulması

The heart's magnetic needle points true.
The cosmos is revealed before us
And the horses' wings flame with love.
The conjunction.
Consciousness gone long ago,
touches mankind.
Our own ascension is in the heart
Our own ascension
takes place in him.

O anda.
Kainat açılırken önümüzde
Atların kanatları aşktan yanarken.
O kavuşma.
Çook önce gitmiş olan bilinç
insanı yoklar.
Bizim miracımız kalptedir
Allahta yer eder
bizim miracımız.

XXII.

So
Man who looked at the sky to find him
Turned to the heart.
To what lived in the heart.
Light pouring from dead stars
Filled the soul.
he is knowledge of the most distant
Knowledge of the most distant
is Belief.

A rusty cluster of stars
Under the waters.

XXII.

Böylece
Allahı çağırmak için göğe bakan adamlar
Kalbe döndüler.
Kalpte meskun olana.
Artık ölü olan yıldızlardan akan ışık
Doldurdu ruhu.
En uzakta olanın bilgisi Allahtır.
En uzakta olanın bilgisi
İnanmak.

Pas tutmuş bir yıldız kümesi
Sular altında.

XXIII.

When I look
I'm aware of all the nights
When the travellers waited.
The horses of time,
of distance.
And letters in the throats of birds,

XXIII.

Baksam
Yolcuların beklediği bütün gecelerden
Duyarım olanı.
Zamanın atları
Uzaklığın.
Ve kuşların göğsünde harfler.

passing north and south,
reaching the heart at last.
From stardust a seed so bitter
so curious
a trace on my neck.
What am I looking at?
What do I sense?
Glowing like a jewel in infinity
Wings let me fly.
Love signs its name.

XXIV.

Now in the heart his time begins.
This metal sheet
Worn thin by the clasp near the heart.
Eternity's testament.
I am there.
Cosmic questions have tired my heart.
I'll draw all infinity into the world.
I'll take it in my palms.
Blood goes wild.

XXV.

When I stargaze
my pulse quickens,
the country of my heart expands.
Now all galaxies are my home.
Listen, can you hear?
I'm closer to him than travellers.
Closer than lovers.
I'm close to the soul

Kuzeyi ve güneyi geçip
Yüreğe ulaştı sonunda.
O kadar acı bir tohum yıldız tozundan.
O kadar merak.
Boynumda iz.
Neye bakmaktayım
Neyi duymakta?
Sonsuzluğun içinde mücevher gibi parlayan
Kanatlar uçurur beni.
Adını aşk koyar.

XXIV.

Şimdi Allahın zamanı başlıyor kalpte.
Kalbe yakın tutulmaktan incelmiş
Bu levha
Gösteriyor sonsuzluğu.
Oradayım.
Kainatın soruları yormuş kalbimi.
Bütün sonsuzluğu dünyaya çekeceğim.
Avuçlarıma alacağım sonsuzluğu.
Kan delirmekte.

XXV.

Yıldızlara bakarken ben
Nabzım genişlemiş.
Ülkesi genişlemiş kalbin.
Bütün galaksiler yurdum artık
Bak duyuyor musun?
Yolculardan yakınım Allaha.
Aşıklardan yakın.
Bir merak ayetiyim çünkü.

for my sign is wonder.	Yakınım ruha...
A magnetic needle true as the faith	Kıbleye dönen bir müminin
of a Muslim who turns to Makkah.	inancı kadar doğru bir ibre
Everything looks to the heart.	Herşey kalbe bakıyor.
We are here now.	Artık andayız.
And only because we are here	Ve ancak anda olduğumuzda
the whole of the cosmos yearns for him.	Bütün kainat Allahı sayıklar.
Where is my homeland?	Neresi yurdum?
Perhaps it is the sun.	Güneş belki de.

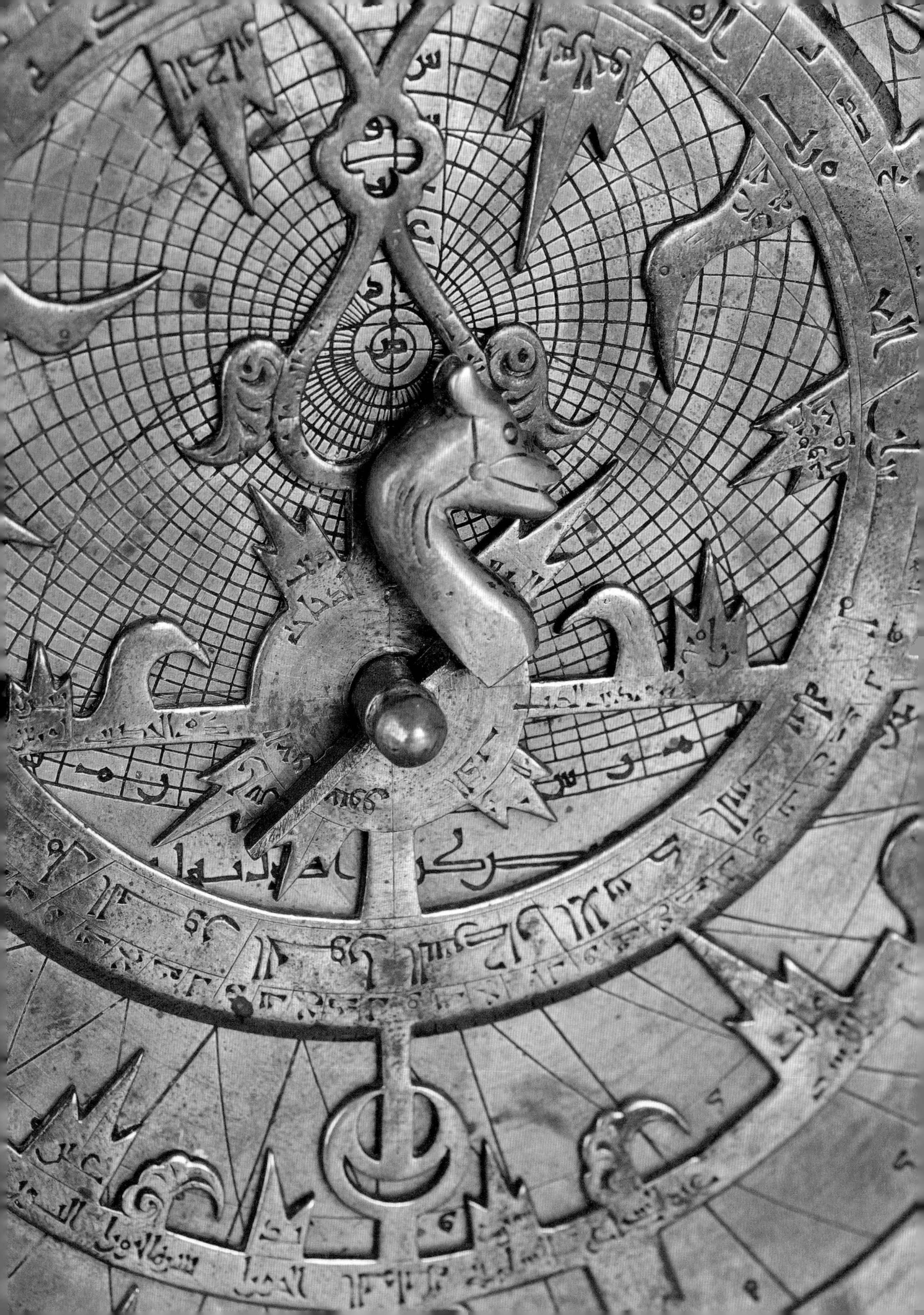

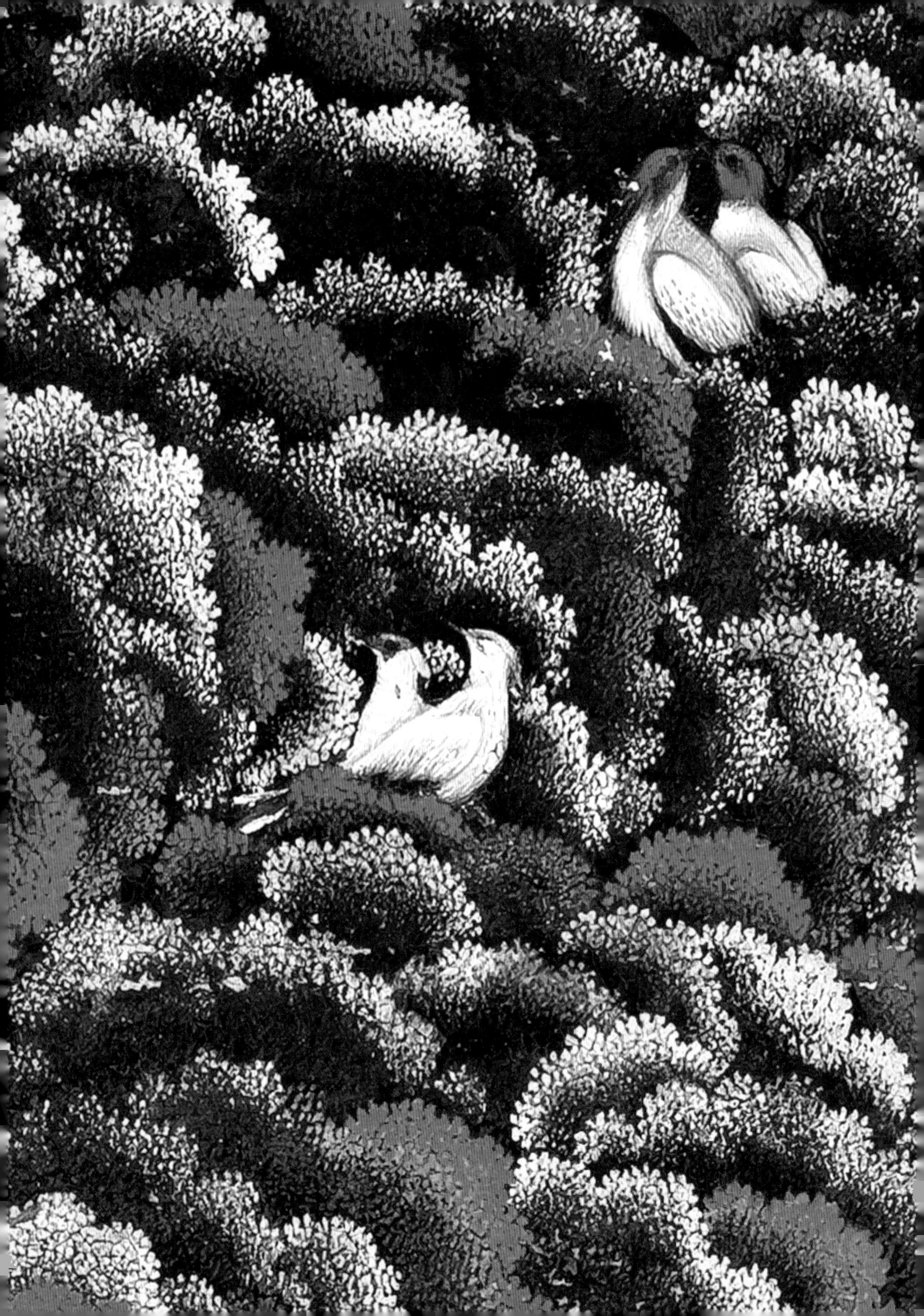

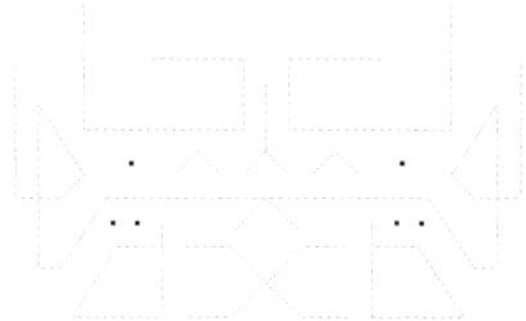

'St Jerome' by Farrukh Beg

Raja Shehadeh

I live in Ramallah in the Occupied Palestinian Territories, ten miles from Jerusalem, the site of one of the most attractive architectural treasures of Islam, the Umayyad-era Dome of the Rock. The Haram al-Sharif is second only – in religious significance – to the two mosques of Makkah and Madinah. I consider myself as shaped by an enduring Islamic-Christian culture, dominant in Palestine since the seventh century when Byzantine Jerusalem came under Muslim rule. Indeed the Dome of the Rock combines Byzantine design and Islamic decorations.

Because of the Israeli occupation in 1967, Jerusalem, the centre of the West Bank and the spiritual capital of Palestine, has been cut off from its context and access to it is restricted. Not long ago I decided to take my nephew and niece, Aziz and Tala, who were then eleven and nine years old, to the Old City of Jerusalem to visit al-Haram al-Sharif. I wanted them to be as proud as I am of their Islamic heritage. It was not easy to get access to the Haram because Israeli guards at the gates forbid entrance to non-Muslims. But we eventually managed. After we joined the pilgrims, worshippers and idlers, and made a tour of the place, we were approached by a suspicious Palestinian guard who proceeded to interrogate us, asking whether we were Muslim or Christian. When we told him the truth he seemed offended: this was not our place. We argued that it did not matter what religion we followed because we are Palestinian Arabs and as such we are proud of our Muslim heritage. This seemed to infuriate him. He could not accept that the Haram was our heritage as well. We later received an apology from the Director of the *Awqaf* (the Muslim Trust that administers the Haram) but the incident was disturbing because it revealed a narrowing of outlook that seems to mark our times.

But it was hardly surprising for the guard to be suspicious when the Mount on which the Dome of the Rock rests is perhaps the most contested of holy sites. This Islamic masterpiece is besieged by Israeli state policies and threatened with destruction by extremist Jews. Yet I have always believed that our biggest challenge in the face of the Israeli occupation is to guard against becoming a mirror image of our oppressors and adopting their ways and attitudes, whether as regards the exploitation of religion for nationalist purposes or making exclusive claims on that which should remain universal and widely shared.

Perhaps it was coming from such a fractious area that drew me to the miniature painting in Doha's Museum of Islamic Art: *St Jerome Representing Melancholy*, an illustration from the Mughal Royal Album, signed by the Muslim artist, Farrukh Beg.

In this painting – done in the style of a Persian miniature – St Jerome is sitting pensively on a wicker chair wearing a green robe, amid a world full of flowers, populated by gambolling cats, suckling goats and sheep. St Jerome is holding a staff and wearing a dagger. His hair is dark green. He is slumped on the chair. His head is tilted as though pulled down by his long straggly white beard. The corpulent and ageing cat on the cabinet on which Jerome rests his elbow is heading for the spilt milk. It might be what he is wistfully looking at. The lion, usual in paintings of this saint, is replaced here by the playful cats.

The painting is framed on one side by a decorative Chinar tree (sometimes called the Oriental plane, an integral part of Kashmiri culture found in almost every village), which also towers over the man's figure. The presence of this tree is common in Farrukh Beg's paintings. It is one of the ways in which the painter made this adaptation of a Middle Eastern saint painted by a German artist his own.

The exhibit is well lit. The strong light illuminates the golden outer border, which makes a strong contrast with the muted opaque colours of the painting. This is another garden in its own right, a gilt-decorated border of sprays of flowers; a garden framing the garden inside the portrait.

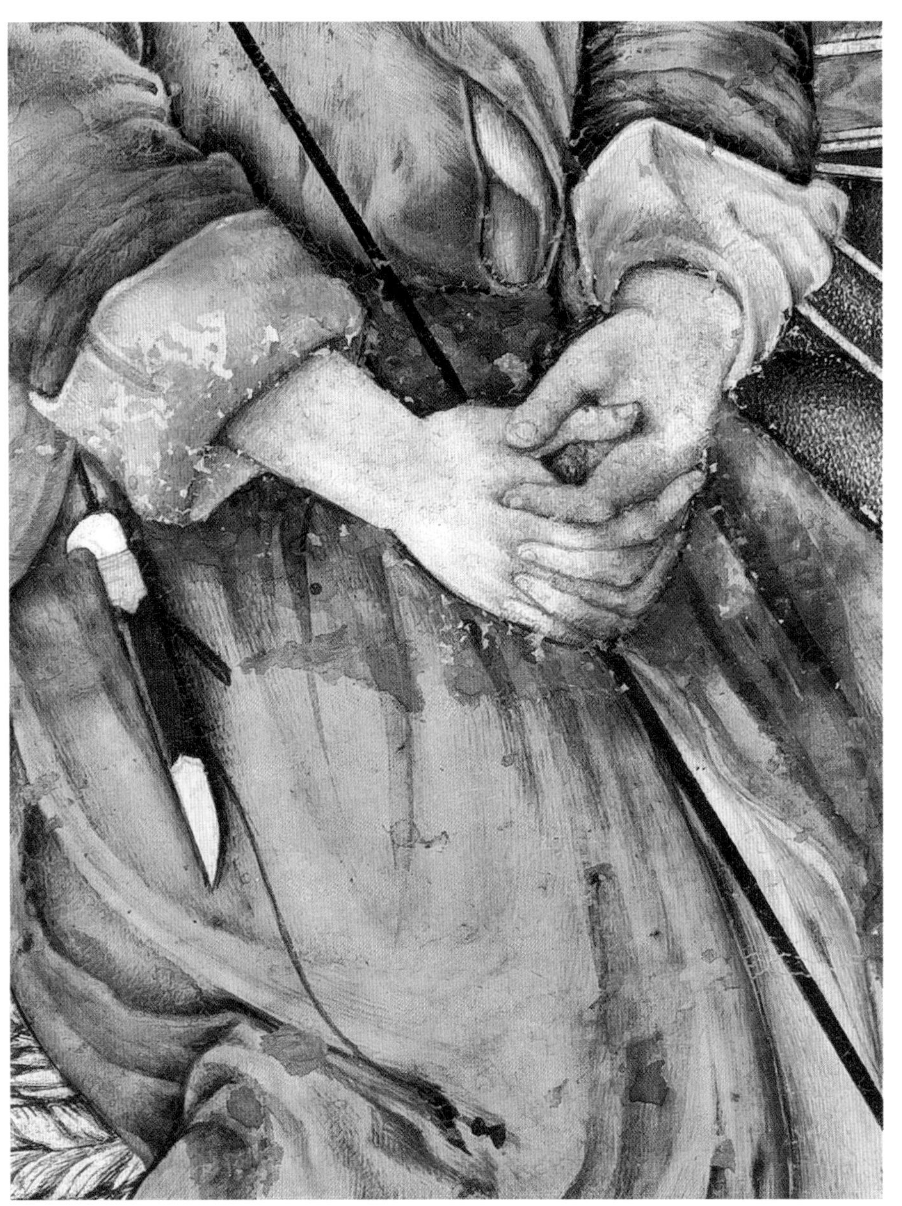

The opaque, predominantly green hues give a settled comforting feel to the painting. Unlike in the engraving on which it is based, here there are no shadows, only bright illuminating light. Yet nothing is striking or stands out; what draws you into the painting is the image of the man: a living being who is part of the rolling life around him. He is not looking at the viewer, trying to tell him something. There is no arrogance or aggression, only humility and peace. It was hard for me to find melancholy in this contemplative figure. Nothing in the way the Saint is presented indicates that he is a hermit; he is more like a rich man sitting in his sumptuous garden. In the eyes of this Muslim artist you didn't need to be a hermit to attain this state of grace. You could have all your worldly things around you and be seated in a glorious garden and yet still have the tranquillity and humility that makes for happiness and contentment. Could this be something that the artist was trying to convey to his patron, a Mughal emperor? Was this why he chose to copy this painting?

From the Farsi inscription in the painting we learn that this is the work of 'the Wonder of the Age Farrukh Beg in his seventieth year inscribed after the opening [the words here are illegible]... in battle in the tenth regnal year Hijri 1024. [1615]'.

It appears that the Emperor Shah Jahan, in whose court Farrukh Beg worked, had a collection of European engravings from which the artist borrowed. Beg was one of the finest artists working at the Mughal court during the reigns of Akbar and Shah Jahan. He was born in 1547 (953 AH), possibly in Kabul, from where he made his way to the Mughal court in the Deccan Plain after a career that took him from Shiraz to Khorasan. The range of experience and exposure to different cultures and styles of painting is well expressed in his work. There was the fusion of four different styles: Persian miniature portraits, Indian style, Christian influence and the Mughal painting and world view. A great artist – like a great civilisation – does not fear borrowing and sharing and is enriched by exposure to other cultures and styles.

To answer the question, what makes this painting of a Christian saint Islamic art, let us compare Beg's painting with that of Marten de Vos's (1532-1603/938-1011 AH) engraving *Dolour*, whose re-interpretation of the Dürer painting of St Jerome was Beg's primary source.

There are a number of common elements in the two paintings. De Vos's is divided into two sections as in the two ages of the saint. Outside, where a woman is stooping, working the soil, and an inside study where the man at the end of his life is sitting – with an open gate between the two sections of the painting. The symbolism is direct and obvious. In Farrukh Beg's painting this narrative is absent. He painted the old man sitting on the wicker chair but placed him in a completely different setting; the outside is represented by the Chinar tree with its infinitely expanding cabbage-like leaves. The study is transformed into a sumptuous garden with flowers and domestic animals, lush and illuminated, more like an arboretum than a study. In this space the vegetable and animal worlds have their own wonder that is highly detailed and illuminated; they have a life of their own, separate from the old man's and not representative or symbolic as in the picture on which this is based. Coming from an artist who was probably born in Persia this is not surprising. The origin of our word for 'paradise' is the Farsi *pairidaeza*, a celestial garden, a heavenly paradise on earth. This, in Persian culture, is the place where a person can reconnect with his spiritual self and take a break from active life to continue a spiritual quest. How appropriate then for a Muslim artist who lived in Persia to have placed the contemplative Christian saint in a lush garden.

So while in De Vos's painting two worlds are represented, both saturated with dolour (melancholy) – the world of work and hardship (the stooping woman) and, beyond the open gate, that of the dying old man – Farrukh Beg instead presents a world unto itself, a self-contained small paradise illuminated and wondrous. In De Vos all the natural elements are employed to focus attention on the old man and his plight. The light comes from the outside and casts a shadow on the section where the old man is sitting. No shadows are in Farrukh Beg's painting where all is illuminated by the opaque light. Unlike in Europe the quality of light in India is strong and direct. Perhaps it was this that determined how the world was represented by artists living there and the prevalence of illuminations. Yet the most telling of the transformations is that St Jerome in Farrukh Beg's painting is not presented as a hermit but rather as an old, retired gentleman sitting in his lush garden, shaded by the familiar Chinar tree. He is surrounded by his various domestic animals. He is a bit tired, contemplative, but without any indication that his reflections are about death or the vanity of human wishes and the transience of the material world. Absent from the painting is the skull; the reminder of death that is so often present

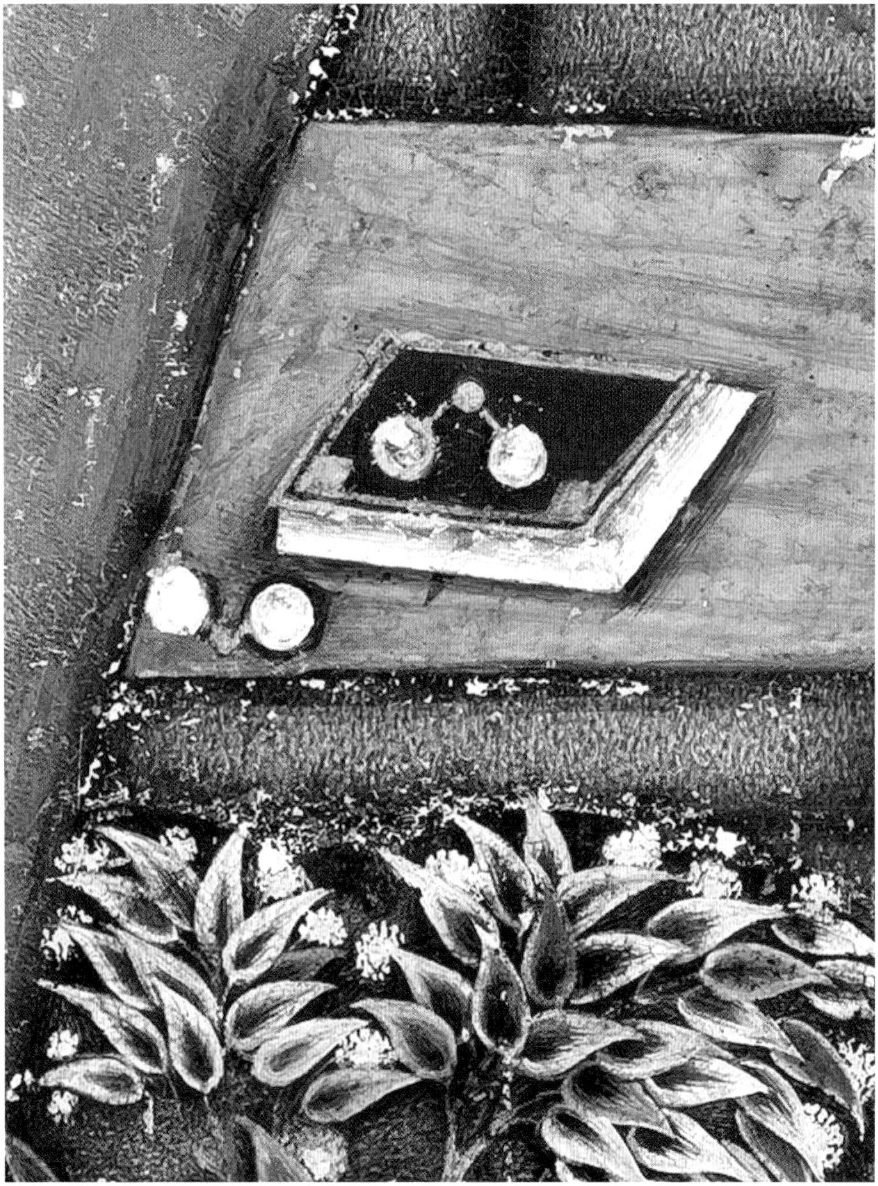

in paintings of St Jerome. No attempt is made here to invoke guilt and fear in the viewer who, unless he be faithful and obedient, will have to face his punishment in the afterlife. Here, life is celebrated while the wisdom and contemplation of the old man is prominently portrayed. In this way Christian saintliness is turned into Muslim Sufism. While the former denounces the material world the Sufi believes that it is possible to draw closer to God and more fully embrace the Divine presence within life. This is what makes this adaptation Islamic even when the subject is at the very centre of Christian iconography.

We are further informed by the Museum catalogue that 'the fashion for copying European prints or borrowing compositional aspects from them began during the Akbar period, when prints were brought to India by Jesuit missionaries, travellers and emissaries'. This fact did not seem to create apprehension in the Muslim Empire. There was no fear then of cultural imperialism; instead we are told that the Mughal emperors had 'an appreciation of the art of other cultures from whom they copied and borrowed'. At the time of the Mughal Empire no restrictions were placed on the choice of subject to be painted. The fact that Christian missionaries were present in India then did not render their subjects prohibited. This is how a confident civilisation looks at and deals with the iconography of another and is happy to adapt and borrow from it. This is one of the important factors that contributed to the richness of Islamic art – as this painting illustrates.

On another floor of the Museum, unfurled in a display cabinet, is an elaborate illustrated medieval *Hajj* certificate dated 6 September 1433 (20 Muharram 837 AH). I read the writing on it, and wondered at the illustrations of places of pilgrimages, and learned that the bearer had completed his pilgrimage by visiting the Dome of the Rock – now out of reach for many Muslims – and I could not help lamenting how shrunken and diminished have become our world and our culture.

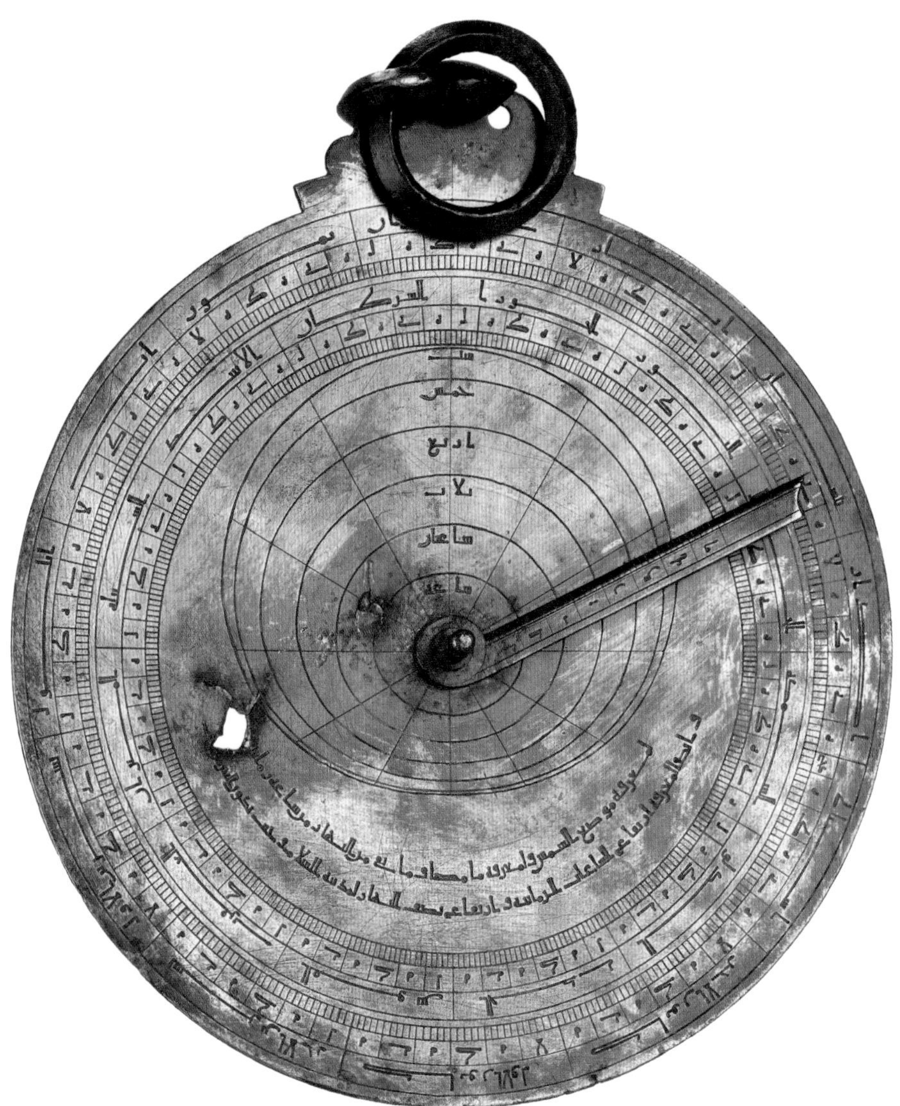

The Cinderella Astrolabe

Jameel al-Khalili

I have often thought that had I not chosen an academic career in theoretical physics I may well have opted for archaeology – leaving aside of course the fact that I harboured what felt at one time like serious ambitions of becoming a rock guitarist or a professional footballer. No doubt, this love of ancient history was born out of my having grown up in Iraq, a country that hides under its troubled skin some 7,000 years of glorious civilisations. But I left, or rather escaped, that country of my birth in 1979 without so much as a backward glance. Now, after a career in scientific research and teaching, immersed in the quantum world of atoms, mathematical symbols, computer programs and abstract ideas, I have started to feel a strong and quite pleasant tug to explore my cultural roots. And, as a scientist, my passions have been mostly aroused by a period of history long neglected in the West: a golden age of Arabic scholarship in subjects such as mathematics, astronomy, medicine, chemistry and physics that began in ninth-century Baghdad under the patronage of the powerful Abbasid caliphs who ruled over the vast Islamic Empire, stretching across three continents.

So my stroll around Doha's stunningly beautiful and serene Museum of Islamic Art was probably inevitably going to lead me to those exhibits that would take me back to this age of rationalism and enlightenment that has been obsessing me for the past few years. Sure enough, after wandering through the many adjoining rooms displaying colourful tiles, pottery, sculptures and examples of early Kufic calligraphy, I finally entered the one at the very end and immediately knew that my object would be somewhere in this room. For I found myself surrounded by dozens of beautiful astronomical instruments: astrolabes, displayed alongside each other in row upon row, all seemingly clamouring for my attention like Miss World contestants, each one more intricate and more shiny than the last. I was struck by their sheer range through space and time: around 1,000 years of craftsmanship that spanned the Islamic Empire, from India to Andalusia.

Having thus decided that my object would indeed be an astrolabe, my next task was to find the one that would speak to me; the worthiest of these wonderful instruments on display; the shiniest, most elaborate and, I suppose, scientific of them all. I know broadly how an astrolabe is used, having researched the subject for a recent book I have written on Arabic science as well as having presented a BBC television series on the subject. And believe me, their workings are not trivial. I had been informed that the Museum's guides struggle to explain this to visitors awkward enough to enquire.

The astrolabe is an ancient astronomical device originally invented by the Greeks, typically made of brass and the size of small plate, although much larger and smaller ones were also made. It was used by astronomers, navigators and astrologers for solving problems relating to the position and motion of the heavenly bodies across the sky. By far the most popular type was the planispheric astrolabe, on which a map of the sky is projected onto the flat plane of the equator. To use an astrolabe, the movable components are adjusted to a specific date and time and, once set, the entire celestial sphere is represented as an etching on the face of the instrument. A typical astrolabe has a circular plate, referred to as the 'mater', with a central peg onto which a set of smaller removable discs, called 'tympans', are placed. Each of these is made for a specific latitude and engraved with a stereographic projection of a portion of the sky. Sitting above the uppermost tympan is a rotating framework, called the 'rete', which is a reference star chart that has engraved on it some of the most important constellations that are matched with the stars on the tympan below it. Above this is a pointer that pivots around the peg marked with a scale showing angles of latitude in the sky. And as if this was not enough, on the back of most astrolabes are further angular markings around the rim along with a rotating sighting arm, or dioptra, called the 'alidade' (from the Arabic *al-'idada*, meaning 'marked ruler'), which is used to make a reading of the angle of inclination of the object being viewed in the sky when the astrolabe is hung vertically.

Given the remarkable achievements of medieval Islamic astronomers, surpassing by far the observations of the Greeks in terms of accuracy and understanding, astrolabes were part of a whole host of pre-telescope instruments that would be found in any one of the many observatories scattered around the Empire. All would have been equipped with sundials with brass gnomons to determine the height of the sun from the length of shadow it cast, along with hand-held sextants and giant mural quadrants (instruments like giant protractors from a school geometry set, cut in half to make a quarter of a circle and placed on their edge so as to measure the precise position in the sky of an object along a sighting rod).

So there I was, standing alone in the cool, softly lit room, trying to decide what criteria I should apply to help me choose the winner of the Miss Astrolabe beauty contest, when I realised I had not really taken in some of the other displays around me. And that was when I found my object on display behind glass in an alcove on the far wall; it really was a sad excuse for an astrolabe and seemed to have been shunned by its more illustrious neighbours.

The poor thing is not even a proper astrolabe, for the caption underneath describes it somewhat blandly as a 'mathematical and astronomical instrument'; and I can sort of see why, since it appears to be rather basic in its function. It consists of a battered and bruised brass disk, about fifteen centimetres in diameter, dating back to late ninth- or early tenth-century Baghdad. Around the plate are engraved notches signifying angles in degrees, and it has a revolving alidade. Saddest of all its features is a small hole punched in it, looking very much like it was made by a bullet, which I know seems rather unlikely, but nevertheless gives the impression of it having been mortally wounded in battle.

But it is certainly not sympathy that led me to choose this particular exhibit. Rather it is the significance I believe it holds in representing one of the most astounding and yet least well-known periods in the history of science. For this instrument would very likely have been used by Baghdad astronomers repeating some of the measurements of the ancient Greeks that they had found tabulated in the writings of the great second-century Alexandrian scholar Ptolemy. Since I cannot be certain how accurate the dating of my object is, I feel I should be allowed the somewhat fanciful notion that it was the property of one of a group of remarkable men brought together during the first half of the ninth century by that greatest of all the Islamic patrons of science and scholarship and son of the famous Harun al-Rashid, the Abbasid caliph al-Ma'mun. What took place during his reign was something quite new in scholarship. A consequence of bringing together for the first time a wide range of different scientific traditions from around the world was that the scholars of Baghdad had at their disposal a far broader world view than anyone before them. Differences in the translations of Persian, Indian and Greek astronomical texts, for instance, each with its own cosmological model, set of measurements and tables of astronomical values, not always in agreement with each other, meant they could not all be right.

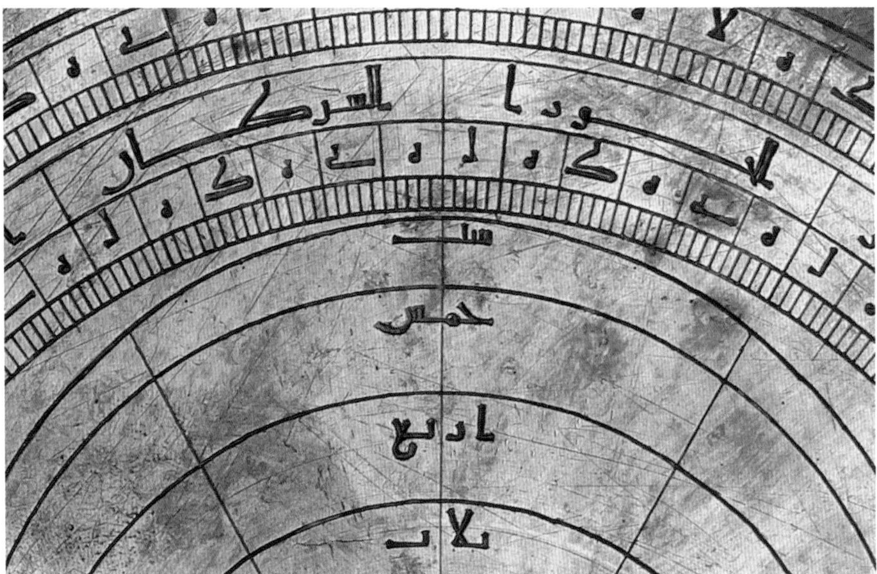

For al-Ma'mun's astronomers, to be able to compare and comment objectively on the many translated texts with fresh eyes and open minds must have been gloriously exciting. Questions started to be asked and doubts raised. Clearly, discrepancies needed to be resolved, and it became apparent that there was an urgent need for a new set of comprehensive astronomical measurements to be made. Some time during the second decade of the ninth century, and associated with *Bayt al-Hikmah*, his new 'House of Wisdom', al-Ma'mun ordered the building of the first astronomical observatory in Baghdad and he put together an impressive team of astronomers. Could my instrument have possibly belonged to one of these remarkable men? Allow me to introduce to you a few of the most important characters, any one of whom might have pondered the heavens by hanging my object vertically and using its sighting arm to measure and record the positions of the celestial bodies in the night sky.

The first of them is Sanad ibn Ali al-Yahudi, an ambitious young man who moved in the right circles of high society in Baghdad. The son of a Jewish astrologer, Sanad, like many bright young minds of his generation had studied the great work of Ptolemy, the *Almagest*, but felt that he needed to be part of the 'in' crowd of illustrious scholars associated with al-Ma'mun to pursue his science further. One man in particular was to play an influential role in Sanad's life. Already highly regarded and a few years older than Sanad, al-Abbas al-Jawhari held regular meetings in his home with a group of scholars. According to one account, the young Sanad convinced al-Jawhari of his impressive understanding of the *Almagest* and was welcomed into the circle. Al-Jawhari also then put in a good word on his behalf with the caliph, and Sanad was soon given work in *Bayt al-Hikmah*.

The senior astronomer in al-Ma'mun's court was a Persian by the name of Yahya ibn abi Mansur. When al-Ma'mun was convinced of the need to repeat the astronomical observation and measurements quoted in the *Almagest*, the two men he turned to were the wise old Yahya and the enterprising young Sanad. They were charged with building and heading up the new observatory in the year 828 (212 AH). While the notion of an observatory was certainly not new – although this would have been the first in the Islamic world – never before had one been created as a genuine scientific institution. The site chosen was in the north-east of the city, in a district known as al-Shammasiyyah.

In order to carry out this ambitious astronomical project, al-Ma'mun called upon one of the greatest scientists in history, the mathematician, astronomer, geographer and father of algebra, the Persian genius al-Khwarizmi. He also enlisted the services of another man, by the name of al-Farghani, who was destined to be among the many Islamic astronomers to influence the European Renaissance. His legacy endures through the great Dante Alighieri, who derived most of the astronomical knowledge he included in his *Divine Comedy* from the writings of al-Farghani, to whom he referred by his Latin name, Alfraganus. Indeed, Christopher Columbus used al-Farghani's value for the circumference of the earth in order to persuade his backers to fund his famous voyage. But al-Farghani's contribution to the Shammasiyyah project seems to have been his expertise with astronomical instruments. His treatise on the astrolabe still survives and provides the mathematical principles of astrolabe construction. Could he have made my instrument?

And so it was that over a period of a year or so around 830 (214 AH), the first critical appraisal of Greek astronomy began in earnest when the earliest systematic astronomical observations in the Islamic world were made at Shammasiyyah. During this time many observations of the sun and moon were carried out and a table with longitudes and latitudes of twenty-four fixed stars is recorded as having been drawn. On completion of all the observations, a new zij, or star chart, was produced for the caliph. It is known as *al-Zij al-Mumtahan*, which translates as 'The Verified Tables'. The group of astronomers involved in producing it were referred to as *Ashab al-Mumtahan* ('Companions of the Verified Tables').

This band of scholars was just the first in a long line of great Arab and Persian astronomers, such as the Syrians al-Battani and Ibn Shatir, the Egyptian Ibn Yunus, the Iraqi Ibn al-Haytham and the Persian al-Tusi. Between them, these men laid the groundwork for the birth of modern astronomy at the hands of European giants such as Copernicus, Kepler and Galileo.

I wonder what role my sad little instrument played in all this, back when it would have been polished and proud, playing its small part in mankind's quest to understand the cosmos.

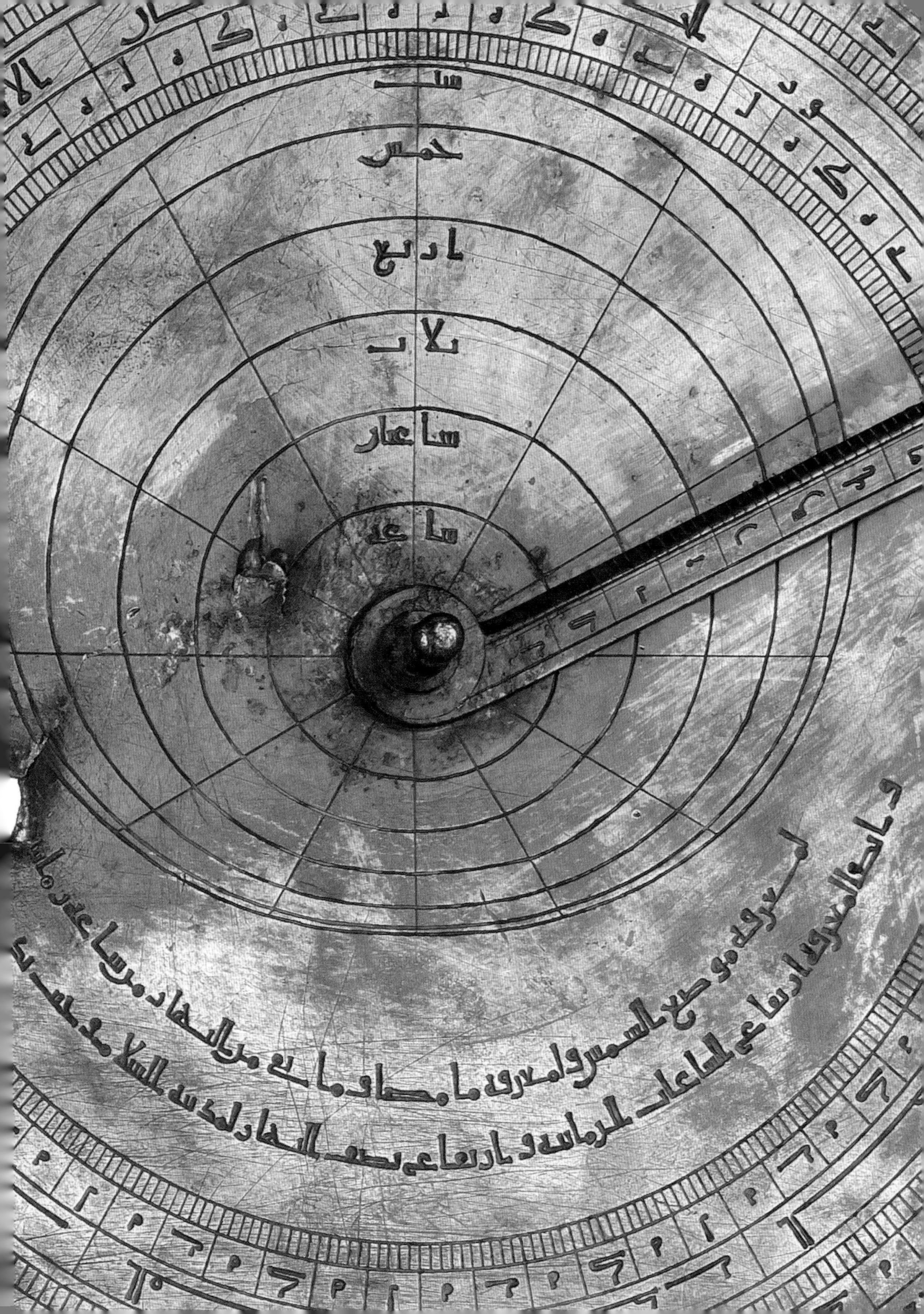

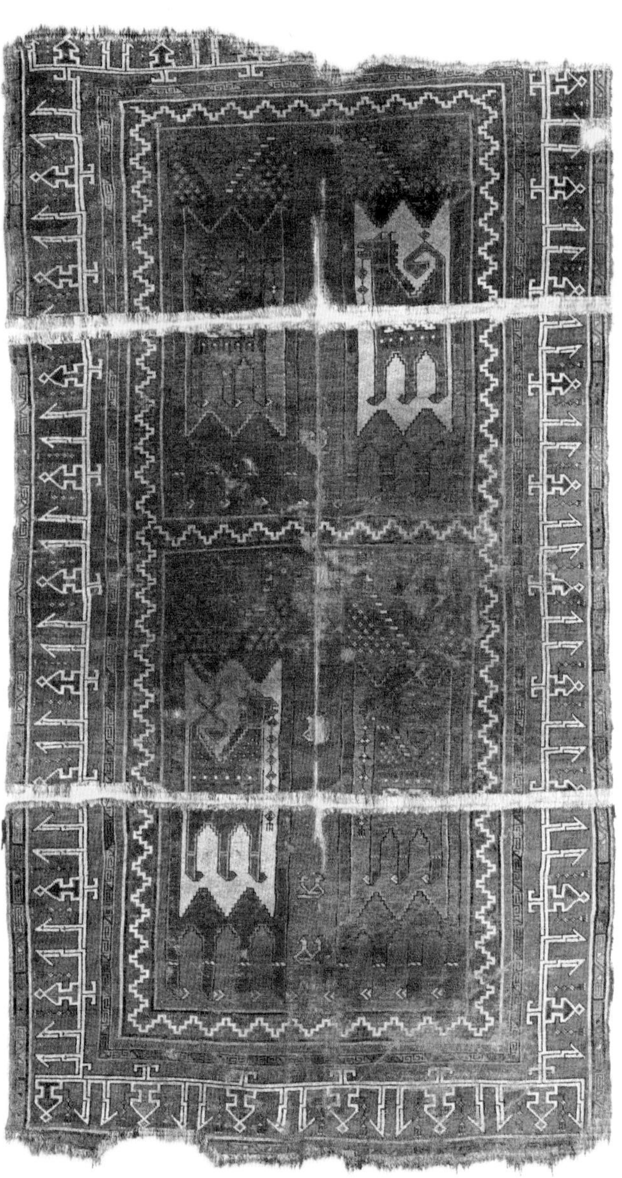

The Divine Flaw

Jamal Mahjoub

It hangs before you, suspended in the luminous air; a sliver of light emerging as the shadows around it recede. A carpet. No longer spread across the floor, for it's in the nature of museums to remove things from their commonplace habitat, and raise them from the banality of ordinary, everyday existence. And so the carpet floats in the dark air before you like an interrogation mark; a doorway to a lost world.

What exactly are we to make of it? The little plaque attached to the wall provides only sparing clues: 'Wool,' it says. 'Turkey.' 'Fourteenth century?' But even this basic detail, coupled as it is with a question mark, appears to shimmer in doubt. Nothing, it seems to tell us, can be taken for granted, not even time. The plaque also informs us that it is a 'Four-animal carpet'. Again, this concedes so little that it constitutes no more than a tantalising crack in the universe, demanding to be explored further. Four animals, but what are they? Certainly, they do not appear to be of this world. They are not the sheep whose wool was employed to make the carpet. They are not of a species known to man; they resemble creatures of legend and lore. They have ruffled wings and coiled tails that taper to sharp points. Birds, then, or dragons? Within each animal there is depicted another, slightly different beast, which suggests that they possess magical powers, like shape-shifters which have the ability to transform themselves at will. The motifs are set up as twins. The duality and symmetry there conspire to create a mirror. But who is it meant to reflect if not ourselves, the viewer?

Poised in the air before us, a rectangle of light dangling in the gloom, the carpet most resembles a threshold. An empty doorframe. A junction between contrasting dimensions: light and dark, good and evil, real and imagined. The significance of doorways has long been recognised, which is why it is common practice to utter a word of prayer, a benediction, at the moment of entering a house for the first time, to placate the invisible occupants, or *ahl al-dar*, as they are known.

So these mythical creatures are intended as guardians, then, to protect us. To ward off malignant spirits. In some places they are known as Senmurv, while elsewhere they are called Simourgh; a name familiar to anyone who has read Ferdowsi's *Shahnameh*, or Book of Kings. In Attar's *Mantiq al-Tayr*, all the birds in the world fly out in search of their king, the Simourgh. Their guide in the journey across the seven valleys to the mountain of Qaf is the wise Hoopoe, who tells of a feather which fell in China one moonlit night, dropped to prove the Simourgh's existence to man. All over the world people tried to imagine the Simourgh's shape and colour. In each heart, the Hoopoe explains, there lies the hidden counterpart to this feather, and so their quest was not only physical but spiritual – a journey within. Borges, in his own encyclopaedic fashion, includes the Simourgh in his *El libro de los seres imaginarios* (The Book of Imaginary Beings). And in his delirium, Flaubert's St Anthony is tempted by the Queen of Sheba accompanied by a glorious bird: the Simourgh.

But wait, there are other, more subtle clues, concealed in the carpet's weave. Look closely. With the aid of a small magnifying glass (and a little imagination) you can detect in the wool the faint blemishes left by the tears of the woman whose heart was breaking while she wove this carpet upon which the man she had longed for all her life was to be wed. No optical devices are needed to spot a row of what appear to be spikes or thorns running around the border; a line of defence perhaps, to ward off bad luck in the marriage? They are interspersed with a repeated symbol that resembles a tree: the Tree of Life, symbol of longevity and fecundity, and a distant echo of the sacred properties of trees in unenlightened times. The woman fled the village the night before the wedding, taking her woven compendium of blessings with her, knotted tightly to her saddle. Her horse's hoofs drumming out the tracks of the tears that fell in her wake as she rode over the hills towards the horizon and the heartbroken existence that awaited her.

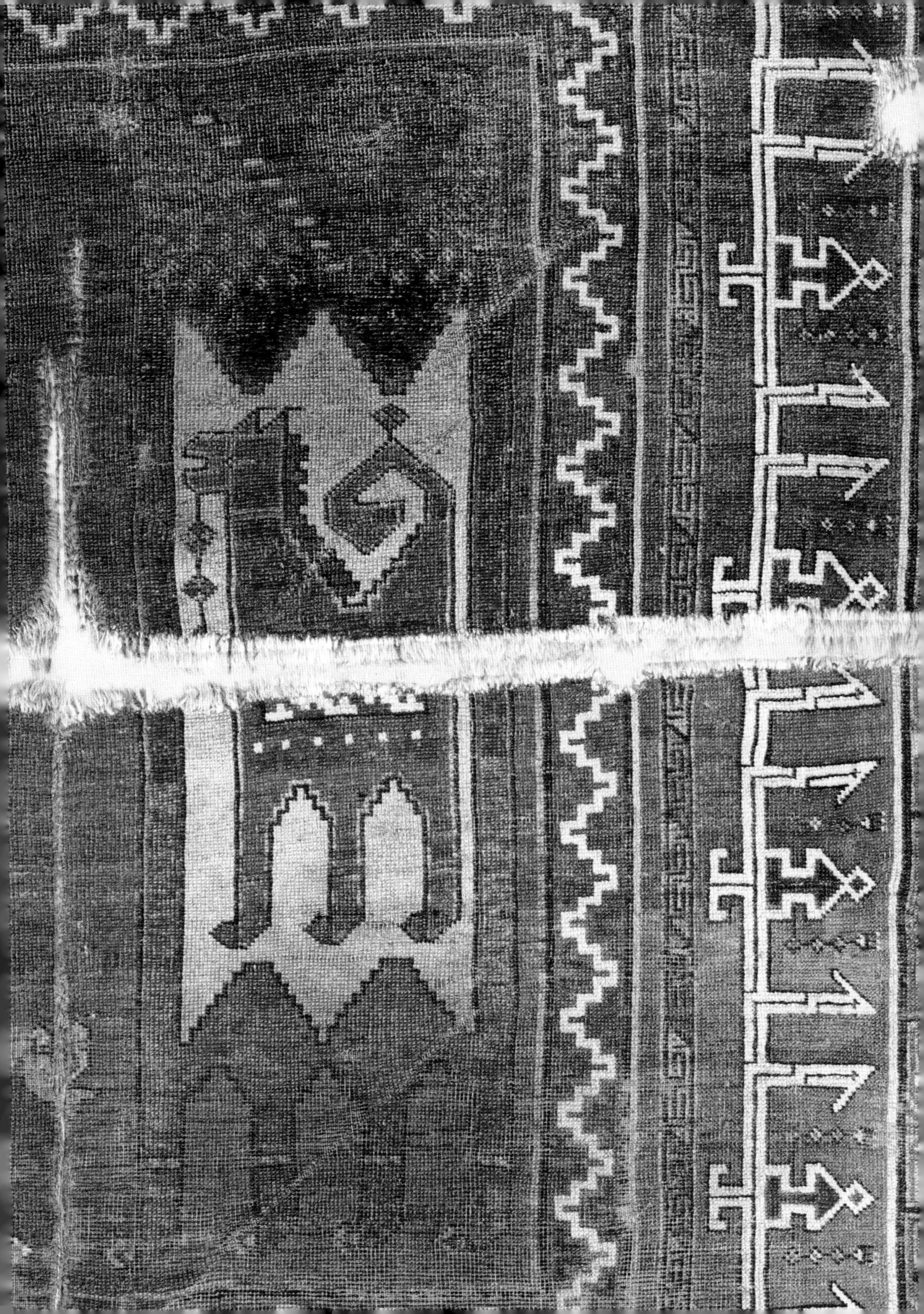

Other clues recount later adventures in the life of the carpet. The faint watermark that fringes both ends testifies to it having been immersed in sea water. Laboratory tests confirm the darker stains in the centre as the blood of a young serving boy who worked in a notorious den of iniquity on the Caspian Sea. Burn marks left by the braziers confirm this period. One evening the boy, made nervous by some ruffians, tripped and spilled the wine they had ordered. The men set upon him and beat him to within a hair's breadth of his life. The proprietor was so scared he dared not intervene. When the thugs came to their senses they wrapped the body hastily in the carpet and carried it down to the water's edge where they threw it in. The boy happened not to be dead, and since in their befuddled state they were unable to tie a decent knot between them, the parcel came undone and he drifted miraculously upon the unfurled carpet for days until it was finally hauled aboard a passing ship, where it subsequently adorned the captain's cabin for several years.

The image of the boy floating over the waves evokes the celebrated story of Prince Husayn, who discovers a carpet with magic properties in a marketplace in Madras and flies home on it to claim the hand of the woman his heart is set upon. According to the mischievous Burton such wonders were already documented long before Prince Husayn's time; he finds a rather dubious reference in the Qur'an, as well as the Talmud, and in medieval literature, he tells us, a certain Duke Richard was conveyed from his home in France to Mount Sinai and back on a carpet lifted by the wind.

In the eighteenth century our carpet surfaces again, this time in Istanbul – a Turkish city with a Greek name (*eis-tin poli*) – a fact which symbolises the dichotomous nature of its character. In tune with this affinity for contradiction, here the carpet was to figure in a number of works by a contemporary English painter. This was easily the most risqué period in the carpet's life. In keeping with the age, the artist draped across it countless nubile females in various states of undress – the better to illustrate the sensuous nature of the Orient, as he saw it – accompanied by men with beards like daggers, swarthy faces and turbans, slyly plucking instruments, smoking hashish pipes or staring back inscrutably.

In these canvases, the carpet is reduced to a mere stage prop. A sharpened talon protrudes here, a wing there. Just enough to hint at its identity. Needless to say, it was ignored by the many experts who lined up to offer their opinions of the paintings over the centuries. Their attention instead fixed on the voluptuous nature of the reclining women and the cruelty of the men who observe them. How well this captured the brutal nature of life beyond the penumbra of Christian civilisation. This was the element that sealed the artist's reputation, after all: his magnificent portrayal of the East as a place drenched in raw sensuality and violence. One can smell the perfume and incense, feel the silken skin of the sultry maidens, shiver at the petrified fury of the glowering men and witness the clutter of past centuries: silver moons and oil lamps, intricate geometrical ornamentation, astrolabes and telescopes, all washed up on the tide like so much junk, along with braying donkeys and sleepy cats.

The carpet sat in the painter's studio for several years until one fine day a colleague observed casually that it appeared in his work as invariably as the cry of the muezzin was heard in the early hours of the morning. A servant was immediately ordered to throw it out, upon which the carpet disappeared for many years.

By now, a certain pattern of ill-fortune appears to emerge, dogging the course of the carpet through history. In its current worn state it is difficult to ascertain, but careful study would reveal that the carpet's weave and the pattern of its motifs are in fact flawless. A testimony to the skill of its maker, you might say, and you would be both right and wrong. It is often said that all master artisans insert one deliberate mistake into their work – a gesture of humility, a recognition that there can be but one Creator of perfection. To do otherwise is to invite misfortune. In this particular case, of course, the culprit was sheer distraction. The trembling of her heart, the anguish and pain which she felt, meant that while her hand swept the loom back and forth with a surety born of experience, the weaver's mind was not fully focused. The gloom which had descended over her existence obscured all else around her. We might forgive her. Particularly given the fact that her own life was terminated prematurely, possibly by this very omission. She lived only for a brief and unhappy time after running away before being set upon by highway brigands and murdered in brutal fashion.

The final fate of the carpet is carved across it in two parallel scars which divide it into three sections. In the jagged burr of the cicatrices which sew it back together, is etched the history of dynasties, the breakdown of family, and the crushing fate of thousands left destitute by the ensuing financial ruin. The death of a father causing a rupture whose echo lands here, centuries later, hung before us on the wall of this gallery, long after all the characters involved have turned to bone and dust. There are other stories, reflected in its worn and faded condition, none of them less important, but all subordinate to the dramatic finality of that severance.

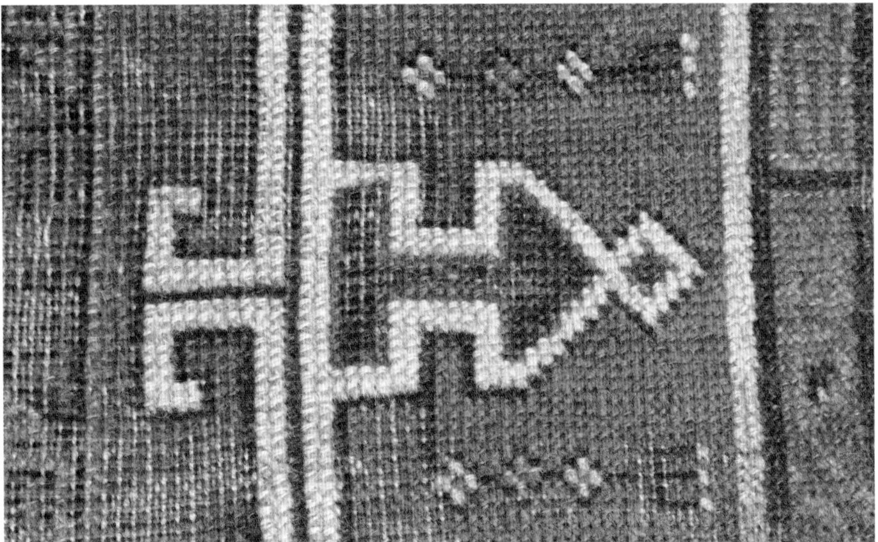

The seed of the closing loop of this tale was sown in Paris in the late nineteenth century when our carpet adorned the study of a wealthy industrialist. Upon his sudden death there occurred a violent falling out within the family. The distraught widow was driven almost out of her mind by the fact that her three children could not put aside their petty squabbles and selfishness for the sake of harmony. To her, the carpet was a symbol of the love out of which this family was created. Indeed, the first-born son was actually conceived on its rough surface one warm afternoon as the tall windows blew open and the summer breeze languorously stirred the branches of the plane tree outside. Now, in her rage she took a pair of garden shears and slashed it into three. None of the children would inherit a penny of their father's fortune until they reconciled their differences. She gave one piece to each and closed the door on them. 'Come back when you have sewn it back together.' They never did. Instead, the three pieces went their separate ways, as did the children. One emigrated to the Amazon, hoping to repeat the success of his father but dying instead of a terrible flesh-eating disease alone in the jungle. Another went east and lost his mind in the company of a tribe of shamans, while the third moved to England and lived out a dull and barren existence in bitter regret.

As day fades and the sun burns itself out, high up in the apex of the building panels of light and shade turn like tumblers in the enormous vault that is this cave of wonders. This is where the story ends, with the coming together of these fragments of history, these bright pebbles cast up out of the sea of darkness that we call the past. What is a museum but a monument to our forgetfulness? Our inability to recall the lessons of history. An inability that condemns us to repeat our mistakes generation after generation, into infinity. Soon the glassy disc of the moon is swimming freely with stars – a benevolent eye gazing down upon us and our futile pursuits. The high window of the Museum's atrium is a black mirror, beyond which the ebony water is bewitched with reflected lights that swarm and dance towards us.

At the end of their arduous journey, only thirty birds make it to their final destination. The rest have given up along the way. As the Hoopoe leads them into the grand palace of the king they are surprised to find the circular hall completely deserted but for themselves. Bright walls of burnished gold surround them on all sides. But where is the king, they cry, where is the Simourgh? And the ever-wise Hoopoe gestures for them to step closer. The words *si-murgh* in Persian mean literally 'thirty birds' – exactly the number of birds remaining. There, he says, pointing at their reflection in the polished walls, this is what you have been seeking.

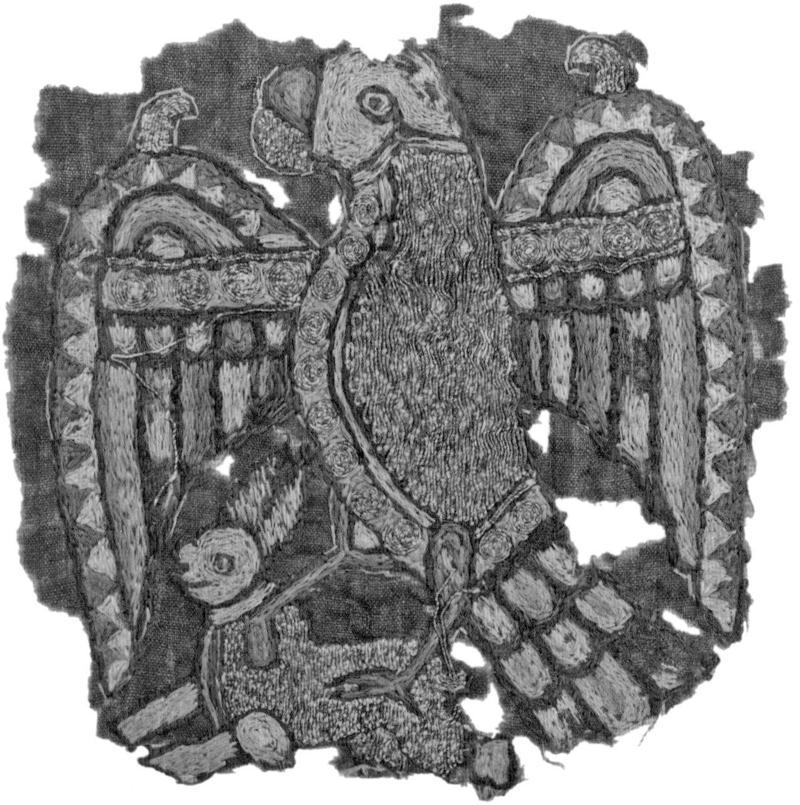

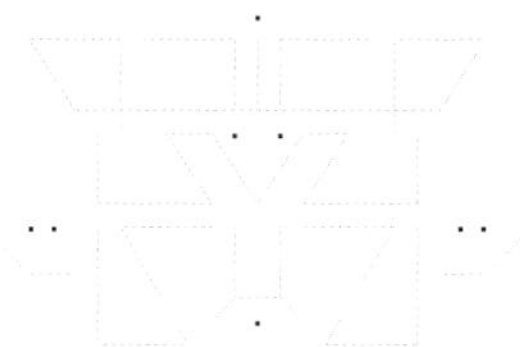

The Shroud of St Lazarus: A Text

Najwa Barakat

The antique dealer said that when he acquired that piece of embroidered silk, he was not sure how to receive it: as an omen of good fortune or one of calamity? He had been told: a rare antique piece from the shroud of a foreign holy man; the first and the last to be offered for sale. He did not have much time to consider, so he bought it. Through intuition not reason, and through something inside him which he could not name, he recognised it.

Well. And now what? He stood in his shop, undecided, afraid for it and afraid of it; it seemed capable of escaping, as though it were tied to an invisible cloud which would soon take off. The shiver that ran through him was not something he experienced often, now, on the threshold of seventy; he saw his shop, overflowing with antiquities. Stripped of their ages they were dried up, withered and constrained so that they occupied only their own dimensions and nothing greater.

He closed the door of his shop, put up the sign indicating his absence for a while, and entered the dark area at the back where a short corridor led to his three-roomed home. He crossed the first room, glanced into the second, and entered the third, where the cabinet was. He placed the embroidered piece among other acquisitions which needed patience and ripening before a mutual recognition could be reached.

And so passed not a few days spent between his home and his shop, looking through the inventories of his precious objects, sipping his coffee in the four-thirty light which visited him after every siesta, talking to people who came to see him, or to passers-by if they passed. And so on, until the day ended, and he entered into the evening, waiting for another day to break. And so on.

Until he was visited by a dream which pierced his soul like lightning; a dream which when recalled turned upon itself like a coil that unceasingly upon itself turned, weaving itself by itself, lengthwise and breadthwise, like a drop spreading into a pool becoming a lake turning into a deep ocean.

And he was not visited by one dream, but three. They were dreams distantly spaced and disparate, not addressing each other except when they met as though they were part of a whole, incomplete and indivisible.

The antique dealer said: I entered, one night, the waters of sleep as is my habit, surrendering to the waves of slumber, comfortable with the passage of an ordinary working day. And while I was drifting away from the last features of wakefulness, there spread around me the sound of weeping muffled and constant, flowing peaceable and monotonous, like a thread quietly pulled. I tightened my closed eyes, listened intently, sharpened my senses and the pores of my hunched, trembling body and found myself seeing two swaying shadows... the shadows of two women swaying, and whispering in an old language I could not understand though it seemed familiar; its letters leaping from the depths of the larynx, and seeping from the lungs. Wailing and beating chests and heads from which the veils had fallen showing faces with eyes like waterfalls pouring forth ashes which turned into sweet fresh water that in turn seethed and yellowed until it appeared like liquid gold.

I was made to understand that they were Martha and Miriam of Bethany, at the mouth of the cave blocked with a stone; the tomb of their brother. And with them was the Nazarene... the Nazarene, I whispered to myself, he is not, then, a foreign holy man?
And I heard Martha say: 'Lord, had you been here my brother had not died.'
And I heard Miriam repeat: 'Lord, had you been here my brother had not died.'
And I saw the Nazarene with tears in His eyes order the lifting of the stone and Martha saying:

'Lord, he has rotted, it has been four days' – and the stone lifted, and the Nazarene calling out in a massive voice: 'Ya Lazarus, come forth' and Lazarus coming out 'his hands and feet bound with strips of linen, his face wrapped in a light veil' and the Nazarene saying: 'Unbind him and let him go'...

When I woke up, I was the one crying like a child, for the dream was overwhelming as an earthquake. And I continued to weep even though I was sure that what I had seen was nothing more than a dream which had led me to the name of the owner of the shroud, not to the shroud itself. His hands and feet bore the marks of wounds, and his face was very pale, his hair very thin, his stature greatly diminished, his voice like that of a boy, and he had eyes wide and deep that shone with the flames of 1,000 candles and rainbows and the many shades of the setting sun.

The antique dealer said that after the dream he knew weeks of disquiet and a fearful heart, followed by weeks of forgetfulness and vagueness, which were smoothed away when he got busy with the traders who returned from their travels carrying rare and mysterious objects which had guarded their secrets for a long time before deciding to bring them into the light.

Until Lazarus came to him in his second dream. He said: Lazarus came to me, sad and reproachful, and said: Have you forgotten that I from death arose? Is this to be my end: that I am returned to life to know what is more cruel than death and more terrible: namely, oblivion? And if my first story ended with a white shroud of linen, cotton and gauze, don't you think that the second should end with a shroud of taffeta and threads of silk, silver and gold, embroidered by the most skilled of craftsmen?

Know, sir, that I was originally from a family of note and position, and that our house in Bethany, near the Mount of Olives, was like a palace and was no further from Jerusalem than five kilometres. Was not my sister, Mary Magdalene, criticised for pouring on the feet of the Nazarene – when he came to our house to stay, to eat with us and to rest – for pouring on his feet perfume beyond price?

After the death of my parents, my sister and I shared their wealth and property. When the persecution of Christ's followers in Jerusalem increased, we were the first victims. The persecutors stripped us of our wealth and set us adrift in a boat without sails or oars, so that we would be lost at sea and die. But something saved us and carried us to the shores of Marseille, where we lived and settled and I began to preach. I soon had followers in the city, and became its first bishop, until I was arrested by the Romans. When I refused to worship their idols they beat me and tortured me and dragged me through the city and threw me into a dark cell where I met my end at the blow of a sword which separated my head from my body. Nobody recorded the date of my death but it was said that I was killed when I had reached a distinguished and advanced age.

During the crusades my relics were moved to Autun for protection. But one of the monks kept my head and stuck a skull not my own to my body. To this day my head remains in Marseille and the rest of me in Autun.

The antique dealer said: Lazarus said all this then vanished before I could ask him this question: And this second shroud, who crafted it for you and where did it come from?

The following night a man came to me and introduced himself and said: 'I am Abd al-Malik bin Muhammad al-'Ameri. Wake up, antique dealer, and bring me the fragment of Lazarus's shroud.' I was not sure whether I was awake or asleep, but I rose, terrified of a shining sword which was held over my own head this time, and of a voice which made the heart quake and the limbs tremble. I opened my cabinet and quickly found the piece, which shone clearly in the dark. I shuddered when I held it, realising now its uniqueness and the concentration of an enormous cloud of times and worlds in its few centimetres.

Abd al-Malik put forward a magnifying glass: 'And now look into this magic eye,' he ordered, 'and tell me what you see.'

So I looked. And I saw the word 'al-Muzaffar' engraved on the belt of a falconer who carried a falcon with a rabbit in its grasp. And I recalled that it was the title of Abd al-Malik al-

Mansur, who succeeded his father and continued his policies, launching military campaigns which brought Christian kings to declare loyalty, as in the battles of Barcelona, Pamplona, Galicia and al-Khrieqah. He was named 'al-Muzaffar, Sword of the Realm' following his victory over the alliance of Christian kingdoms under the troublesome leader of Castile, the Count Sancho García.

As I gasped into the palm of my hand, so that my ignorance would not betray me, or startle the bearer of the title, the question I asked myself in secret was: what is the connection between Lazarus and his shroud and this man? Is it possible that he came to me to retrieve a small piece of embroidery? Or had Lazarus's shroud been made in one of the Spanish-Arab workshops at this prince's request? And why not? For it was written of him that he was 'watchful of his god, grieving for his sins, loving of the righteous, desirous of blessing, generous with rewards, demonstrating justice and showing compassion to his subjects'. And he had reduced the people's tax by one sixth.

I was about to ask him the question, but before I could allow my mouth to speak the imprisoned words I remembered that he was also said to love liquor, and that when he drank to excess he turned into a killer, issuing cruel sentences as he caroused and ordering hideous murders while he was out of his senses. Terror took hold of me and silenced me; I was not so acquainted with him as to know his sobriety from his drunkenness, or his tolerance from his tyranny.

And then another thought: could a king of the Christians have gifted him the shroud as proof of loyalty? And could the shroud of that poor saint, resting for ever with his head apart from his body, divided between two cities, two civilisations, two deaths, have been given to a Muslim, even though this Muslim was al-Muzaffar, Sword of the Realm, Abd al-Malik ibn al-Mansur?

Al-Muzaffar commanded again: 'Observe!' I looked and saw... my God, Córdoba! Water and greenery and cotton clouds swimming in the air, and gardens and walkways and buildings tinted in the colours of sunset, spheres of luxury and vibrant life and breezes dancing with the scent of jasmine.

I found myself standing in one of the embroidery workshops of the Court, in front of me a large piece of silk, with a blue background, stretched on a leaning frame, while the music of the qanun, the oud and the ney guided hands that plied needles and lavished upon the cloth silk thread and thread sheathed in gold.

When I understood what I saw I stepped back, gasping at a scene so magnificent that it filled me with awe – could there be a connection between that awe which inspires reverence and that which inspires terror? The fabric was embellished with circles of pearls, connected by ornamental drawings of plants and flowers. Inside the raised circles with their pomegranate border, bearded knights on a hunting trip, some carrying leopards behind them, or raising a falcon, or a spear, or a braided stick, such as the Umayyads carried in Córdoba. The rows of raised circles each holding two knights alternated with rows of circles containing sphinxes, and there were star-shaped objects containing falcons with rabbits in their claws, or others with their wings fully spread, as in the piece that I owned. The total effect was of order and geometry and rhythmic precision: the knights and the sphinxes all facing left, with their right feet raised.

And when I lifted my eyes from the fabric to the faces of the embroiderers I saw that they were all blind; their eyes fixed to the sky, their inner sight addressing colour, stitch, thread and design. Persians and Turks and Arab and Spanish Andalusians, with slim fingers racing over the textured taffeta trembling under the piercing of double-pointed needles. Blue undulating like the sea, threads drowning in it then surfacing like fish that stiffened instantly on the surface of the water. And the colours! In my long life I had never seen their like; as though they were from the dawn of creation, from the bursting forth of the first day.

I went to the only sighted person amongst them – their foreman, to ask him to explain the whole matter. He said: They cannot see, yes, but they judge. This is our tradition here so that the colours remain pure, clear, bright, untouched by human eye. Embroidered by the blind so that the colours retain their essence, their radiance and wildness, or let's say their non-human magic. How do they judge? I asked him. And he replied: They are guided by melodies: the improvisations of the oud for gold thread, the ripple of the qanun for the silken red, and the beat of the duff defines the stitch. Don't forget that you're in the workshop where time is fashioned, time, which covers with its weave every blind memory.

And I went to seek the help of one who could better find a connection between my three dreams. He was an honest friend, a retired master of history, and an expert enthusiast of Andalusia, its news, peoples and sects, and I hoped that he would tell me the truth and reveal to me finally, what the connection was between poor Lazarus of the two deaths and al-Muzaffar, Sword of the Realm.

He said: He is 'Abd al-Malik ibn abu 'Amer Muhammad ibn 'Abdullah ibn 'Amer ibn abu 'Amer ibn al-Waleed ibn Yazeed ibn 'abd al-Malik al-Ma'afery. He came from the green isle to Córdoba seeking knowledge and his intelligence won him the guardianship of Prince Hisham, who was no more than eleven years old. Later, in Hisham's reign, he became 'Guardian of the Realm', empowered in all matters of state, and called himself al-Malik al-Mansur.

I interrupted him to say: You speak of his father, but what of the man who claims the piece of embroidery in your hands as his own?

He replied: It could be that the Caliph Hisham al-Mu'ayyad b-Illah gave him this valuable piece at the time that he also bestowed the title of al-Muzaffar on him.

I said: How could that be when the Caliph's mother, Subh al-Bashkanjeyyah, having first supported al-Muzaffar's father, al-Mansur, turned against him when she discovered his intention to exclude all but himself as ruler?

He said: But al-Mansur sent his son, 'Abd al-Malik, to Córdoba to tell the Caliph Hisham about the monies smuggled by his mother Subh.

I said: And the meaning of all this?

He said: That Hisham was under the influence of 'Abd al-Malik and wished to please him.

I said: And Lazarus, what of him?

He said: What of him?

I said: How could the piece of embroidery at the same time be his shroud?

He fell silent. And so did I.

I stood up and thanked him and took my leave. He shook my hand and said:

'Reorder your thoughts and don't fall prey to the chronology of time; it may trick you.' He continued: 'Valuable Andalusian silks have been mentioned in the inventories of the Vatican since the ninth century AD...'

On the way home I walked with a heavy heart, my thoughts dimming my sight, my head filled with shapes of ice, accumulating then melting. The next morning, I was still in the same condition, so I said I'll get rid of my confusion, of these dreams and puzzles, and advertise it to be sold at auction.

And so it was. Not much time passed before its buyer came, and I wrapped it well and handed it to him. His eyes laughed as he said: 'To a place of safety.' I smiled sadly: 'Who? It, or I?'

And the years passed. And my dreams left me. And my shop left me.

Only the image of Lazarus remains, signalling to me from afar, every time I contemplate my shroud, rested in the cabinet, in the second drawer to the left.

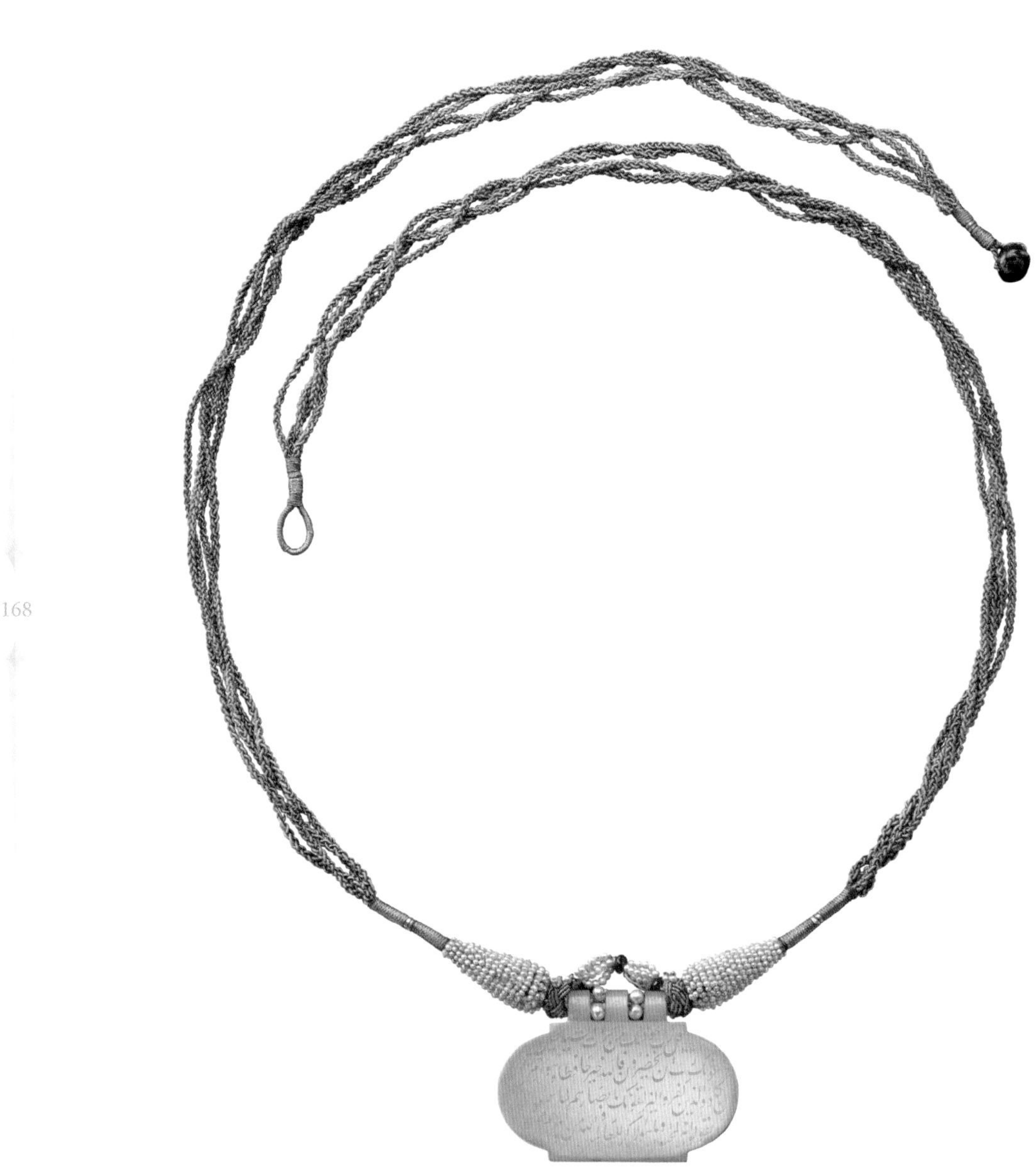

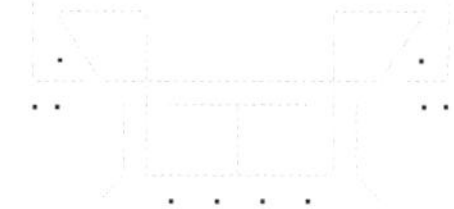

Heart of Empire

Sonia Jabbar

A few weeks after my eighteen-year-old brother was killed in a motorcycle accident in Calcutta, my father hurriedly tied a protective amulet around my neck. It was a tiny box of beaten silver, which housed verses from the Qur'an. I didn't like it much. The edges scratched my chest and unlike my middle brother, who wore his proudly at the base of his throat like a roadside Lothario, I wore mine longer, hidden under my clothes. It wasn't just that I was embarrassed by the uncharacteristic display of superstition in my urbane, educated father; I knew with the unerring instinct of a ten-year-old that though it might help me dodge a capricious fate, the amulet was powerless against the sudden storms that rose and raged within me. This, because by the time the *tabeez* was tied I had already learned to distinguish between sadness, experienced thus far with the breaking of a toy or the death of a rescued fledgling, and grief, that dull, miserable feeling that welled up inside and stained our lives for ever.

I hadn't thought about that long-discarded amulet for decades and it was only while wandering around the Museum of Islamic Art in Doha that the memory returned. Among the dazzling displays I came upon something similar: a small and rather simple object. It was a pale jade tablet no larger than a potato chip, unadorned, and unlike the other priceless jewellery on display, neither gilded nor embellished with precious stones. Unlike my *tabeez*, the verses from the Qur'an were etched upon it, but the engraving was so unostentatious that viewed from a certain angle it looked more like a play of shadow and light than elegant calligraphy. It was such an unassuming thing that I imagined it sitting on a dervish's chest. The caption accompanying it revealed very little: 'Calligraphic Jade Pendant (Haldili), India, dated 1631-32 (1041 AH), Jade (nephrite), JE.85'.

Why was such a plain object displayed in a museum that housed some of the finest renderings of Islamic art? I got myself an audio guide hoping to learn more. It advised me to look at the inscription on the *haldili's* lip. Astonishing. Far from the obscure mendicant that I had imagined, it proclaimed the owner to be no other than, 'Shah Jahan Padshah son of Jahangir Padshah son of Akbar Padshah.' Further, the disembodied voice informed me, the *haldili* was supposed to 'calm heart palpitations caused by strong emotions such as grief'.

I was intrigued. My first thought was, why did my father not give me the far more useful *haldili* instead of the *tabeez*? The second was surprise that an object so simple had belonged to the Emperor Shah Jahan. Had it been his grandfather's, the brilliant, mercurial Akbar, who delved into the heart of Sufi mysticism, I would not have been surprised. But Shah Jahan, born Khurram, renamed 'King of the World', was quite different. For one he was the richest, most powerful man of the seventeenth century, East or West, whose reign was marked by the most flamboyant display of wealth. If he wore amulets they were more likely to be the magnificent hexagonal 73.2-carat emerald inscribed with the Throne Verse from the Qur'an (looted from the Baghdad Museum in 2003).[1] If he sat on a throne, it could be no less than the *Takht e-Tavus*, the Peacock Throne, made of gold worth 14 million rupees and jewels worth 86 million rupees. If he needed a capital, the Agra of his ancestors would not do, and he would build himself a spanking new Shah Jahanabad in Delhi. And if his dead wife needed a tomb, well, she would get nothing less than the Taj Mahal. Indeed, a note in the published Museum's guide links the *haldili* with the romance of the mausoleum: 'He would have worn this amulet next to his heart whilst he was building the world's most famous public monument of a man's love for his wife – the Taj Mahal.'

Emperors are known for conquests of territory, not of the heart. But Shah Jahan's claim to fame continues to be his romance with Mumtaz Mahal. The emperor himself encouraged this storyline. Known for personally censoring every written word and vetting every painting produced at his court, he nevertheless allowed his biographers to dismiss his other wives as having 'nothing more than the status of marriage'. Of Arjumand Bano, who became Mumtaz Mahal, Ornament of the Palace, in 1612 (1020 AH), they exulted: 'The mutual affection and harmony between the two had reached a degree never seen between a husband and wife among classes of rulers, or among the people. And this was not merely out of sexual passion: the excellent qualities, pleasing habits, outward and inward virtues, and physical and spiritual compatibility on both sides caused great love and affection and extreme affinity and familiarity.'[2] Shah Jahan ascended the throne in 1628 (1037 AH), but Mumtaz Mahal was to be Empress of India for only three short years. As she lay dying at the age of thirty-eight in Burhanpur, far south of the Mughal capital at Agra, the court gossips alleged that she extracted a promise from her husband to build her a mausoleum that would leave the world breathless.

I have visited the Taj complex at Agra half a dozen or more times over the years and have absorbed the perfect symmetry of the *charbagh*, the *baoli* near the mosque, the *naubatkhana*, the perfection of the calligraphy adorning its gates and, of course, the grace of the building itself. I have strolled around early in the morning, at noon, in the late afternoon in winter with the light angling in and the rose-ringed parakeets screeching raucously in the gardens. I have contemplated it at length at dusk and then again at dawn from the sandy banks of Babur's Mahtab Bagh across the Jamuna, now dull grey and treacly with pollutants. I have idled many hours in its gardens. And yet, something eludes me; something doesn't ring true despite the protestations of the most eloquent of Agra's pot-bellied tour guides. It's not just that of all Mughal buildings I have a predilection for the red sandstone of Akbar's Fatehpur Sikri, that charming city of tiered pavilions and elegant cupolas, or for the muscular grace of Humayun's Tomb in Delhi. Nor that if I were to choose from among the marble edifices I would rank the creation of Shah Jahan's bête noire, Noor Jahan's, tomb for her father a notch higher than the Taj. No, there's something inherently cold in its flawlessness, soulless in its symmetry. It's like a woman whose perfect beauty disguises a congenital neurosis or a man whose physical perfection cloaks a streak of cruelty. And where is the celebrated love in this cool, white mausoleum? Where is the passion?

It is true that Shah Jahan loved his wife; in fact he loved her to death. In the nineteen years that she was married she bore him fourteen children, the last of whom killed her in labour. By the seventeenth century birth control was not only known, but actively practised in the Mughal court. Only select consorts were allowed to bear children; mistresses, courtesans, lesser wives of the seraglio aborted their foetuses with herbs and potions no sooner than they were impregnated. So why, when there were sensible options, did Shah Jahan and Mumtaz Mahal embark on this entirely foolish display of his virility and her fecundity? Why, when she did get pregnant, did he insist on her accompanying him on his arduous expeditions and military campaigns all over his father's empire? And then, when she died why did he, who is supposed to have loved her as much as he did, bury and exhume, bury and exhume her body four times?[3] I may be forgiven for suspecting this love.

The court chroniclers insist (and the tour guides love to repeat) that Shah Jahan grieved so much for Mumtaz, his beard turned white overnight. But either the emperor was sloppy in his censoring or too vain, for events recorded by miniature painters long after Mumtaz Mahal's death show a handsome, robust, black-bearded Shah Jahan not some drab, wilting widower.[4] The twenty-six years that passed between Mumtaz Mahal's death and Shah Jahan's is not something that romantics would care to dwell on; not only did Shah Jahan live the life befitting an emperor – waging wars, bestowing *mansabs*, receiving emissaries, hunting, holidaying in Kashmir, marrying off sons – he married twice in the intervening period, to say nothing of the numerous concubines who warmed his bed until his death at the ripe old age of seventy-four. Europeans at the Mughal court whispered that the stranguary that killed him resulted from his experiments with various aphrodisiacs. Bernier writes that not only was the Emperor 'fond of sex', but he even developed an incestuous relationship with his daughter, the Princess Jahanara. Though this was 'difficult to believe', the court mullahs turned a blind eye by declaring, 'it would have been unjust to deny the King the privilege of gathering fruit from the tree he had himself planted'. From Bernier we learn of a jealous Shah Jahan who barges into Jahanara's apartment one night. The unmarried princess, who had smuggled a lover into her chambers, quickly hid him in a capacious bathing cauldron. Revealing nothing, the Emperor casually suggested that his daughter should bathe, commanding her attendants to light a fire under the cauldron. According to Bernier, Shah Jahan 'did not retire until they gave him to understand that his wretched victim was no more'.[5]

Licentious, cruel, sadistic, selfish; was the builder of the world's greatest monument to love really capable of love? One of the many words for love in the Muslim world is *ishq* (Arabic, Persian and Urdu), which means passionate love or rapture. It is the closest one can get to divine love. One whose heart has been touched by true love is one graced by the presence of God. The ideal lover is utterly selfless: a man like Majnoun, who wanders the desert like a madman for his Laila, or Ranjha who swallows poison for his Heer, or Farhad, the sculptor who moves a mountain for his love, Shirin; not a vain, old emperor who boils his daughter's lover to death. And yet, as I regarded the *haldili*, something within me softened towards Shah Jahan. This small, simple object that promised the one who wore it refuge from the storms of his heart was greater proof of love than all the grandeur of the Taj Mahal; it was the manifestation of the private grief of a very public emperor. It is dated 1631 (1040 AH), the year Mumtaz Mahal died, but I find myself hoping that it continued to protect the man well into the time when he would taste the poisonous fruit of a love he could never adequately return.

'You never loved me!' raged his third son, Aurangzeb. At the time he was forty and Shah Jahan sixty-six, an age that fathers and sons are, at worst, reconciled. But that was never to be. Sent away from Agra on difficult military campaigns from the time he was a teenager while his eldest brother was cosseted at court, Aurangzeb rarely received approval from his father. Away from the luxury and sophistication of the Mughal court, he grew into a severe, thickset man who found comfort in the most conservative interpretation of the Qur'an. Shah Jahan treated him with contempt, often ignoring his requests for funds to maintain and upgrade his army, mocking him for military failures, which were really caused by his own poor strategy and humiliating him in public. Aurangzeb was to wait many years before exacting a terrible revenge.

In the burning, sultry June of 1658 (1068 AH), having defeated his eldest brother, Dara Shikoh, in the battle of Samogarh, the challenger to the throne laid siege to the Agra Fort, cutting off the channel which brought the river waters into the ramparts. Shah Jahan was desperate: 'My Son, my hero,' he wrote in a letter to the man he despised, 'Why should I complain of unkind fortune, seeing that not a leaf falls without God's will? Yesterday I had an army of nine hundred thousand; today I am in need of a pitcher of water! O prosperous son, be not proud of the good luck of this treacherous world!' Aurangzeb sent the letter back with an impatient scribble: '*Karda-i-khwesh ayed pesh*' – as we sow, so we reap![6] He was not wrong. Shah Jahan had rebelled against his father as a young man and when he became emperor, had all his rivals, including two brothers, cousins and nephews, executed for good measure. Aurangzeb followed in his footsteps doggedly, justifying his rebellion in letters to his father: 'Although I heard that disturbances were being raised... I refused to lend credence to hearsay and remained loyal to you... till I knew for certain that you did not love me...'[7]

Beware the wrath of the unloved. Manucci reports that after ordering his execution, Aurangzeb sent his brother's head to Agra to be served to the imprisoned Emperor in a covered dish when he sat down to dinner. 'On withdrawing the lid, he discovered the face of Prince Dara. Horrified, he uttered one cry and fell on his hands and face upon the table; and striking against the golden vessels, broke some of his teeth and lay there apparently lifeless...'[8] Aurangzeb had more horrors in store for Shah Jahan as he dispatched his rivals one by one: Prince Shuja's assassination in Burma, Murad's in Gwalior and Dara's son Sulayman Shikoh's slow poisoning into madness and death.

His rage unslaked by the blood he had spilled, Aurangzeb then turned on his hapless subjects. He re-imposed *jaziya*, the tax on Hindus, which Emperor Akbar had revoked in his time, and banned music, art, wine, dancing and entertainment. The luminaries who had found patronage at the Mughal court and made it the wonder of the world – the artists, designers, poets, jewellers, architects, sculptors, calligraphers, sufis and philosophers – moved on to greener pastures. The state treasury drained steadily into the new emperor's relentless military campaigns. As if the lineage inscribed on the lip of the *haldili*, ending with Shah Jahan Padshah, was a prophecy: for from here began the slow decline of the great Mughal Empire. Unconsoled, unloved and alone on his deathbed, Aurangzeb wrote a final letter to his son, Kam Baksh: 'Soul of my soul... I am going alone... Every torment I have inflicted, every sin I have committed, every wrong I have done, I carry the consequences with me. Strange, that I came into the world with nothing, and now I am going away with this stupendous caravan of sin! Wherever I look, I see only God... I have sinned terribly, and I do not know what punishment awaits me...'[9]

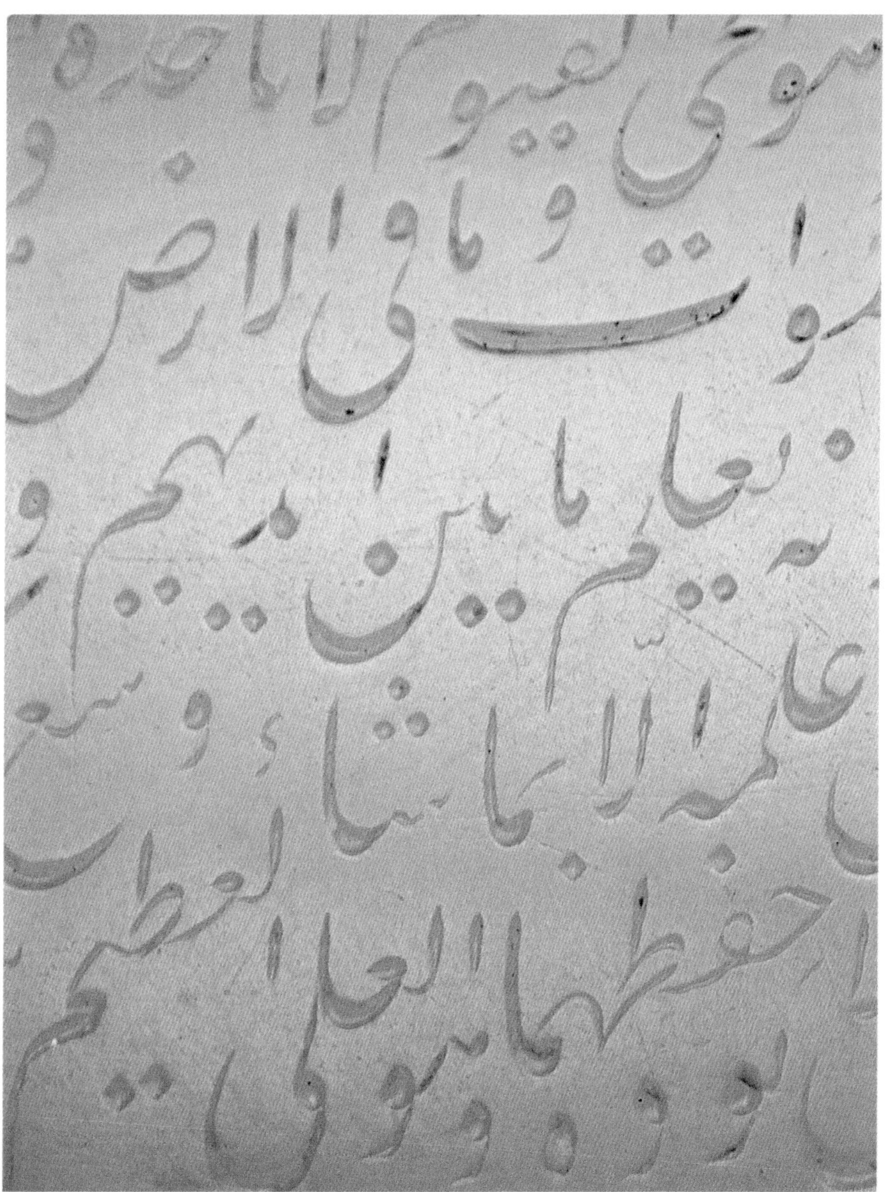

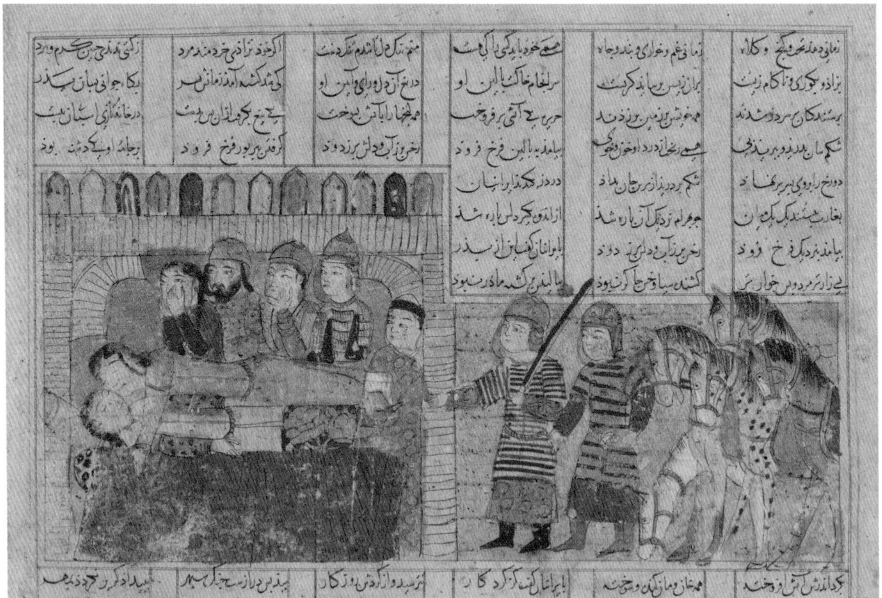

Some Mother's Son

Shirin Neshat

She woke with a start, with a pounding heart, the neighing stampede of horses hurling her into a waking life through the womb of a nightmare, soaked in blood, swallowed in flames. In that fleeting moment of first consciousness she knew her boy would die that day. She opened her eyes and looked upon the face that bore such aching traces of a father long dead; the crescent of his brow, the slope of his nose, the long black lashes resting on the soft skin that covered the hard bones of patriarchal geography, the human face bordered and bound to kith and kin.

The quarrels of men gathered at her gate. She watched her boy step into its vortex and return to her arms with a sealed fate, his body laid out on a cold white slab, his heart pumping out of synch. She held her face close to his mouth and felt the breaths expelled: one, two, three, then no more. In one broad stroke the living son succumbed to symbol.

A shift in her womb like a plate tectonic split the singular continent of mother and son and as he drifted away from her into the horizon of myths and legends, images and icons, symbols and stories, she looked upon this perpetual tale of wailing women and warring men, setting it all afire as she stepped inside, climbing the slab where her dead son lay, a blade in hand she opened her belly, enveloping his body, taking him back to the womb of the world where all mankind is nothing more and nothing less than some mother's son.

The nightmare is now branded on a young man's core, words written on the image, but beneath the word and behind the picture, a living hand once rested on a beating heart. Now stilled.

Text by Rabeah Ghaffari

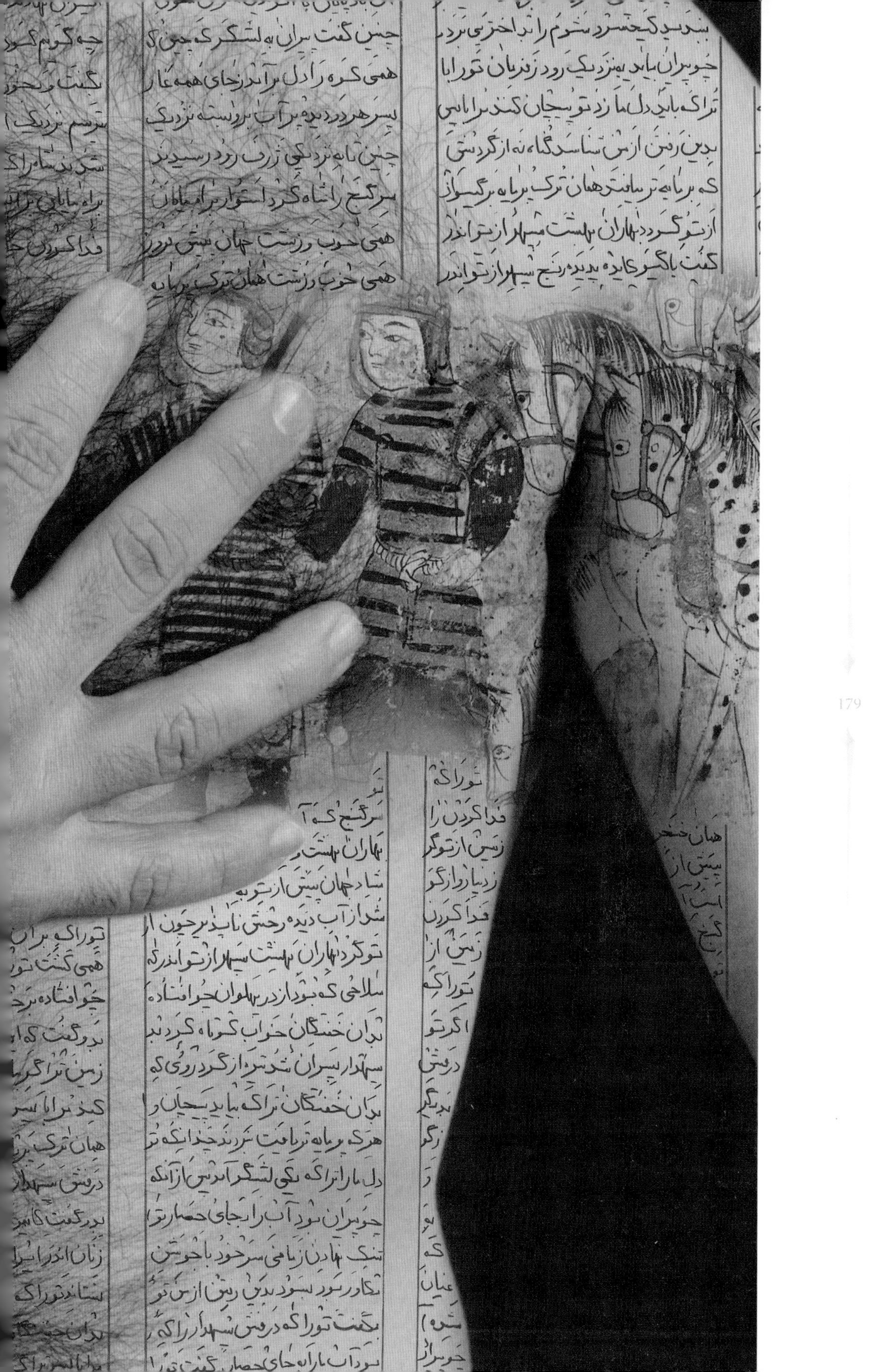

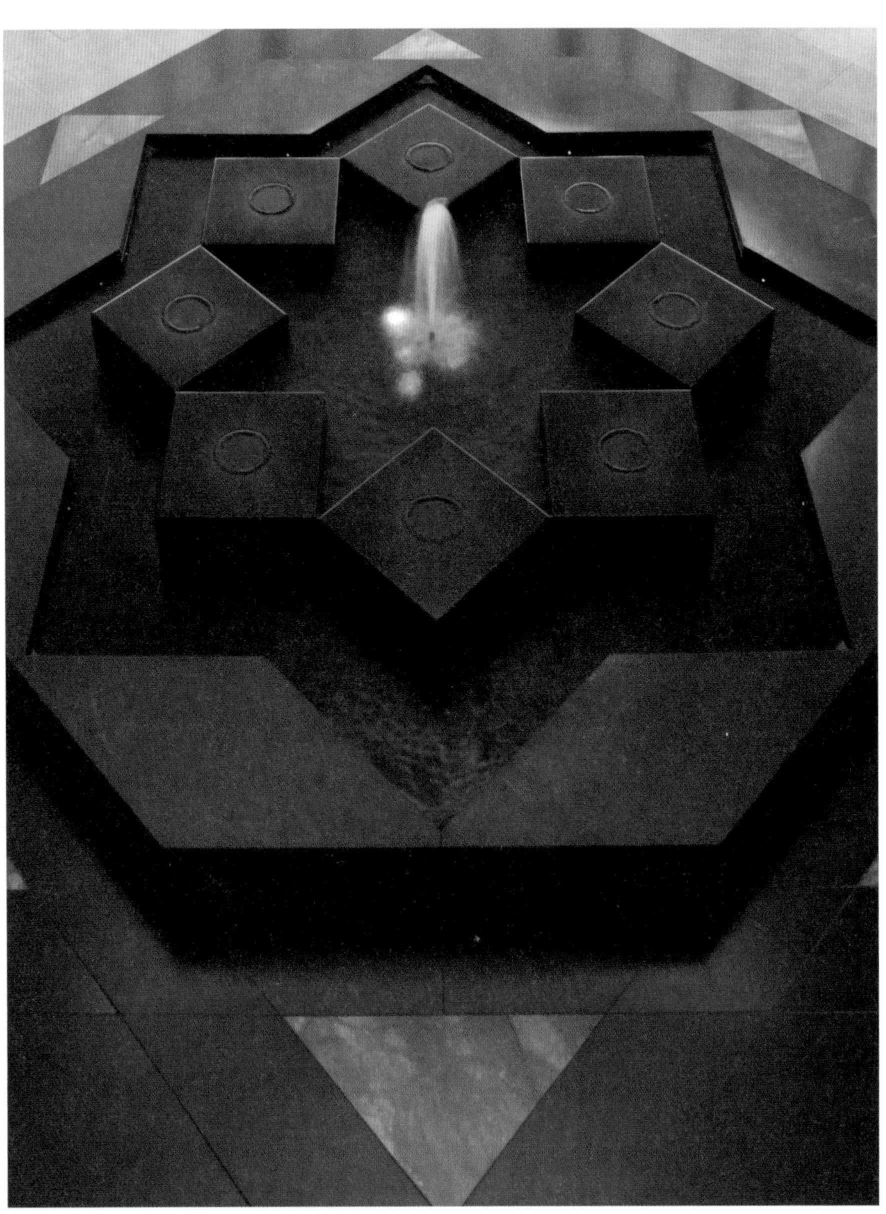

The Nightmare of the Translator

Anton Shammas

In a dimly lit, muted corner, encased behind thick glass, painfully small in size, totally outside the visitors' attention: a golden belt-buckle, abandoned and solitary in its fragility, far away from fourteenth-century Granada. It was the intricate, blue enamelled, eight-pointed star at its heart that first drew my attention; a distant Andalusian echo, reverberating in the background. I remembered I'd just seen that star from the bridge overlooking the atrium of the Museum of Islamic Art; seen it in the eight-pointed star-fountain that I.M. Pei has placed at the heart of the MIA as an aqueous, architectural statement: that the murmur of running water and the eight-pointed star are the most prevalent motifs of Islamic art. The husky voice of Paco Ibañez would come to me later, singing the ballad of Rafael Alberti about 'the one who never went to Granada', about the 'chains around the murmurs of her fountains'.[1] But now there it was, Nasrid Granada itself, quintessentially present in this small golden buckle, and I felt I no longer needed to 'set foot in Granada'.

Yet for a buckle, I thought, to be worthy of the name, it needs to establish a connection of sorts between two ends; that is its mission, its purpose. For each thing, we are told, insofar as it is in itself, endeavours to persist in its own being – in this case, being a buckle. And there was the nightmare of the buckle: to cease being an object whose raison d'être is to connect together the two ends of the royal belt and, as a re-assigned signification, become an artefact in a museum, for idle yet utterly grateful visitors like myself to contemplate and adore. Was this the original, concealed intent of the Granadan goldsmith who forged this buckle in his workshop, probably for the Sultan himself? Did he mean for the buckle to outlive its bearer and the lassitude of his kingdom, to carry over into a new context his 'izz, his glory (or his *farr*, as Ferdowsi would have said – but that, too, would come to me later), across centuries and countries and climes? 'Beauty,' Kant has been telling us, 'is the form of the purposiveness of an object so far as this is perceived in it without any representation of a purpose.' The purpose of a buckle, then, is to connect two ends of a belt, to horizontally accentuate and adorn the human waist, maybe that of the Sultan himself. But now the buckle is bereft of its belt, distant Granada bereft of its Sultan. Now, the buckle, which otherwise would have found no meaning and no sense in not being itself, does not display any representation of a purpose but, rather, its now purposeless beauty, is encased behind glass. Otherwise how could I have seen it, without ever setting foot in Granada?

The words in relief, *'izz li-mawlana al-sultan*, an echo of the calligraphy that adorns the walls of the Alhambra alongside the more famous *la ghalib illa Allah*, 'God is the only victor', assert in enamelled white, red and green: 'Glory to our lord the Sultan.' At first, I wanted to mistake the 'glory' of the first word, 'izz, for *'ud*, or 'return,' as the 'z' and 'd' in Arabic calligraphy look sometimes beguilingly alike, and I wanted to think that the words were actually saying: 'Return to our lord The Sultan!' as if the royal buckle was carrying its own 'return address', as it were, in a self-referential loop; that no matter where destiny and fate would take it, it would always return to its master, the Sultan, in fourteenth-century Granada; yearning to hold the crumbling kingdom together, even after that last stronghold of 'izz and glory had been diminished for many centuries and been turned into a nostalgic Andalusian poem. That is when I remembered what a friend had pointed out about the word 'buckle' being an auto-antonym: as well as holding things together, it can also mean falling apart.

The goldsmith forged this perfect buckle around the perfect number eight and its variations, the inner core of Islamic art, when the artist and the mathematician used to be one. Eight points to the enamelled star in the middle, which is formed by eight intertwined blue lines; eight filigreed and granulated spheres in the attenuated thumb-piece at the bottom; and sixteen letters, all in all, for the calligraphic inscription. But the tiny, almost inaudible seven-pointed star of the boss at the top, takes us, should we so desire, a century ahead, to one end of the imaginary missing belt, to a World Map that depicts, as a mathematical echo, the seven climes of the world.

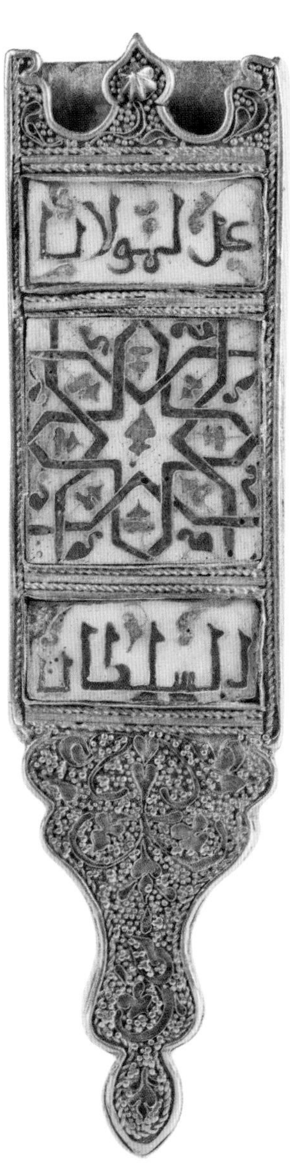

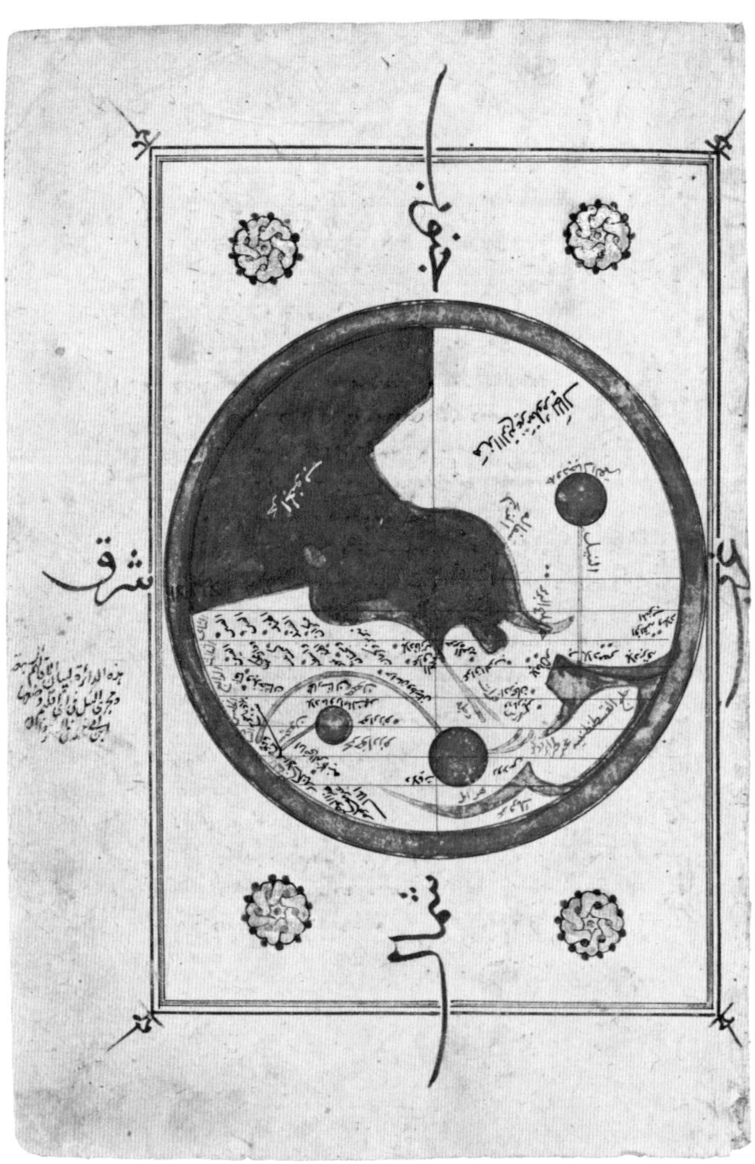
شرق

And one's first reaction to this rather abstract Map of the World, from a now dispersed manuscript, is total disorientation. Similar to that of, say, the fifteenth-century Arab cartographer responsible for it; the cartographer whose South was at the top of the map, and who would look at 'our' upside-down maps not knowing that self-proclaimed superior Europe, for the past 500 years or so, has consistently positioned itself at the top of the world, giving North the upper hand, looking down on the rest of Earth with the arrogant coloniser's gaze, believing that you can have sovereignty over whatever territory you can map out. This wasn't the case in the fifteenth century. When he drew this map, most likely in Egypt, our cartographer (or the copyist drawing on the work of our cartographer), couldn't make up his mind between South and North, and so positioned South at the top, as was the custom among Arab cartographers, but then decided that – to read the writing and make out the division of the northern hemisphere into seven climes, or regions, marked in parallel, red horizontal lines – the reader would have to turn the manuscript upside down. And then there were southern parts of Africa and northern parts of Asia that had not yet been mapped out, some terra incognita, so he added a neatly scribed notation saying: 'This territory is unknown/uncharted'; unlike his European counterparts, who assumed terror in unknown territories and marked them with monsters and other imaginary beasts. But the real cartographic nightmare was what lay on the flip side of the map, what lay behind the edge of darkness. Later in that century, the other side of the map, the New World, was allegedly 'discovered' by Columbus, who took with him on his first voyage west an Arabic interpreter, because he was sure Arab cartography and the Arabic language inhabited the Eastern world where he was heading, and he needed that interpreter to converse with that world. But that didn't turn out to be the case, and so Arabic was rendered obsolete in the New World, as was this map that, much like the buckle, has lost its geographic purpose and has been turned into a work of abstract art.

My own minor nightmare, however, was different from the cartographer's. It didn't have to do with the flip side of the world but, rather, the hidden and 'uncharted' verso side of this disarticulated folio – what was the manuscript for which this map had been commissioned? In other words, if the map doesn't show us accurate details of the world, as we now know it, what can it tell us, then, about itself? Unable to see the verso, and perhaps even not that interested, I was more intrigued, being an amateur cartographic detective, by the possibilities of unravelling the secrets of the map based exclusively on its own 'text'. I wanted simply to decipher its concealed codes – on its own terms. But the framed, enclosed map, hauntingly beautiful as it is, revealed contradictory clues at best and, as is the case with its South/North confusion, it sent mixed messages about its possible origin and date of composition. For if it is indeed a fifteenth-century map, as we are informed, then why isn't it, for instance, as detailed as the more famous map of al-Idrisi, based on his twelfth-century 'image of the world', in which the southern part of Africa, unlike in this one, extends eastward, giving the Indian Ocean a very long southern coast? Al-Idrisi's influence on future Islamic cartography, we are told, as an explanation of sorts, was minimal and, moreover, there was always a large gap between geographic theory and cartographic practice in Arab culture. So cartography in a certain age didn't always reflect the geographic knowledge of that age, hence the seeming abstraction of this particular map; its being almost out of tune with what had cartographically preceded it.

And then later, when I was re-reading the map, something else caught my attention – a three-line notation, an afterthought, outside the frame, written in black on the left margin of the map: 'This circle is to illustrate the seven climes / and the course of the Nile in each clime as established by / Ibn Abi... in...' The rest of the third line could hardly be made out; the full name of that mysterious author, and his book, were made obscure by a quill whose ink seemed to have run dry as it struggled to reach the end of the line. So the major clue to the map's origin was obfuscated by a moody quill, and I lost hope. But then a colleague told me he had seen a very similar map in Gotha, Germany, in a manuscript of *Halbat al-Kumayt* (The Racecourse of the Bay Horse), a famous fifteenth-century encomium on wine, written in Egypt by one al-Nawaji (1383-1455/784-859 AH). In the twentieth chapter of his book, al-Nawaji suddenly abandons his major theme of wine-drinking and its etiquette, and sets out to write a geographic treatise on Egypt and the Nile, and he quotes copiously from the fourteenth-century manuscript *Kitab al-Sukkardan* (The Book of the Sugar Bowl), by Ibn Abi Hajalah (1325-75/725-76 AH). And now looking again at the semi-erased third line of the marginal notation, things fell into place, the third word appeared to be clearly 'Hajalah', and it followed that the last word should read '*al-Sukkardan*'. So the notation was pointing out that the inclusion of this map in this particular manuscript is merely to add an illustration to the chapter on the seven climes of the world in Ibn Abi Hajalah's *Kitab al-Sukkardan*.

'Praise be to Allah,' Ibn Abi Hajalah writes at the outset of his manuscript, 'who by his might ordered the seven rivers to flow, and who made our lord the Sultan sit on the throne as the seventh among his [twelve] brothers... And since seven is the noblest of numbers, and since its manifestations are very common in Egypt... I have written this book in seven chapters.' He then gives a very long and detailed list of all things he can think of which revolve around, or are connected to, the number seven. There are seven elements, seven colours, and seven doors of hell; there are seven verses in the first surah of the Qur'an, seven flowers in Egypt, and seven is the number of years that Joseph spent in Egypt at the house of Potiphar before he was tempted by his master's wife, and seven is the number of years he spent in prison, etc. But above all, Ibn Abi Hajalah elaborates on the Ptolemaic idea of dividing the northern hemisphere into seven climes, or climates, and gives a very detailed geographic description of the land of Egypt and the Nile, being in the Third Clime. And that is, presumably, what al-Nawaji is quoting at length on the verso side of this folio, which I believe is a page from another dispersed copy of *Halbat al-Kumayt*.

Persian cartographers preceded the Arabs in thinking about the division of the northern hemisphere into seven regions, but instead of using the parallel lines, they represented their view in what they called the *kashvar* system: a central circle, with Persia (Babel) at its centre, is surrounded by six other circles, representing the other climes. So the *kashvar* is, in effect, a six-pointed star. And if you look at our map again, you will notice that at its corners, in gold, red and blue, there are four six-pointed stars that usher us straight into another nightmare – *The Nightmare of Zahhak*.

In *The Nightmare of Zahhak*, a painting from a manuscript of the *Shahnameh*, commissioned by the Safavid Shah Tahmasp in the sixteenth century, the artist, Mir Musavvir, has to grapple with a multilayered nightmare of his own. The *Shahnameh*, Ferdowsi's masterpiece and the national epic of Persia, was composed at the beginning of the eleventh century, and now, five centuries later, the painter chooses to represent a moment in the narrative, when Zahhak, the evil king who ruled for 1,000 years, wakes up from a nightmare, some forty years before the end of his reign, and the whole palace is in turmoil. So it is not the nightmare itself that Mir Musavvir chooses to represent but, rather, its aftermath, resonating around the different spaces of the palace. And as we are tiptoeing on the meticulously ornamented tiles – that are all variations on the six-pointed star motif – we notice that Mir Musavvir has slyly planted some nightmarish clues here and there. First we have to jettison all we know about perspective and the art of representing three-dimensional space as it was practised in that same century in Europe. Perspective was reinvented by al-Hassan Ibn al-Haytham ('Alhazen', as his name was translated into Latin), in his *Kitab al-Manazir* (Optics), which he was embarking upon in Cairo some years after Ferdowsi had finished, in 1010 (400 AH), his *Shahnameh*, over which he had laboured for thirty-five years. But Mir Musavvir has his own perspective: exploring the subtleties and symmetries of the two-dimensional space. We enter the royal palace from the lower right, as if we were reading a Persian text, and we know it's night-time because the two *qizilbash* (sentries) who accompany us, wearing the Safavid headgear, with the red upright *taj* (bayonet) stuck in their turbans, like all the other sentries in the scene, are holding torches, and there's a crescent, timid moon in the narrow sky between the upper two sections of the palace. But we also know that the headgear of these sentries places them actually at the sixteenth century court of Shah Tahmasp, not Zahhak's, and the palace is structured in the present, like a dream whose interpretation might apply to both kings – the mythological Zahhak, and the Shah who commissioned this very manuscript. And we know that Shah Tahmasp himself has his own nightmares of intrigues and poison plots and betrayals by his brothers and devotees. But now, the nightmare has just slipped away into the night, leaving its traces for the artist to capture.

The artist's first challenge, it seems, is to represent this complex structure: four levels of both wings of the palace, and its foreground, crowded with fifty-four figures (a multiple of six), three of whom are still fast asleep and the rest are at sixes and sevens, as it were, reacting to the shriek coming from the royal bedchamber. On the middle floor on the left, in front of a relatively large wall in blue, King Zahhak in his bedchamber, shoulders cursed with one snake each (that feed on human brains; the devil's curse),face that has lost its *farr*, eyes squinted in terror and fixed on the orchard at the right entrance to the palace, hands stretched out in a helpless gesture that does not suit the ruthless king – is telling his wife, Arnavaz, her fair head adorned with a golden crown, what he has just seen in his nightmare. And in his nightmare, the ruthless king has seen three warriors entering his palace. The youngest among the three was walking in the middle, his face radiating with royal *farr*, his hand holding the ox-headed mace with which he will kill Zahhak. Arnavaz calms down the

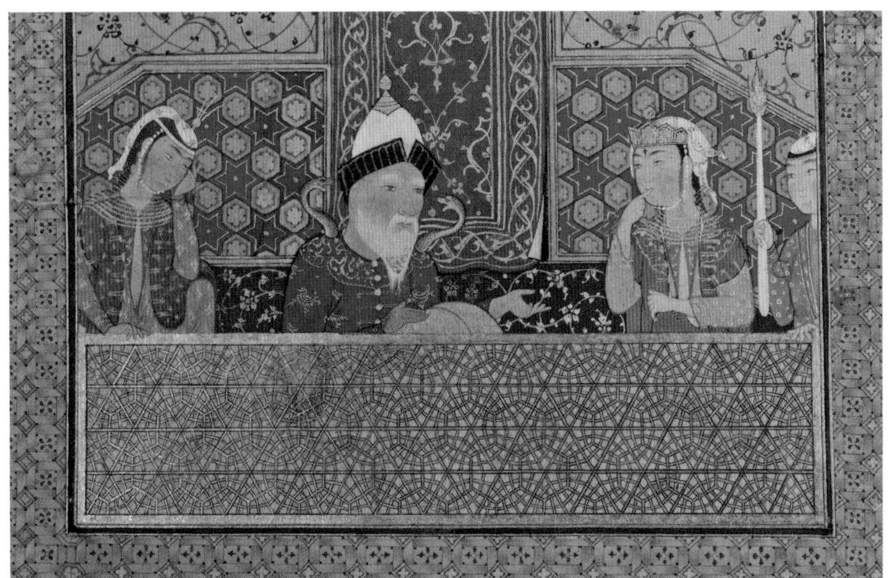

King, telling him that he has nothing to fear, 'the seven climes are yours to rule, and animals, men and demons watch over your safety'. But Zahhak doesn't feel safe at all, and summons his sages to interpret the nightmare for him:

Who will come after me? Say who will own
This royal diadem, and belt, and throne?

And he is told that the young man he has seen in the nightmare coming after him will indeed come after him. His name will be Feridoun, but he is not yet born, and when he is, in three years' time, a sacred cow named Barmayeh will nurse him, but the King will slay her, and kill Feridoun's father, and that will be why the young man will, in due course, come after the King with his ox-headed mace, seeking revenge, and will cast the royal belt into the mud. (Feridoun will actually order a cow-headed mace to be forged for him, in memory of the martyred Barmayeh, who is depicted in the Tahmasp *Shahnameh* as a horned cow. So it's not an ox-headed mace the King sees in his nightmare, as traditional scholarship has it, but a cow-headed one, the proper weapon for avenging Barmayeh's blood.)

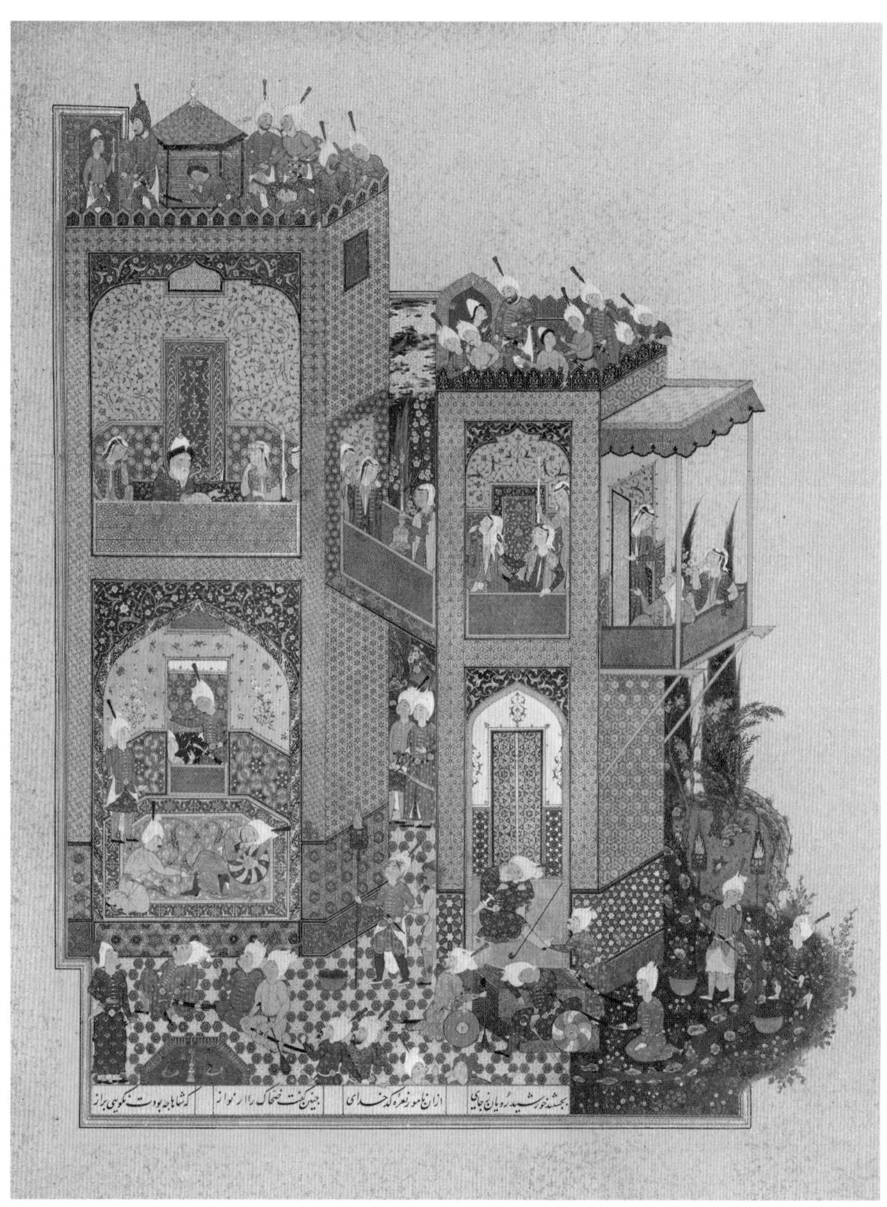
بجنبد خورشید رویان ز جای
ازان نامور نعره کدخدای
چنین گفت ضحاک را ارنواز
که شاها چه بودت بگوی براز

We enter the palace from the lower right, then, walking through the orchard, which Mir Musavvir has put there to remind the evil Zahhak that, instigated by the Devil, he had killed his own father, King Merdas. The King used to go before dawn every day to his orchard, and there he would wash and pray, accompanied by a servant carrying a torch. The Devil dug a pit into which the King, not seeing because his servant did not bring a torch that day, fell and died. And now Mir Musavvir puts two sentries with torches in the orchard that Zahhak may contemplate.

But pay attention to the sleeping *qizilbash* immediately above the first calligraphy panel on the right, dressed in blue, resting his head on his bent right arm, and probably sleeping so deeply that he doesn't wake up to the commotion caused by the sight of the cow-headed mace in Zahhak's nightmare. Feraydun is not born yet, and the cow-headed mace is yet to find the skilled blacksmith who will forge the lethal weapon for the future king. But then, maybe, there it is: in the left hand of the sleeping sentry, guarding the entrance, possibly, to Shah Tahmasp's palace, but at the same time posing a threat. First you think his hand is holding the grey head of a horned ox or cow, but then you realise that artful Mir Musavvir is playing hide and seek with his images, with the monsters of Zahhak's unconscious, with the future Feridoun and his blacksmith, with his own Shah Tahmasp, but above all with you, the onlooker: the hand could be holding a slipping grey piece of cloth that's artfully concealing the image of the secret weapon that will bring about the realisation of the nightmare. But then again, maybe it's a projected image from a sentry's counter-dream.

Imagine, then, the Museum of Islamic Art structured like a dream. Inside the space of that dream you, a visual thief, sleepwalking between darkness and light, are assigned to pick a single artefact, and translate it into words. But you cannot help yourself; you pick up three: a buckle, a map and a nightmare, in that order. And you find that all three are unconsciously strung and buckled together, by association, according to the logic of dreams, that they form variations on the numbers eight, seven and six, respectively; and you find out that turning breathtaking beauty into breathing words is, after all, the ultimate nightmare of the translator; when original and translation are no longer buckled up, and language buckles and falls apart.

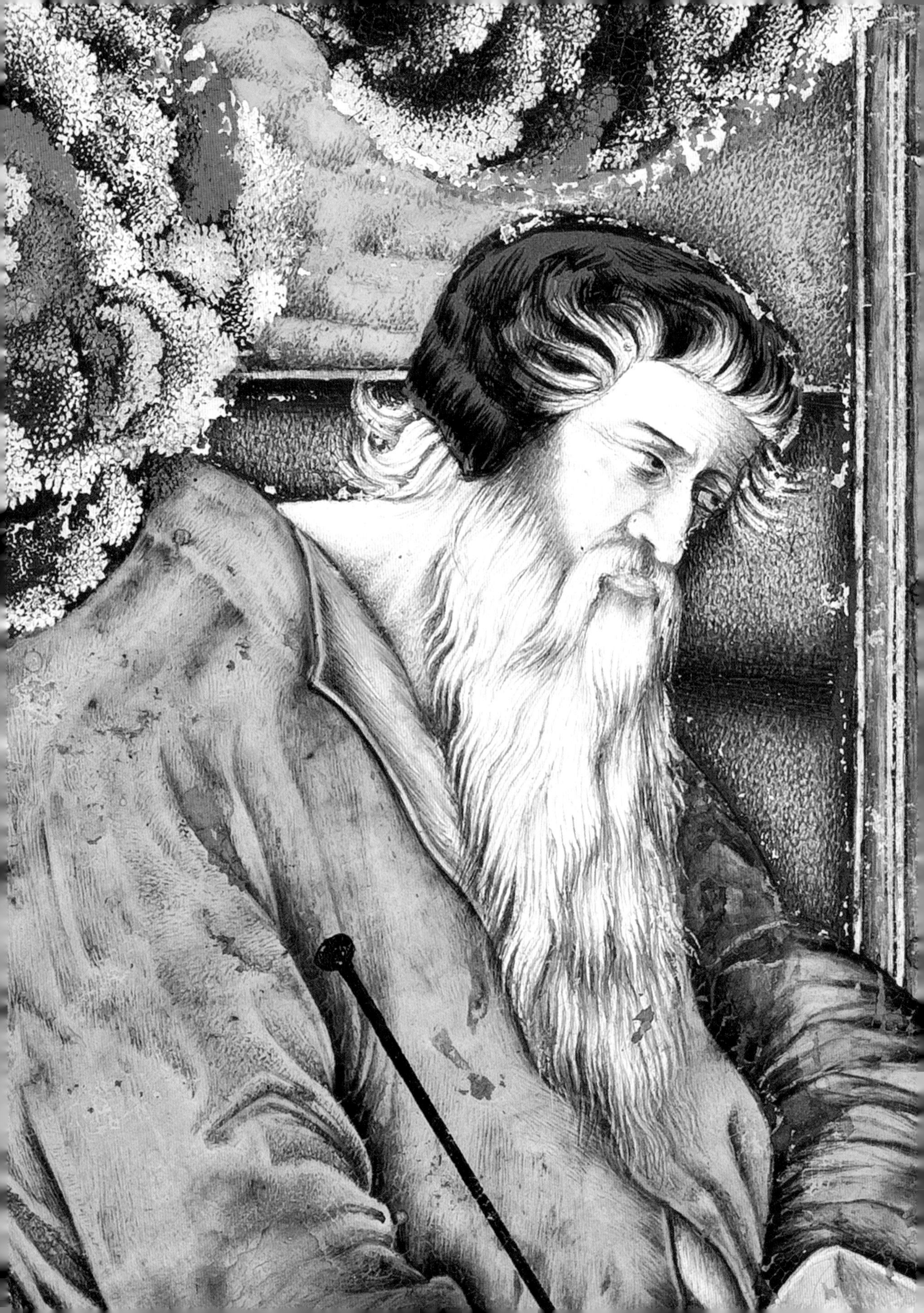

'St Jerome'

Adam Foulds

The cat laps at the spilling milk and St Jerome sits and stares. But perhaps he does not see the cat at all. His gaze is that of a person lost in concentration, who sees inward. Moreover, it is possible he can't see: his spectacles, two pairs of them, lie on a shelf behind him with a book. From this we know that at this moment his great scholarship has been laid aside. Maybe his eyes are filled with the colours of memory; an old, white-bearded man remembering his youth as a prize student in Rome or his time as a hermit in the Syrian wilderness, those austere devotions. *After my copious weeping, after fixing my eyes on heaven, I sometimes felt myself mixing with the ranks of angels, and I would cry with joyful exultation, 'I run after You in the fragrance of Your perfumes.'* He knew union then, knew transcendence. Now he is an old man in an old body sitting in a precisely painted, earthly and factual wicker chair. But then... *I see a strangely brighter light; here I rejoice to throw off the burden of flesh and soar to the pure radiance of heaven.*

Flesh looks like a burden to the old and famous man, the translator of the Bible. Of course it is possible that his work is what is on his mind, a question of translation, and it might be profitable for translation to be on our minds also as we stand in this corner of the Museum and look at this miniature by Farrukh Beg, painted for the Mughal emperor Jahangir.

The Oxford English Dictionary provides extensive definitions of the transitive verb 'to translate,' among them, *bear, convey or remove from one person, place, time or condition to another,* and, *expound the significance of something not expressed in words; interpret, explain.* Also, *express in terms of something else, or by a different medium or mode of expression.*

In Farrukh Beg's painting the translator has been translated, conveyed in space from northern Europe to India and expressed in a new mode. The sombre resonance of the Dürer engraving on which the painting is based, its sharp, close lines of black ink that vibrate in the eye to become shadow and form, are here transformed into the vivid, compact, harmonious colours of a Mughal miniature, colours that recall silks, gemstones, the wings of birds.

Before he entered Dürer's imagination, depicted Jerome had already been conveyed for 1,000 years, translated from a real man born in Dalmatia in the fourth century to a new amalgam of man, saint and fable. An established father of the church. A scourge of heretics. A saint in heaven. The man who had pulled a thorn from the paw of a lion and was accompanied by the creature for ever after. The man who'd undertaken the terrifying task of translating the Bible from Hebrew, Aramaic and Greek into Latin.

Dürer made several images of Jerome, a popular subject of Renaissance paintings and engravings which usually show him as an emaciated hermit in the wilderness or quiet and contemplative in his study, a scholar at work in deep, clear silence. Dürer's engravings were of the scholar. Later they were copied, or at least liberally borrowed from, by the artist Marten de Vos. It is De Vos's image that Farrukh Beg knew. Altering and adapting much else, Beg copied closely the grave, bearded face of the saint. That face was conveyed intact all the way east from Dürer's studio to Mughal India.

Which brings us to the question of place. Where is Jerome exactly? Sitting still, his posture unmoved, his facial expression unchanging, his clothes have been transformed, colour has filled every point of his monochrome surroundings, furniture has moved, a tree has grown, animals have appeared. In this place Jerome seems to be simultaneously inside and outside. The desk in De Vos's engraving has come with him, a rigid geometrical structure of straight lines angling into space in strong Renaissance perspective, complete with vases, that bottle of spilling milk and the lapping cat. But now it sits ambiguously athwart a stone wall and appears to be floating. The shelf behind Jerome, where his spectacles and book rest, also hovers across or within this surrounding wall. Two kinds of space, the hard and geometrical and the soft and enfolding, seem to be at odds with each other. The effect, however, is not awkward.

There isn't the jolting clumsiness of a mistake. Rather there is the gentle pressure of suggestion, of psychological connotation. It reminds me of how perspective is actually experienced in life, solid and mathematical in immediate focus but afloat and unstable in peripheral vision or with eyes defocused by concentration. We are offered perhaps Jerome's vision, the disintegration of his physical surroundings as he sits lost in deep thought. The real and the perceived, objective and subjective, are alloyed in the supple space of Beg's miniature. A similar combination of outward appearance and inner reality is to be found in the tree that flourishes behind Jerome, rising up over his leaning head. It is exquisitely painted. The modulation of colour and shadow around the smooth trunk is so fine it amazes. The sharply drawn leaves billow in strange, stereotyped growth. They are colourful and vivacious but their form is oddly, unnaturally pure, as though the principle of growth itself has been illustrated. The leaves multiply like the repetitions of a fractal. The tree is a force of nature, of creation, Jerome would say, revealed. The contingent appearance of nature has been translated into a clearer phrase, its meaning disclosed.

In that metaphysical tree sit two pairs of birds. At Jerome's feet lies curled a sleeping dog. Behind Jerome, under the tree, a cat licks its left paw. Two goats with two kids, one of which suckles from its mother, are also present in this inside outside place. The old translator sits in his wicker chair, thinking, and around him all these animals lead their bodily lives. Animals in European Renaissance art usually serve a symbolic function, representing with their earthly forms the transcendent realities of Christ's story, but these animals seem unencumbered by such meanings. They seem free as they bleat, lick, suckle, sing. It is Jerome, the human, the master of language, who seems burdened. Poets, who live by language, who struggle for words and through words, have often noticed how they contribute to the privileged and painful isolation of man among the creatures. W.H. Auden wrote of people as animals' 'lonely betters'. The Russian poet Osip Mandelstam wrote of the wordlessness of animals in verses that precisely chime with the note of pathos in Farrukh Beg's lonely Jerome, the sage and teacher.

How sad and exemplary
Is an animal's dark heart!

It has no urge to instruct
And no use for words,
And swims like a young dolphin
Among the grey gulfs of the world.

Yes, that unconscious, oceanic freedom is denied to Jerome and he seems to feel it. This painting is sometimes entitled *St Jerome Representing Melancholy*. Its date, 1615 (1023 AH), certainly places it in the age of melancholy. Farrukh Beg's painting is a mere fifteen years younger than Hamlet. Melancholy itself was not much older, a modern condition, often associated with the solitary life of the scholar. As an athlete's body suffers muscular strain and joint injuries, so the scholar's exerted mind suffers the injuries of melancholy, from which it struggles to recover. Dürer's most famous engraving is an image of Melancholy that makes explicit its connection with intellect. She is a beautiful angel seated in anguishing apathy amid the possibilities of mental activity, mathematics and construction. Unused behind her is a ladder to climb up out of this desolation. Historians tend to associate the advent of melancholy in European culture with the Reformation and the founding of Protestantism, which placed a new emphasis on the interior life of the individual. Where Catholicism had ritual, Protestantism had the fraught internal drama of intellectual assent to Jesus as saviour and other considerations of faith. A new space was created inside the mind in which it was possible to lose one's way, to fall prey to despair.

But Farrukh Beg was not a Protestant. He was a Muslim, a Sufi, his usual subjects sheikhs; elderly Sufi adepts who share with Jerome his inward gaze. Beg will have been more familiar with the inward struggle of yearning for mystical union with God than with the new European melancholy. *I sometimes felt myself mixing with the ranks of angels, and I would cry with joyful exultation, 'I run after You in the fragrance of Your perfumes.'* It seems that in translation Jerome has been both translated and returned to the company of mystics, the company he kept in Syria. Beg's Jerome sits thinking in the beautiful room where ascetic Christianity and Sufism overlap. Perhaps he is thinking as a Sufi, thinking of the *dhikr*, the repetition of the names of God. Jerome, knowing many languages and all of the Holy Scriptures, knows many names for God and knows that God exists within and behind these names. God is in the language of the Holy Scriptures and separate from it like the meanings inside words, like the soul inside the body. Perhaps this is Jerome's thought as he sits here: he is thinking about God's shimmering manifestation in language and His disappearance from it. He is thinking of the soul in his aged body and its approaching translation to the next world.

Wordless in front of him, perfectly content, the cat laps at the spilling milk.

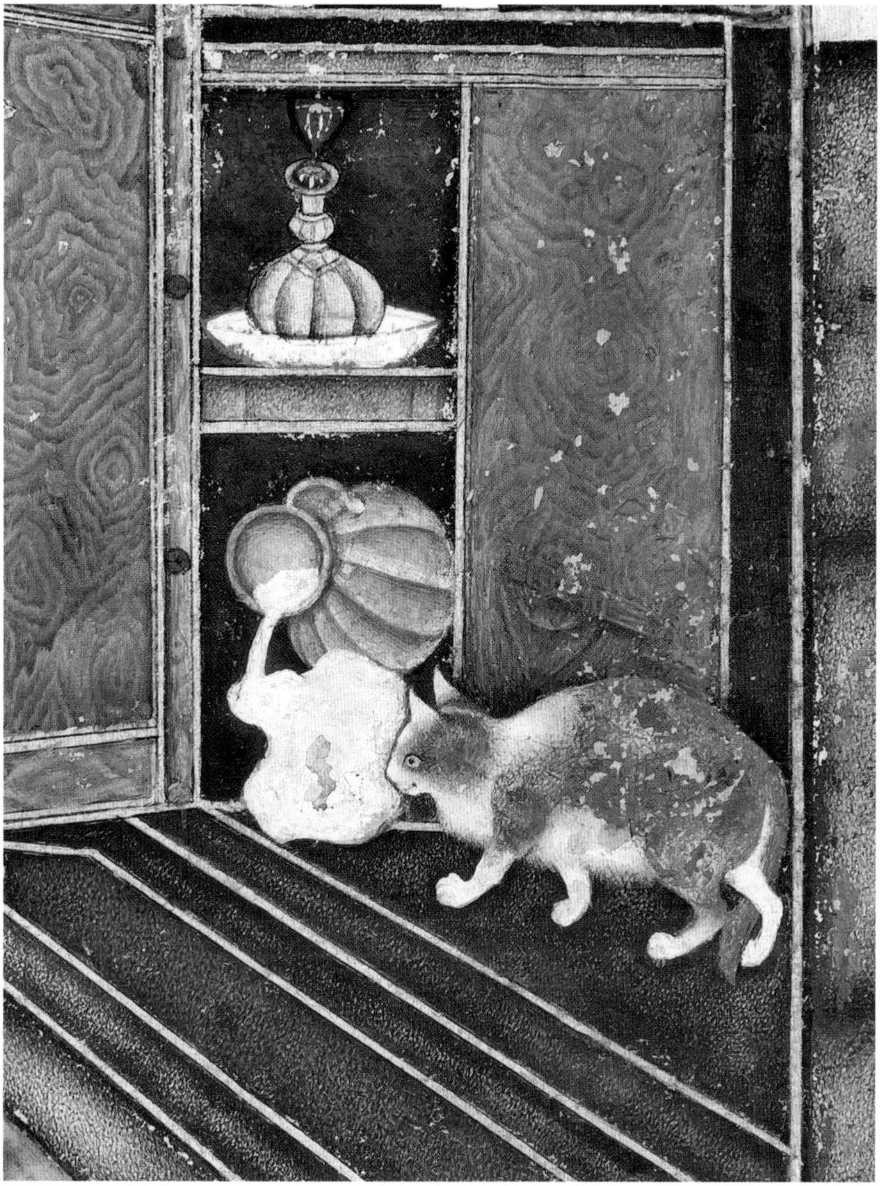

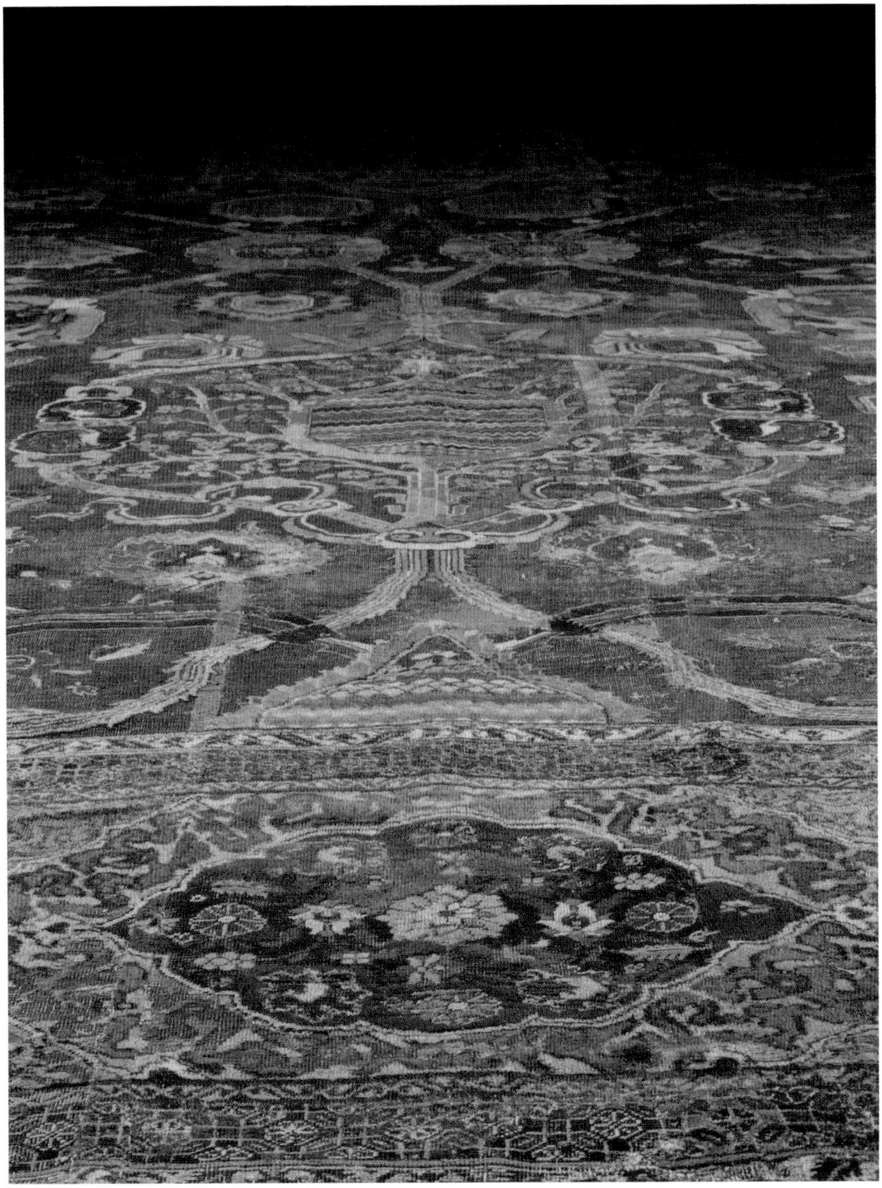

A Great Carpet Fragment and a Great Carpet

James Fenton

I remember as a child lying on a rug in front of the fire, and gazing at its design, trying to make some kind of sense of it, following its repetitions and its inconsistencies and dreamily wondering what they could mean, what it could represent. But that particular rug represented nothing, and it was the fact that such Eastern rugs represented nothing that so appealed to our Western ancestors. They were rich and complex and elusive, these designs, like problems which could never be solved, unless by some rare flash of insight. That was why, for Henry James, the expression 'the figure in the carpet' stood for the ungraspable key to a writer's whole philosophy. 'As soon as [Delacroix] touched on colour, abstract colour,' his friend Maxime Du Camp recalled, 'he became marvellously ingenious. I've seen him, one evening, near a table on which there was a basket full of strands of wool. He took the strands, arranged them in groups, criss-crossing them and dividing them according to their shades and in this way producing extraordinary colour effects. I've heard him say: "The most beautiful pictures I have seen are certain Persian carpets."'

His friend suspected that Delacroix was not entirely sincere in saying this, but the remark suggests that the love of abstract art – abstract colour, as Du Camp calls it, but also abstract design – found its way into Western taste through the appreciation of Eastern or Islamic carpets. But it is also true that the great carpets of the past could be representational as well, although sometimes the theme of the representation had been passed from hand to hand, from country to country or people to people, until it became hard to decode.

The art of these carpets is quintessentially portable. It passes along trade routes. It is sold in bazaars. It travels great distances – the greatest distances some of the makers of these carpets could conceive. Imagine making a fine silk rug in sixteenth-century Isfahan, destined for a noble house in Poland. What would far Poland mean to the weaver at the loom? What would a Polish coat of arms have meant in distant Isfahan? Yet this particular class of rugs – known as Polonaises, because it was once believed that they must have been woven in Poland – must once have been large.

I have read somewhere that fifty of them survive to this day. And if fifty survive, there must once have been many, many more than that. Most of them have lost certain of their colours – the darker silks, the rich reds, proved unstable over time. What I love about them is the sharpness and intricacy of their design. I know that, for the most part, the effect of soft green and gold in the old Polonaise type of carpet is an accident of history and exposure to light. It is like the blueness of old tapestries, which is what is left when the greens have faded. But the Polonaise rugs in the Museum of Islamic Art in Doha are much better preserved than the majority of their type. They set an elusive standard.

The carpets travelled, and found their uses and their homes, and in due course they, most of them, must have disintegrated and been thrown away. I was amazed to read that of all the earliest antique Persian rugs practically none were found in Persia itself. The rugs that survived in the mosques of Turkey were laid on the floor and piled five high. But worship in the Persian mosques was conducted in the open air, and a different kind of floor covering was used. In the days when the Western connoisseurship of rugs was just beginning, one would have been more likely to find an old Persian rug in an English country house, or an Italian church or palazzo, than anywhere in Persia.

Those early connoisseurs, those nineteenth-century scholars who set about learning the types and designs of the old rugs – they hugged their knowledge close to their chests, so that they could build up their collections without the inconvenience of rivals. And it is wonderful to think of them looking at the work of the great painters of the Renaissance specifically and only because they wanted to see how early or how late certain kinds of rugs were being traded

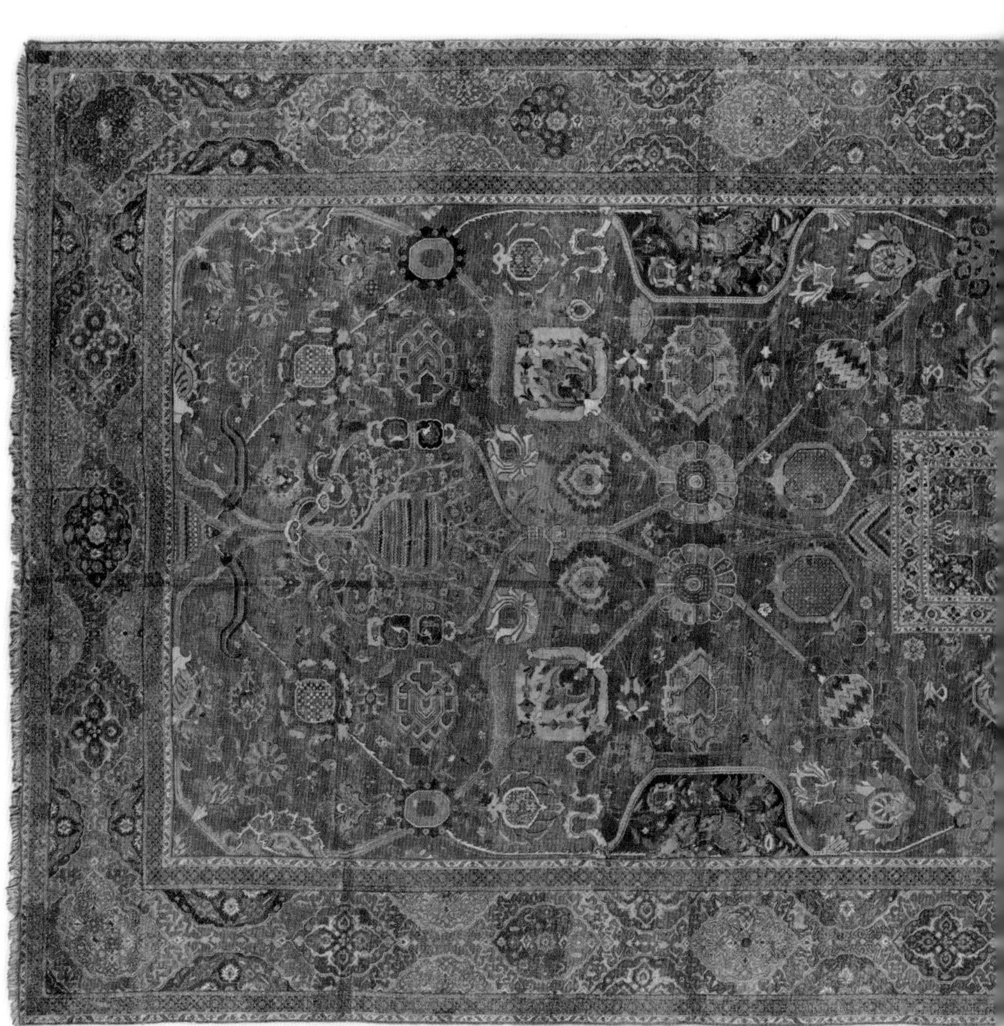

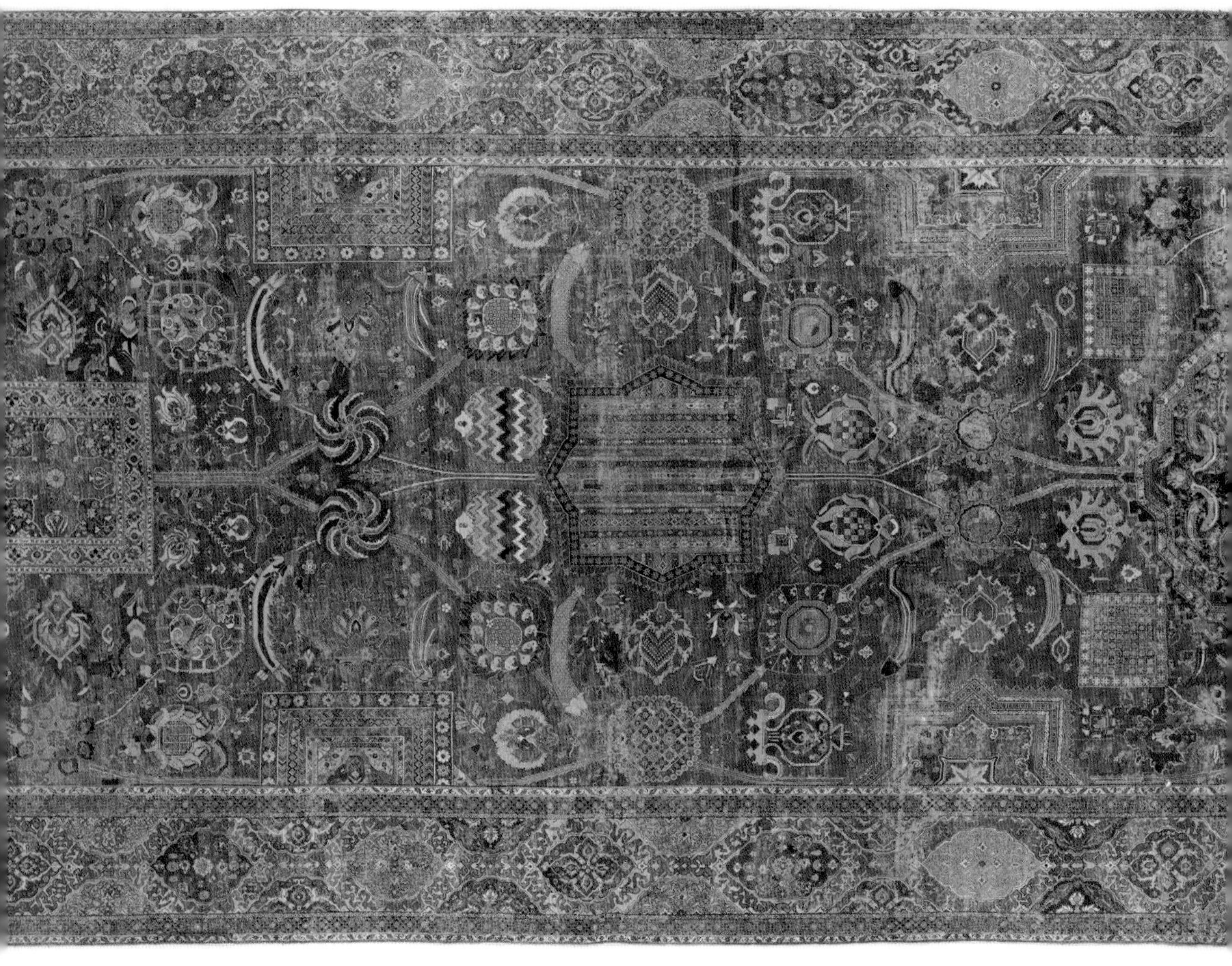

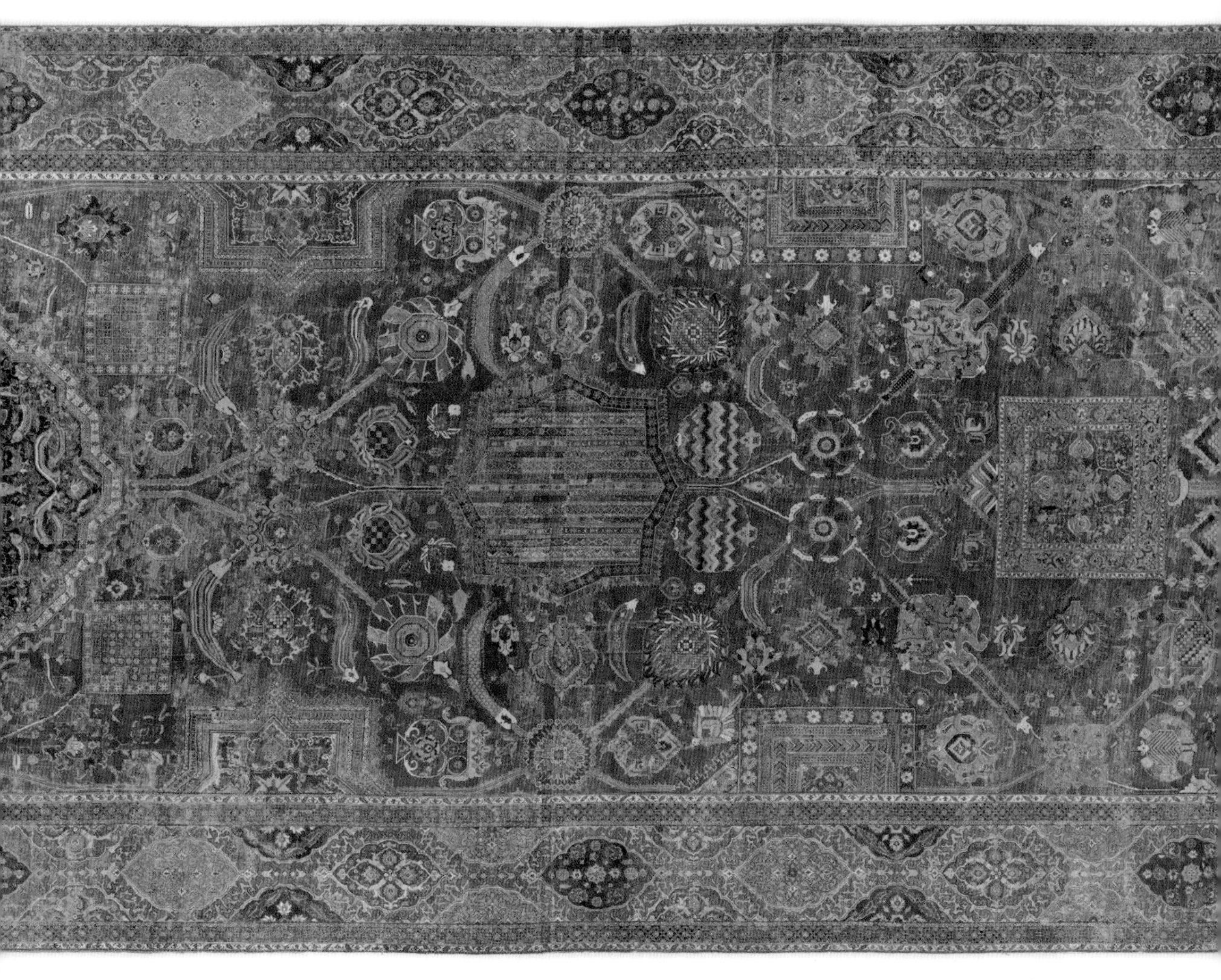

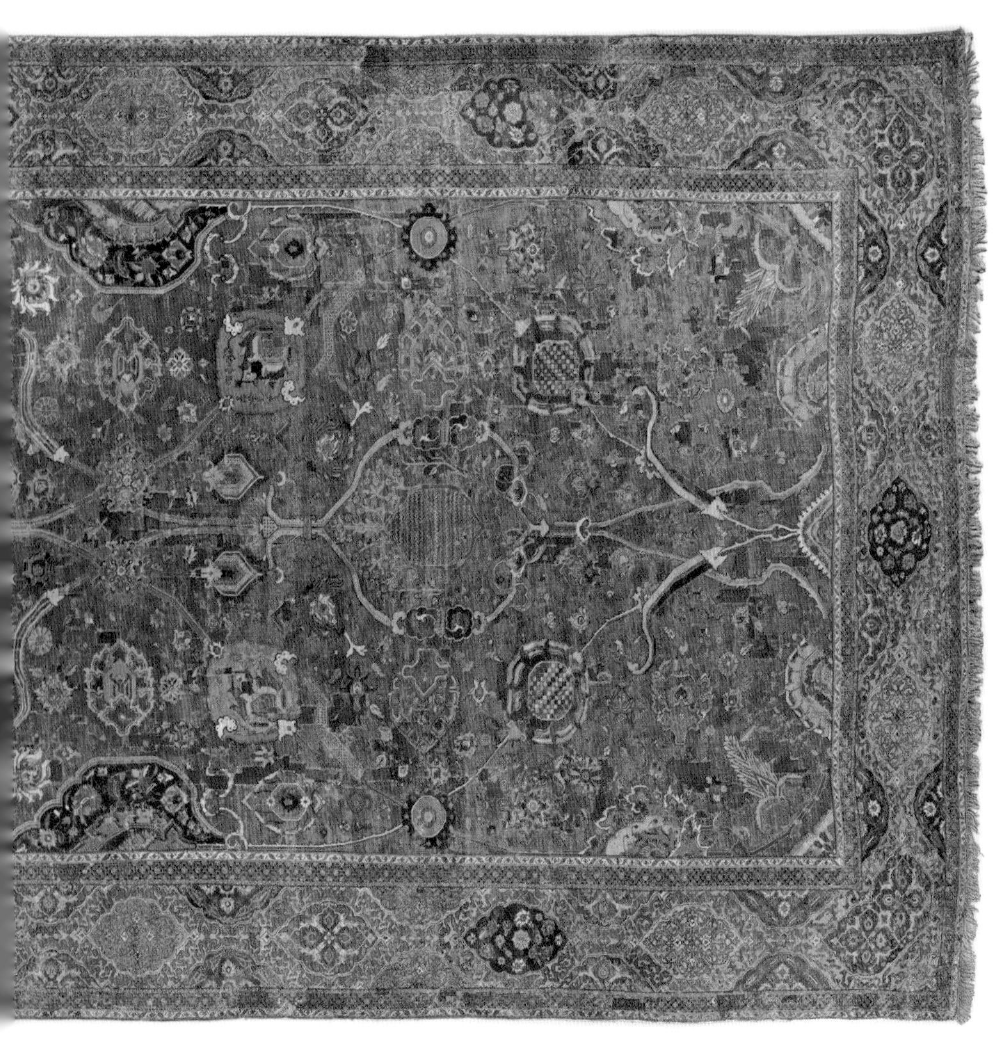

into Europe. And that is why still, to this day, some types of rug are – in the West – named after the Old Masters – Holbein and Lotto.

I had expected some great carpets in Doha. A dealer I met in New York told me that every single important rug that had been sold in the past fifteen years had found its way to the Qatar museum. He described making a fruitless trip to London, to bid on behalf of a client, for a rug that had appeared in a sale, and for which his client was prepared to pay... many times the estimate. But not, it turned out, as many times as the competition.

As it happened, I had seen this rug and could remember one thing about it. 'Was it that beautiful blue rug?' I asked. My friend looked pained. Yes indeed it had been that beautiful blue rug (it is not yet on display) that had been noted as exceptional.

The great exceptional carpets are like the great violins: they have names, as here in Doha – 'The Rothschild Polonaise', 'The Schwarzenberg "Paradise Park" Carpet', 'The Kevorkian Hyderabad' and so forth. They sound like fabulous objects from the adventures of Sherlock Holmes – 'The Mystery of the Kevorkian Hyderabad'. And they all have histories. They did not, generally speaking, appear out of thin air. They have been known and watched for generations, and scholars have taken their measurements, and counted their threads, and speculated on their origins.

The great carpet fragments are correspondingly rare, spread far and wide around the world's richest collections, but watched again, compared and noted for the evidence they give of masterpieces long disappeared. The scholars collate the fragments, tracing and plotting their designs, much as if they were dinosaur bones. They make their calculations. They whistle softly to themselves as they contemplate the result.

For an enormous carpet implies an enormous loom, and a large group of workers with expensive materials to hand. An enormous design indicates that there once must have been some kind of large cartoon, from which the weavers worked. And then of course an enormous carpet tells us there must have been an enormous space where that carpet was laid – a palace, a court, not some tiny yurt – and a grand occasion to require such splendour. But what that grand occasion would have been, nobody knows for sure. Some kind of audience or durbar is supposed, which is why these great carpets, when they are Indian, are known as durbar carpets.

A great fragment leads us to imagine a great carpet, a great carpet to posit a great occasion, but at that point we are left alone with our imaginations. We think of the Emperor Akbar, and of his court at Fatehpur Sikri, with its 'one hundred offices and workshops each resembling a city, or rather a little kingdom', with their 'studios and work-rooms for the finer and more reputable arts, such as painting, goldsmith work, tapestry-making, carpet and curtain-making, and the manufacture of arms'.

This is the romance of the Carey Welch fantastic-animal fragment, one of around fifteen remnants of probably the earliest known Indian carpet. These fragments are instantly recognisable, and bear no resemblance at all to any other carpet or carpet fragment in existence. The carpet they imply would have been over sixty-five feet long, but it is conceivable that there were two carpets of just half that length. Just as the Italian art dealers used to cut up old altarpieces and sell them as fragments, so it would seem some dealer in Paris, a century ago, was cutting up the remains of this unique rug, and releasing the ensuing fragments to the trade. It is a sobering thought that the Western market in Oriental rugs was responsible both for this sort of destruction, and simultaneously for the restoration of antique rugs, where that occurred. The ground colour of the Carey Welch fragment is a wine red, typical of Mughal carpets. What is unique is the design, depicting grotesque animals devouring each other: a fox or a hare caught in the mouth of a whale, a bird with six heads, leopards gobbling down birds. Or is it that these birds and rabbits and foxes are being born out of the mouths of these leopards and oxen and sea creatures? The situation is ambiguous, and the draughtsmanship is crazy. Someone – some Indian James Thurber – seems to have laughed a great deal while devising these animals, and perhaps the whole team laughed as they worked. Whoever saw a turtle eating a snake?

The art critic David Sylvester wrote about Oriental carpets that 'Showing them properly would not stop at displaying them on the ground (and unglazed). They cannot be fully experienced if they can only be walked around: to be unable to stand in the middle of a carpet is to be insulated from its full impact as one would be from that of a cathedral where one was not permitted to move down the nave. The aesthetic of the carpet demands that the spectator needs to be – or at least to feel – surrounded by its form and colour (which is why fragments of carpets tend not to work as well on the floor as on the wall). In a public gallery the nearest practical substitute for standing on the carpet is to be able to view it from a higher level.'

Sylvester had thought hard about this subject because he had been involved with two major Arts Council carpet exhibitions in Britain, in 1972 and 1983. One of the star items in the latter show was the Kevorkian Hyderabad, which then belonged to the dealer John Hewett. I asked a friend the other day what he remembered about this carpet. He said at once: 'It's beautiful. It's a carpet for walking on, not for hanging on the wall.' Both Sylvester and my friend would appreciate, I think, the solution that has been found at the MIA, where this immense and much repaired old masterpiece dominates its own gallery from a raised platform on the floor, and where – once the upper level is opened – one will be able to view it from a level above.

It is almost sixteen metres long, a size that argues for royal patronage. Any of the seventeenth-century Mughal emperors – Jahangir, Shah Jahan or Aurangzeb – might have been on the throne. The design has been described as an 'eclectic production, with elements derived from many sources' – most notably Persian vase carpets.

Here is part of a technical description: 'On the red ground great thorny stems in three different colours curve and intersect, forming three enormous curvilinear lattices; other thinner stems coil among these. All the stems carry blossoms in the style of Persian vase carpets and leaves in the shape of fish, which also occur in the Persian prototypes; there are also a few vases... The sixteen-lobed central medallion is full of fish, like the pools and canals depicted in garden carpets; other medallions are in the form of eight-pointed stars, squares and pointed ovals.'

The design lends itself to this sort of description, but the description hardly begins to account for the overall effect of the carpet, which when closely examined turns out to consist of innumerable variant shades, reflecting its long usage and the many interventions in the pile. 'A carpet for walking on,' as my friend said; but its days for being walked on are over now, and the Kevorkian Hyderabad has come to rest in the most distinguished company of carpets – with its vases, its flowers, its fishponds and its canals – speaking of the lost, abstract splendour of the Mughal court.

I suppose what is awakened in me, when I look at the great antique carpets of the Islamic world, is some memory of that old childhood romance, an aesthetic romance because it came with a story, a story whose authenticity I have never liked to check. It is the story of the weaver who liked to introduce a mistake into the design, since to presume perfection was to show arrogance before God. For the day-dreaming child, lying on the rug in front of the fire, following the pattern to those moments that could be identified as pious imperfections, you could say that the figure in the carpet did indeed have a meaning, even if the design was not representational. I suppose that the man who wove the carpet – for I always imagined him to be a man – was the artist who both strove for perfection and knew he must always fall short. And this pious man, this wise individual with his humble approach to the Almighty, in whom alone perfection is to be found – this is my first imaginary Muslim, my Muhammedan, my Mahometan friend.

The fire burns down. The tea grows cold. The butter has leaked from the crumpets and onto the rug, where I trace the line again to the point where the compromise has to be made. For the miscalculation means that the figure must be cut in two. God is perfect. We are not. I doze off among the tea-things on the abstract rug.

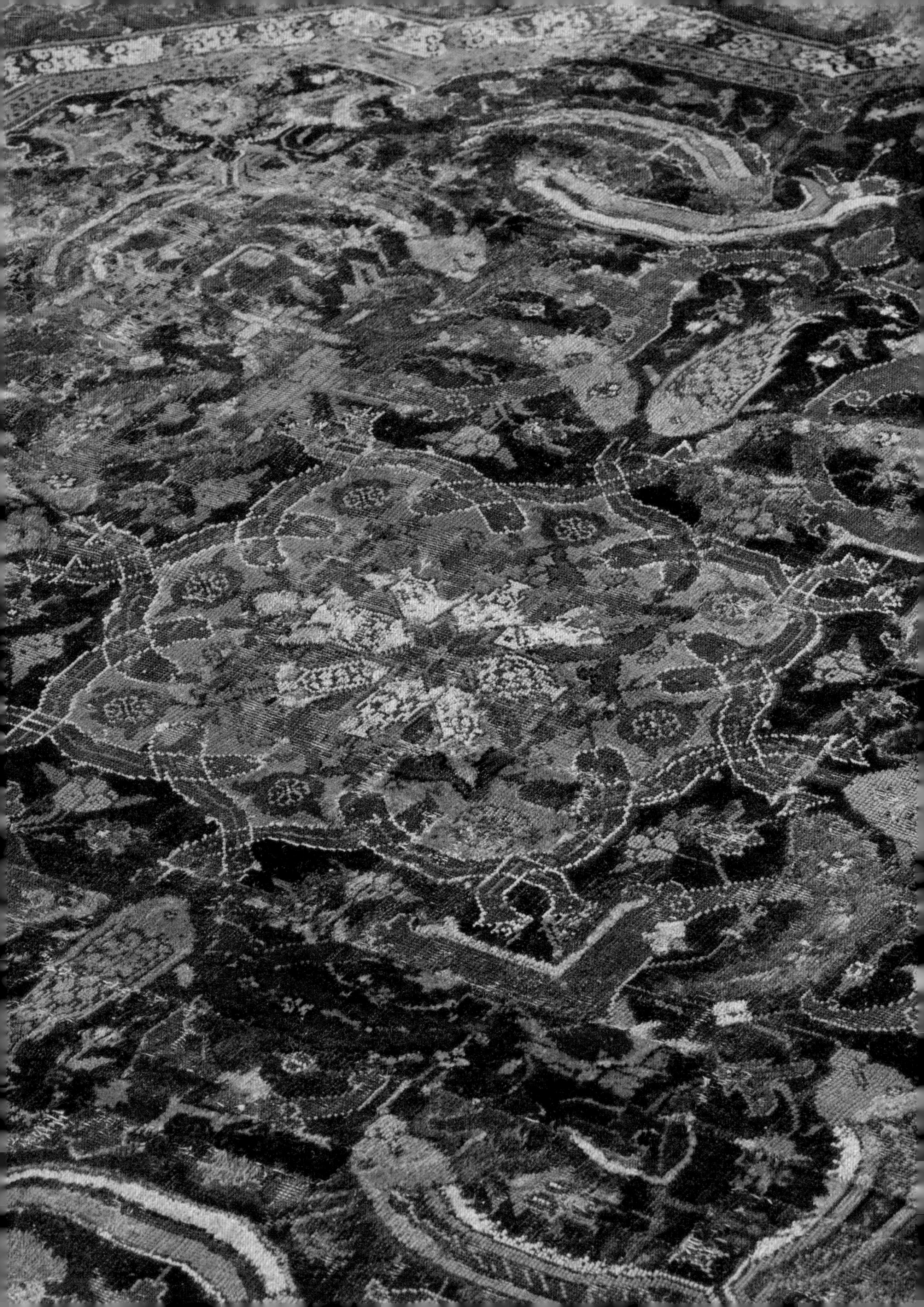

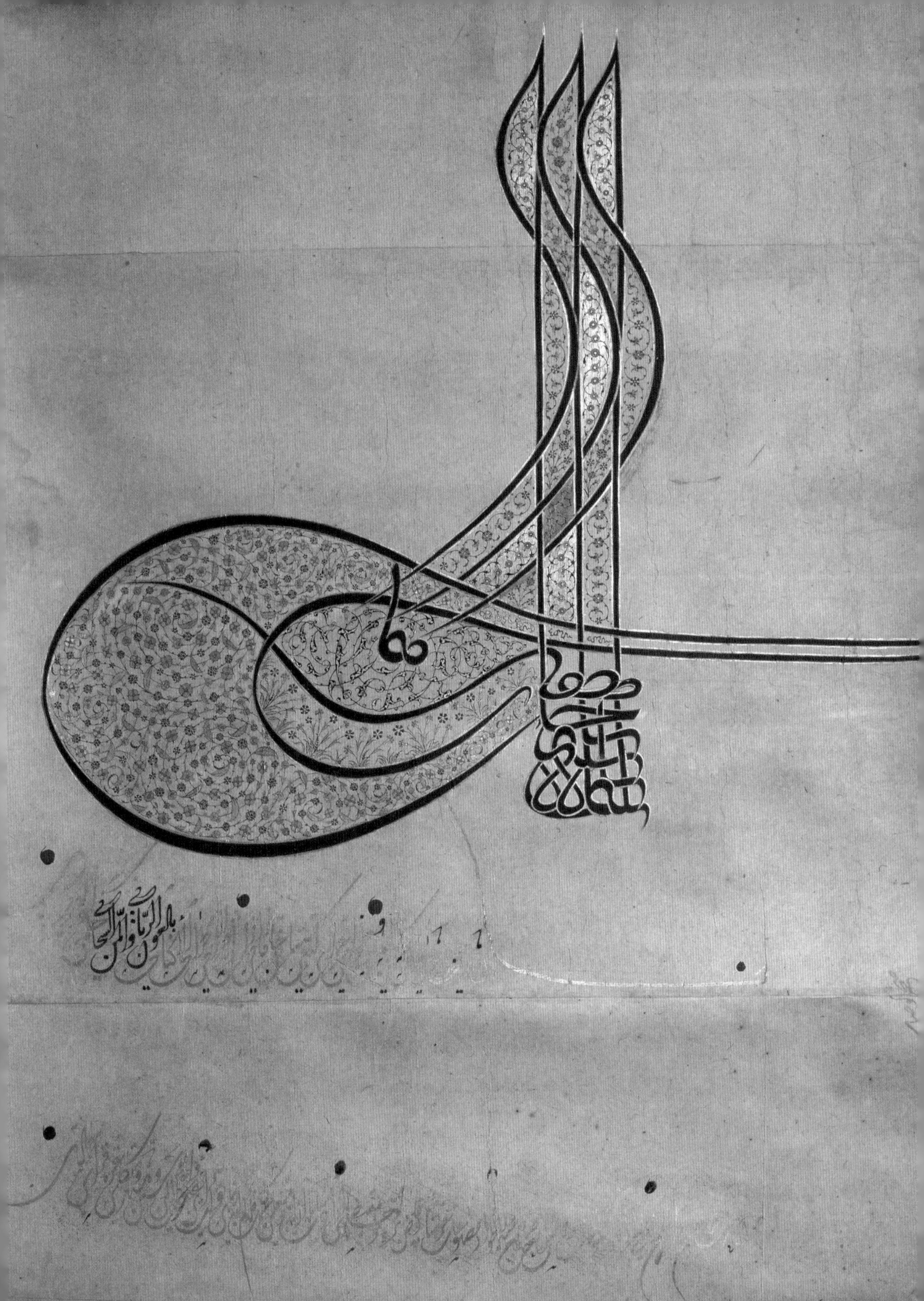
بالعون الربانی والمن السبحانی

Parable of the Tughra and the Mobile Phone

Youssef Rakha

And then I dreamed of Abdülhamit II (1842-1918/1257-1336 AH). The Red Sultan, so called because of his averred love of gore, turned out to be pale and palsied. Stooping and baby-paced, he looked brittle as he wobbled into the Second Empire-style salon with the incredibly high ceiling where I was waiting for him...

It had been three years since I started researching the Ottomans in the course of writing my first novel, also set in 2007. I was nearing the end of the biggest literary task I had ever embarked on, wholly immersed in the history of the Sublime State. Partly because the story involves messages transmitted through sleep, I was very drawn to Osman I's dream, the legendary prophecy out of which that State is sometimes believed to have sprung (and the subject of various Anatolian folk epics).

While still a relatively modest feudal lord in the late thirteenth century, the man who gave the dynasty its name is supposed to have seen a tree grow out of his belly-button and spread its shade over three rivers, so marking the world's three known continents. Of course, it all came promptly true. Depending on your historical-cum-ideological perspective, my ancestors in the Nile Delta were either pawns or beneficiaries.

The book I was writing is about Cairo, and its protagonist, Mustafa Çorbaci, is trying to draft his own subjective map of the megalopolis. Mustafa is visited by the ghost of Abdülhamit's younger brother Mehmed VI Vahdettin (1861-1926/1277-1344 AH), the last sultan and the penultimate caliph, and their meeting gives previously unknown meaning to every aspect of Mustafa's life, down to his name and his cartographic pursuits.

After each journey he makes in the course of three weeks in Cairo – the period during which the events of the book take place – Mustafa traces his route across or adjacent to the Nile; he draws with his eyes shut, in order to avoid the influence of reality. At the end, having renamed the relevant neighbourhoods the better to claim them for his story, he combines his drawings to end up with this:

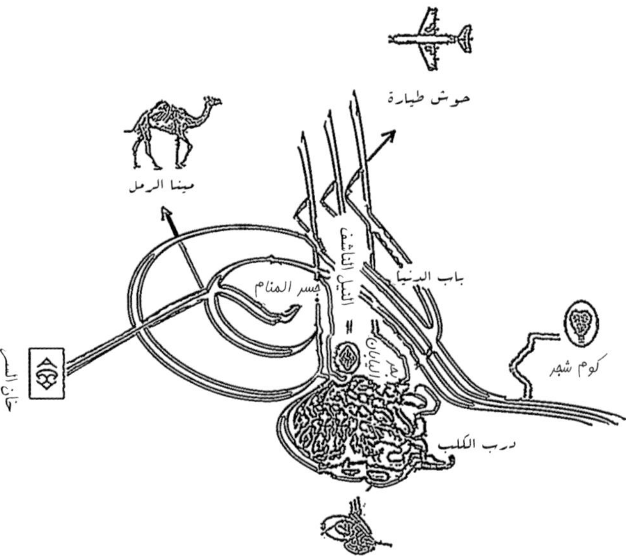

As it turns out, Mustafa's city, the post-millennial Cairo haunted by Islam's last ruling caliph, looks like a *tughra*: the calligraphic emblem of the *Osmanlı* which first appeared in the time of Osman's son Orhan I (1284-1359/682-760 AH).

Each 'sultan, son of a sultan' – so I found out, in time – had his own individual *tughra*, a basic design that altered only slightly every time it was inscribed, which spoke his name and worked as both signature and seal. It was created by the Chief Court Calligrapher directly after enthronement, and continued to grace official documents and state paraphernalia until the end of that sultan's reign, when the new sultan's name required a new design – often by a new Chief Court Calligrapher.

A magnificent triumph of the Arabic script, the form combines the Text, Islam's principal reference point, with the Image: abstract but evocative, semiotically loaded but instantly and globally functional. In the sixteenth century, at the height of Ottoman glory when, besides Makkah, Madinah and Jerusalem, both Cairo and Constantinople had been secured, giving the *Osmanlı padişah* as Caliph of Islam an authority unmatched in Ottoman history, the *tughra* – a work in progress for centuries by now – took on its definitive shape. Like much else in the empire the *tughra* was later to calcify into something uncreative and prescribed, looking all but identical from one sultan to the next. But no matter.

Though significantly different from the later *tughras* on which the map is modelled – both Abdülhamit's and Vahdettin's being examples – of all the specimens I had seen online and in Istanbul, it was that of Sultan Süleyman al-Qanuni (1494-1566/899-973 AH), the appropriately named 'Magnificent', that held me in its thrall.

The first time I went to Qatar, I did not know I would find my beloved *tughra* there, but a digital reproduction of its image already adorned my mobile phone screen. That was many months after I started working on the novel, when I lived in Abu Dhabi. There, I spent a strangely removed year helping to launch and then writing for an English-language newspaper. My first experience of Arabia, which has had neither precedents nor has happened again: that year is a sort of spatio-temporal pocket in my adult life. Anyway, in the autumn of 2008, a week or so before the official opening of the Museum, I was assigned to raise the curtain on the event, handed a plane ticket and allowed two cheap hotel nights in Doha.

By then, having bought the mobile phone in question at the Wahda Mall off Abu Dhabi City's Old Airport Road and transferred the low-res image onto it from Wikipedia, I was convinced that Arabia was as much as anything a low-tax consumer paradise, technological commodities not excluded. And this seemed to me profoundly un-Islamic. To my satisfaction, therefore – counterbalancing that role – the Gulf was evidently also becoming a hub of Islamic art acquisition and display.

On arriving in Doha I was given a private tour of the Museum. I remember little beyond the phenomenally unexpected moment when I made it out: the familiar, blue-and-gold mythical creature, enormous, suspended above beautiful text that slanted inexplicably uphill in a sea of layered grain. It was one of those times when, for a moment, the whole world suddenly makes sense: my novel, my love for this *tughra*, my job at the newspaper, my presence in this part of the world at this point in human history.

I have been to Qatar only twice. Each time, at the heart of my visit was this specific, original *tughra*: MS.1 at the Museum of Islamic Art, sealing the 1559-60 (966-67 AH) *ferman* in which Süleyman bestows an Istanbul palace on one of his granddaughters. Each time, having stayed no longer than ninety-six hours in total, I left with greater confidence in the secular accomplishments of Islam: its art, its science, the beauty of its formalism.

The second time I went to Qatar was to write about an object of my choice for this book; and what else on earth was it going to be!

But I had something on my mind besides excitement to be part of the project and gratitude for my superb hotel room and the opportunity for a reunion with the *ferman*. The night of my departure in October 2010, back in Cairo, I had made the acquaintance of the latest iPhone model: I happened to walk into a mobile phone shop with a bill-paying friend and there it was, attached to the display table by an elastic cord, but working. I coveted it. I thought back to the kind of paradise I had experienced Arabia to be, I registered the fact that I would be in Arabia again, and I made up my mind to get the phone there.

Let me not wax loquacious about my second, closer encounter with the *ferman*. My knowing the *tughra* would be within reach made the prospect of seeing it no less exciting. The *ferman* is impressive, of course, and it was meant to be. But what struck me about it now was how intimate it was, how something could be at once regal and mellow, approachable, almost personal in its appeal, without losing any of its commanding authority. The gold seemed to seep out of the brown paper like a natural exudate, the curves of the writing to reflect the figure of a friend.

The next day, after lunch at Souk Waqif, I asked to be dropped off at the nearest mall and started scouring the premises for the object of my desire. Eventually I found it, cheaper than it was in Cairo and, unlike its Cairo counterpart, independent of the sim card to be placed in it.

The limit on my credit card is less than US$1,500; this keeps my spending sprees in check and when I am out of Egypt it reminds me how little I live on by World Bank standards. Still, I knew there was enough credit to cover the bill. So I felt fear and loathing when the cash machine declined my request for QR3,000, reporting that my credit card was dysfunctional. I thought of grabbing the iPhone and running, I thought of phoning my bank. In the end, back at the hotel, the Museum catalogue soothed me into a long nap before another engaging evening with authors and organisers.

Only later, on my way to the airport, did I realise that the hotel had blocked precisely the amount I was seeking in case I incurred expenses while staying there. Thus it had deprived me of the iPhone for good; I knew I would never summon up the oomph to buy it in Cairo, especially since my existent Nokia Express Music is all I actually need, there would be no Gulf-Ottoman-mobile phone mélange to justify the excess.

Now I could develop this into a Sufi parable about abstinence, materialism and God's mysterious ways; I will not. Thinking of the two roles of the Gulf, I just feel I was somehow saved from something...

Old, old man, I thought when Abdülhamit II materialised in the distance, back in that literary-historical dream of mine. And then, while he approached: *This guy could not injure a fly if he tried.* And when we were facing each other: *Nonetheless, what dignity! Seven centuries of blueness do rarefy a man's blood, whatever else you see in him.*

I was not sure if I thought that last statement or said it. I tried to gauge out the Padişah's expression to see if I had committed a faux pas; he looked perfectly impassive, the bare outline of a smile still brushing his thin lips. Yet when he extended his hand and I shook it, it did not occur to me to bend over and touch my mouth to the royal skin, as I had already established I should do.

'*Alem penah*,' I started to address him: Refuge of the World. But my Ottoman Turkish bobbled and the Caliph of All Muslims did not seem to understand.

So, 'Cigarette?' I beamed, consciously defiant of the EU-inspired anti-smoking laws I had recently encountered in Istanbul. The Sultan nodded. As I flashed a packet of Marlboro Lights level with his enormous beard, which in its greyness seemed somehow more solid than the rest of him, I – for an instant – realised I was slurping rice pudding with the angels, as Egyptians say of dream-filled slumber.

For an instant before I sank back into the sweet, milky madness of the encounter, I wondered whether or not I might be having a quasi-divine revelation.

Dreaming of the Prophet Muhammad (of whom, in Sunni Islam, even a scheming Turk becomes the rightful heir once he has been declared Caliph) is a perennial trope of spiritual experience. According to the Messenger of God himself, to dream of him is to meet him in person: probably the greatest reward possible in this life.

I suspect I am too secular and agnostic to ever be blessed in this way, but like millions of post-millennial Muslims – I also suspect – I remain concerned with what it means, culturally if not theologically, to have a religious identity at all.

Secular or devout, it seems necessary to convince myself at least that, while it is true that they have contributed little to human civilisation for some six centuries now, Muslims might nonetheless have more to them than the Wahhabi motifs of misconstrued Jihad with which the creed is increasingly identified: beard, *burqa* and bomb.

There must be ways to assert Islam in the twenty-first century beyond mindless militancy and rituals long since struck with rigor mortis, rejection of difference or anachronism. And while integration into the rat-race of smoke-free capitalism – the one that produces iPhones – is quite clearly not one of them, Islamic art just might be. Reason, science, and art are perfectly valid aspects of the Muslim legacy, after all; and there is no doubt that Muslims contributed to their evolution.

But by now all this is liberal-democratic cliché. What I mean is: when I dreamed of the last important Ottoman sultan, it felt like the historical analogue of the canonical Dream. And this served my purpose almost as well as the novel I was in the throes of completing when I had the dream.

The generic dreamer – a worshipper whose ideas have not evolved since the twelfth century – was replaced by an individual; a novelist whose research into the Ottoman Empire as the last more or less universally recognised Caliphate yielded a creative, I would even say poignant, variation on the same theme.

I was being rewarded if not for righteousness then for curiosity. Instead of the Prophet, I was visited by the last of the fighter monarchs, the Gazis: warriors of the faith, Mediterranean-farers, conquerors of Byzantium. And perhaps I was deprived of owning an iPhone the better to remember the true significance of Qatar in my life.

The night he appeared in my sleep, Abdülhamit II spoke to me in impressively fluent Egyptian Arabic. I do not remember what he spoke about, just how delighted I was that I needed to use neither Ottoman Turkish nor Qur'anic Arabic; implausibly but in line with Mustafa Çorbaci's experience, the great man knew my dialect. Then, bearing a bright red satchel on his shoulder, he exited the salon on his way to the end of both Osman Gazi's and my dream.

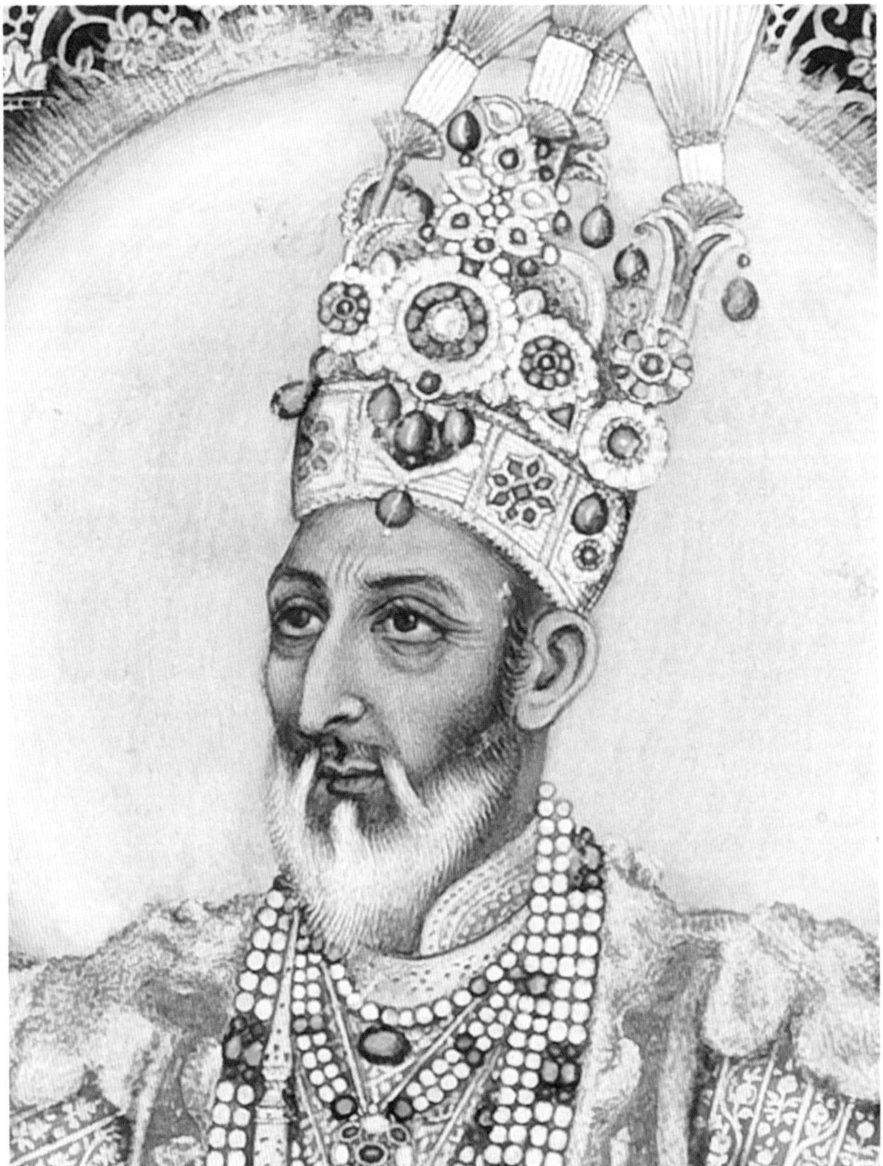

The Coronation Portrait

William Dalrymple

Not far from my farm on the southern edge of Delhi there lies the ruin of the summer palace of the last Mughal Emperors. It is named Zafar Mahal, the Palace of Victory, and sometimes, on winter afternoon walks, I wander over there to sit amid the broken doorways and shattered cusps of the Mughal arches.

Delhi has always been a phoenix of a city, destroyed and rebuilt century after century. 'It has a feeling about it of "Is this not the great Babylon?" all ruins and desolation,' wrote Emily Eden in her diary when she first visited in the late 1830s. 'How can I describe the desolation of Delhi,' agreed her contemporary, the poet Sauda. 'There is no house from which the jackals' cry cannot be heard. In the once beautiful gardens, the grass grows waist-high around fallen pillars and ruined arches. Not even a lamp of clay now burns where once the chandeliers blazed.'

Zafar Mahal, built and lived in during the period when Sauda and Emily Eden were both writing, is today a deeply melancholy spot. Somehow it still retains the quality of tragic ruination that marked the last days of Mughal Delhi in the eighteenth and early nineteenth centuries, that period known as the Delhi Twilight, just before the British destroyed both the Mughal dynasty and the syncretic culture they had created there. Despite its crumbling beauty, the old summer palace receives little protection from the government and has now become the preferred gathering place of the ne'er-do-wells of Mehrauli: gamblers, drunks and heroin addicts haunt its gutted courtyards. Junkies sneak behind the pillars of the Durbar Hall with their silver foil and brown sugar and boxes of matches; in the former Elephant Stables the afternoon drinkers knock back shots of Bagpiper as they throw down their cards. Teenagers looking for somewhere to play cricket bat their balls into the delicate Mughal lattices of the zenana quarters. Every few months another pillar is knocked over or another fragile screen is broken.

Nowhere in this sad monument is sadder than the imperial tomb enclosure, which lies just behind the white marble palace mosque. Here four Mughal marble sepulchres are covered in subtle and sinuous *nastaliq* calligraphy. They are arranged in two groups of two, with the gaping socket of an empty grave lying between them.

The empty grave was intended as the resting place of the last Mughal Emperor, Bahadur Shah II, known from his penname as 'Zafar', and it was after him that the palace was named. Zafar was the direct descendant of Genghis Khan and Timur, of Akbar, Jahangir and Shah Jahan. He was born in 1775 (1188 AH), when the British were still a relatively modest and mainly coastal power in India, looking inwards from three enclaves on the Indian shore. In his lifetime he saw his own dynasty reduced to humiliated insignificance, while the British transformed themselves from vulnerable traders into an aggressively expansionist military force.

Zafar came late to the throne, when it was already impossible to reverse the political decline of the Mughals. But despite this he succeeded in creating around him in Delhi a court of great brilliance. Personally, he was one of the most talented, tolerant and likeable of his dynasty: a skilled calligrapher, a profound writer on Sufism, a discriminating patron of painters, an inspired creator of gardens and an amateur architect. Most importantly, he was a serious mystical poet, and partly through his patronage there took place the greatest literary renaissance in modern North Indian history. Himself a *ghazal* writer of accomplishment, Zafar also provided, through his court, a showcase for the talents of India's greatest lyric poet, Ghalib, and his rival Zauq, the Mughal poet laureate, and Salieri to Ghalib's Mozart.

While the British progressively took over more and more of the Mughal Emperor's power, finally laying plans to remove the Mughals from the Red Fort and banish them to Zafar Mahal, the court spent the hot monsoon months in the summer palace busying itself in obsessive pursuit of the most cleverly turned *ghazal*, the most perfect miniature painting. Indeed it was one of Zafar's principal achievements that he helped bring about a great revival of painting – an art that had been semi-dormant in Delhi for a century – and one of the greatest masterpieces of his reign is the Coronation Portrait, now in Doha's Museum of Islamic Art. The painting was commissioned from the artist Ghulam Ali Khan when Zafar finally came to the throne on his father's death in 1837 (1252 AH), when the poet-prince was already in his mid-sixties.

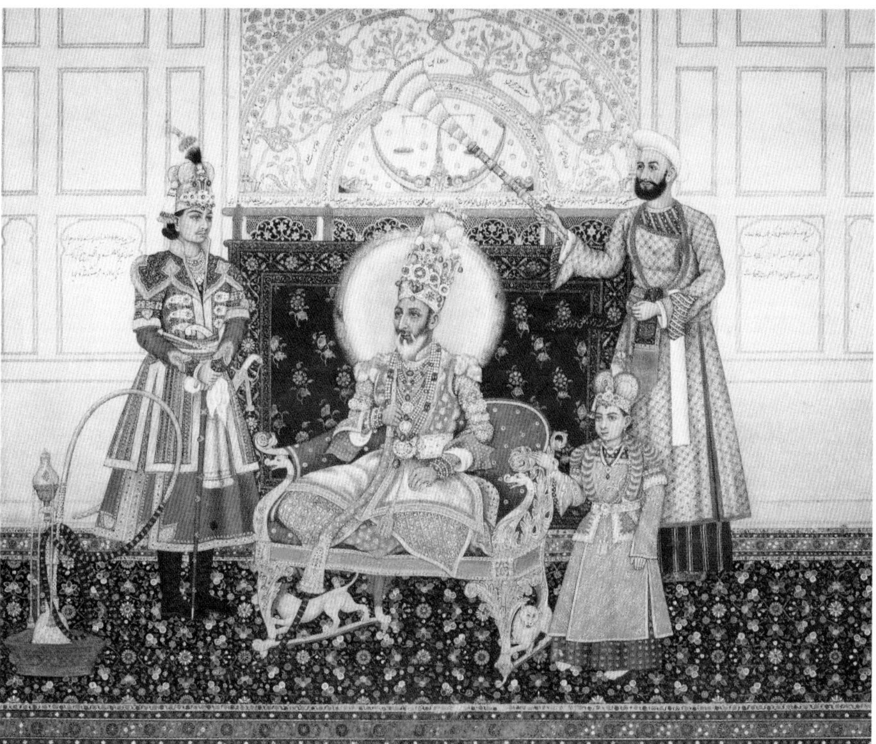

In the picture, although Zafar is painted as Emperor against the Imperial Mughal scales of justice; and although weighed down with enough diamonds and pearls to form almost a jewelled armour over his torso, his face is nevertheless that of a Sufi ascetic. Indeed his bearing is as ethereal and other-worldly as a desert father from the apse of some Coptic monastery.

His huge brown eyes are looking away from the viewer, as if lost in a trance, and he seems almost to be floating over his throne, subject to the laws of gravity thanks only to the weight of the crown anchoring him to the terrestrial world. Ghulam Ali Khan very deliberately created an image of a man who was both king and saint. Indeed Zafar was regarded as a Sufi *pir*, and used to accept pupils or *murids*. The loyal *Dihli Urdu Akhbar* even went as far as calling him 'one of the leading saints of the age, approved of by the divine court'.

The artist describes himself in an inscription on another version of this picture as 'the hereditary slave of the dynasty, Ghulam Ali Khan the portraitist, resident at Shah Jahanabad' and elsewhere he signs himself 'His Majesty's Painter'; but although his family were in the process of becoming hereditary painters to the Mughal throne, the truth was slightly more complex. Zafar no longer had sufficient funds to employ Ghulam Ali Khan exclusively, and to survive the painter had to moonlight as an architectural and portrait painter to several other members of the court, notably the Nawab of Jhajjar, whom Ghulam Ali Khan painted astride his pet tiger. Ghulam Ali Khan also had to take work from the British, including the Rajput-Scottish mercenary James 'Sikander Sahib' Skinner and the Daniels brothers, whom Ghulam Ali Khan may well have assisted with their celebrated architectural lithographs when they came to Delhi. He also took commissions from British Residents at the Mughal court, including my wife's ancestor, William Fraser, who by the 1830s became the painter's principal patron as part of the Fraser Album project, as Fraser's purchasing power eclipsed that of the Emperor he was sent to watch over.

The reaction to increasingly aggressive British encroachment during the late 1840s and early 1850s finally came on a May morning in 1857 (1273 AH), when three hundred mutinous sepoys from Meerut rode into Delhi, massacred every Christian they could find in the city, and declared Zafar to be their leader. Powerless as he was in so many ways, Zafar was still widely regarded as the Khalifah, God's Regent on Earth, and the focus of political legitimacy in Northern India. When Delhi people made an oath, rather than reaching for the scriptures they swore 'by the throne of the Emperor'. As the Doha Coronation Portrait records, he was thought of across Hindustan as 'His Divine Highness, Caliph of the Age, Padshah as Glorious as Jamshed, He who is Surrounded by Hosts of Angels, Shadow of God, Refuge of Islam,

Protector of the Muslim Religion, Offspring of the House of Timur, Greatest Emperor, Mightiest King of Kings, Emperor son of Emperor, Sultan son of Sultan.'

For this reason many ordinary people in North India responded to Zafar's appeal to rise up against the arrogant merchants and bureaucrats of the East India Company. All this came as something of a surprise to the British who had long ceased to take Zafar seriously. Seeing only his powerlessness, the British had ceased to recognise the charisma that the name of the Mughal still possessed for both Hindus and Muslims in North India. Mark Thornhill, the British collector in Mathura, recorded his own surprise in his diary immediately after the rebel capture of Delhi:

'Their talk was all about the ceremonial of the palace. They speculated as to who would be Grand Chamberlain, and who were the fifty-two Rajahs who would assemble to put the Emperor on the throne... As I listened I realised as I never had done before the deep impression that the splendour of the ancient court had made on the popular imagination, how dear to them were the traditions and how faithfully, all unknown to us, they had preserved them. There was something weird in the Mogul Empire thus starting into a sort of phantom life after the slumber of a hundred years.'

Zafar was no friend of the British, who had shorn him of his patrimony, and subjected him to almost daily humiliation. Yet he was not a natural insurgent either, least of all in his eighties. It was with severe misgivings and little choice that he found himself made the nominal leader of an uprising that he strongly suspected from the start was doomed.

The great Mughal capital, caught in the middle of a remarkable cultural flowering, was turned overnight into a battleground. The Siege of Delhi was the Raj's Stalingrad: a fight to the death between two powers, neither of whom could retreat. Finally, on 14 September 1857 (25 Muharram 1274 AH), the British assaulted and took the city, sacking the old capital and plundering its palaces. Zafar Mahal was burned to the ground, and most of the Red Fort was demolished to create a British barracks.

Those city dwellers who survived the killing were driven out into the countryside to fend for themselves. Delhi was left an empty ruin. Though the royal family had surrendered peacefully, most of the Emperor's sixteen sons were tried and hanged, while three were shot in cold blood, having first freely given up their arms, then been told to strip naked: 'In 24 hours I disposed of the principal members of the house of Timur the Tartar,' Captain William Hodson wrote to his sister the following day. 'I am not cruel, but I confess I did enjoy the opportunity of ridding the earth of these wretches.' One of the three was Mirza Mughal, the little boy to the right of Zafar in the Doha Coronation Portrait.

Zafar himself was put on show to visitors, displayed 'like a beast in a cage' according to one British officer. Among his visitors was the *Times* correspondent, William Howard Russell. 'He was a dim, wandering-eyed, dreamy old man with a feeble hanging nether lip and toothless gums,' wrote Russell. 'In silence he sat day and night with his eyes cast on the ground [although] some heard him quoting verses of his own composition, writing poetry on a wall with a burned stick.'

The following month Zafar was put on trial in the ruins of his old palace, and sentenced to transportation. He left his beloved Delhi on a bullock cart. Separated from everything he loved, brokenhearted, the last of the Great Mughals died in exile in Rangoon on Friday, 7 November 1862 (14 Jamadi al-Awal 1279 AH), aged eighty-seven. He was buried in an unmarked grave, and the empty socket among the imperial graves in Zafar Mahal has remained vacant ever since.

With Zafar's departure there was a rapid and complete collapse of the fragile court culture he had faithfully nourished and exemplified. Today, more than 150 years later, Delhi feels as if it is fast moving away from its Mughal past. In modern Delhi an increasingly wealthy Punjabi middle class now live in an aspirational bubble of fast-rising shopping malls, espresso bars and multiplexes. This emerging middle-class India is a country with its eyes firmly fixed on the future. Everywhere there is a profound hope that the country's rapidly rising international status will somehow compensate for a history widely perceived as a long succession of invasions and defeats at the hands of foreign powers. The result is a tragic neglect of Delhi's past. Occasionally there is an outcry as, when for example, the tomb of the poet Zauq was discovered to have disappeared under a municipal urinal; but by and large the losses go unrecorded.

Sometimes, sitting in the ruination of Zafar Mahal, I think of that melancholy other-wordly, oddly detached face on the Coronation Portrait and wonder what Zafar would have made of all this. Looking out over the Sufi shrine that abuts his palace, I suspect he would somehow have made his peace with the fast changing cyber-India of call centres and software parks that are now slowly overpowering the last remnants of his world. After all, realism and acceptance were always qualities Zafar excelled in. You can see it in that haunting, haunted, eternally patient face. You can also see it in the spirit of make-do which defines that portrait. The perfect Persian carpet on which the throne, the sons, the courtiers and the hubble-bubble all stand covers a ruined water channel – when the picture was painted the Nahr-i-Behisht, or stream of paradise, was no longer flowing, and the Emperor seems to have rigged up some sort of platform in order to be depicted in front of the scales of justice, symbolic of the most important duty of a great Muslim ruler. This was very much Zafar's way, to continue to do what he could in impossibly adverse circumstances, and to remain a bastion of duty, justice and goodness for his people as the Mughal era reached its final neap-tide. For all the tragedy of his life, Zafar was able to see that the world continued to turn, and that however much the dogs might bark, the great caravan of life continues and moves on. As he wrote in a poem shortly after his imprisonment, while Mughal Delhi lay in ruins around him:

Delhi was once a paradise,
Where Love held sway and reigned;
But its charm lies ravished now
And only ruins remain.

No tears were shed when shroudless they
Were laid in common graves;
No prayers were read for the noble dead,
Unmarked remain their graves

But things cannot remain, O Zafar,
Thus for who can tell?
Through God's great mercy and the Prophet
All may yet be well.[1]

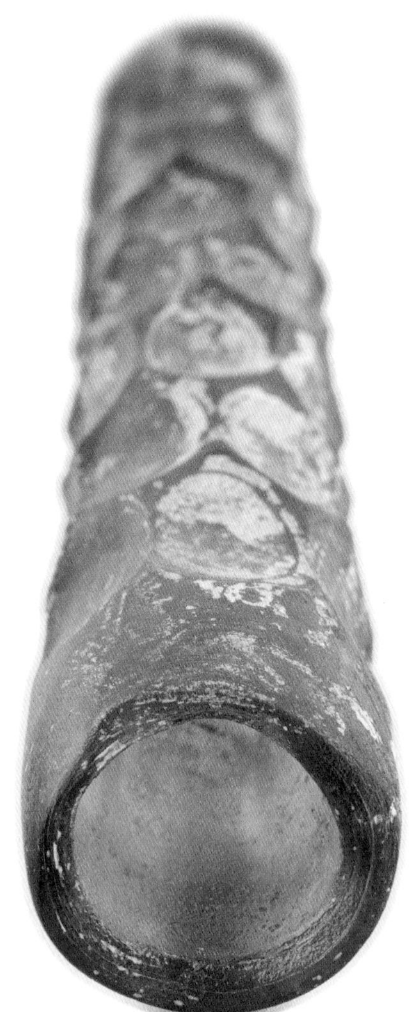

Glass Document Holder

Sarah Maguire

I
Cylinder of seagreen beachglass,
its façade

a honeycomb
of hexagonal facets,

wheelcut,
(each pool the size of a fingerprint);

weathering – like meal –
sketching the abrasions.

II
Imagine the papyrus
    furled
in a tight scroll

    then eased
into its sheath,
    tamped into place.

The ends capped,
    sealed off
with sealing wax.

III
This is the alchemy of the furnace:
ash and dust transfigured
into pellucid poured stone.

IV
Core-formed fusion of sand
and the washed ashes of saltwort:

a handling-rod thickened with clay
plunges into incandescence –

seething in a bath of molten glass
that clings to and coats the clay core.

Withdrawn, the vessel slowly anneals,
hardening as it cools;

then cored, and cleansed,
it is opened and ready.

V

Slung in a saddlebag, documents
depart from Nishapur to Merv –

the commandments of empire
are sheathed in glass:

visible, impermeable, intact.

VI

Isolate,
kindled in a pool of white light,

far from home,
far from all the messages

once coiled in your throat.
Cold glass pipe,

hollowed by air,
cored clean of words now –

of all the secrets you once housed,
not a whisper remains.

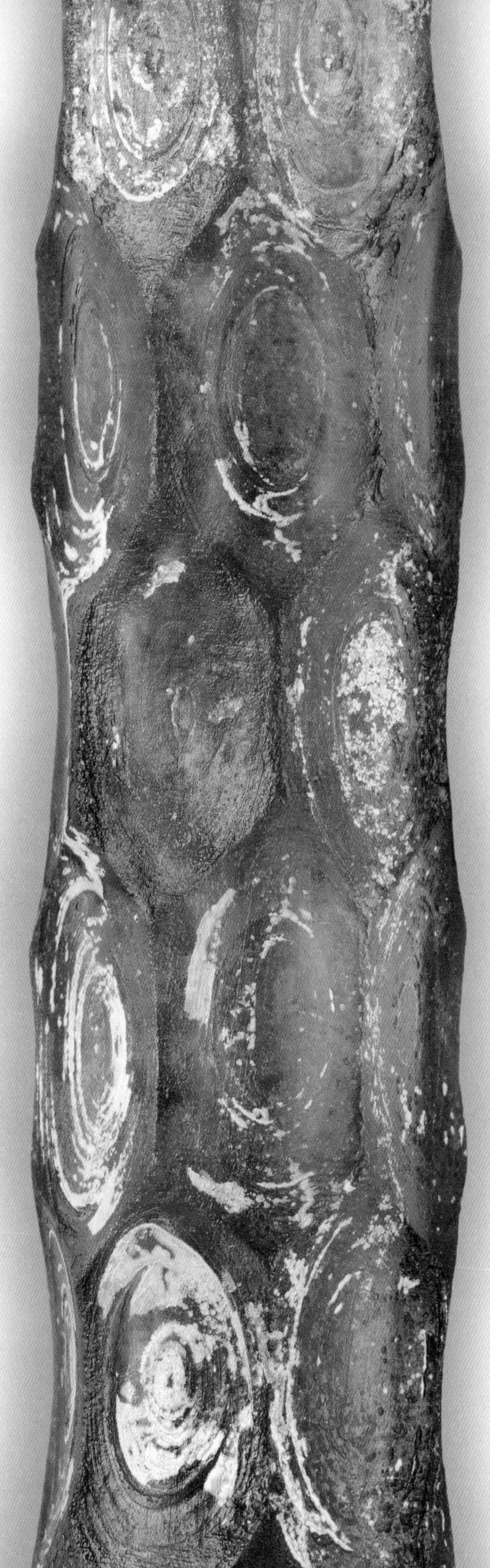

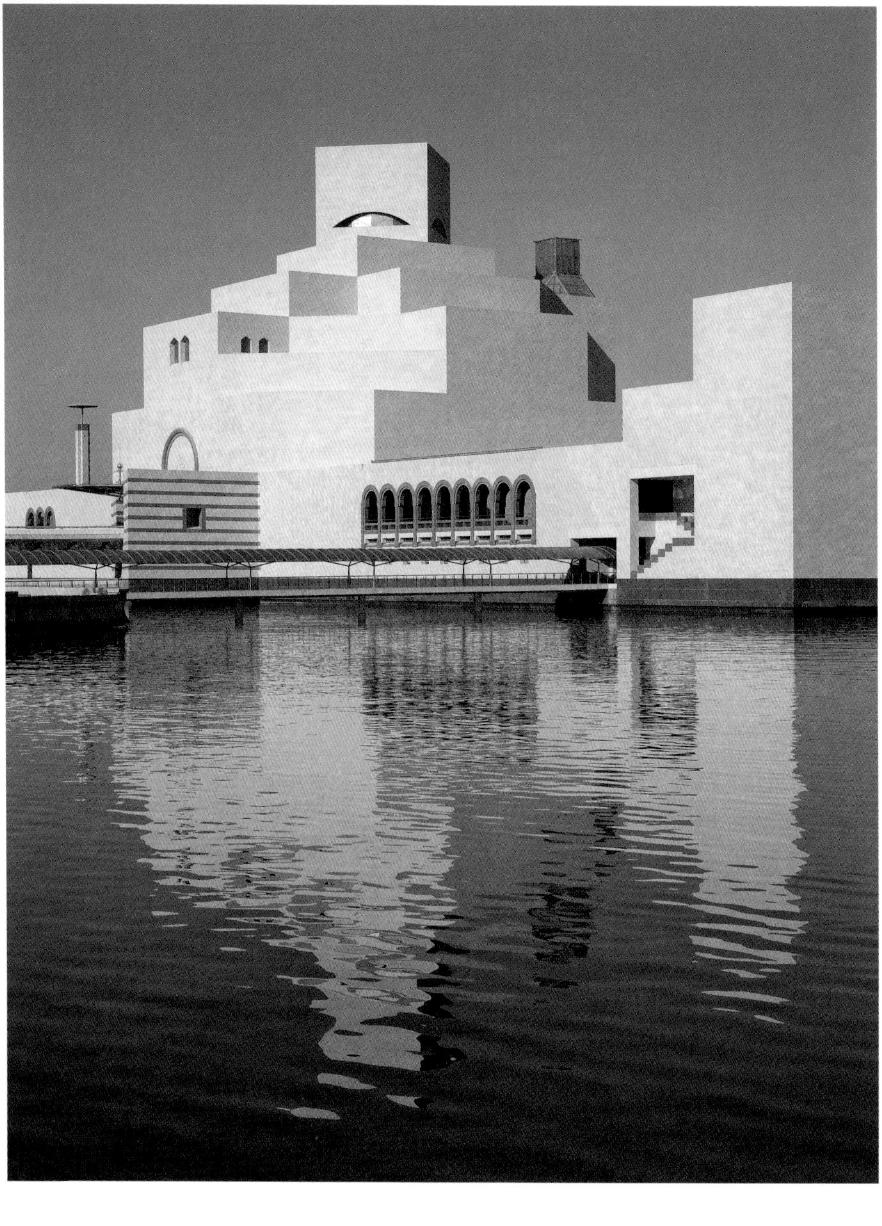

MIA and the Memory of Ibn Tulun

Nasser Rabbat

In the middle of the Mosque of Ibn Tulun, I had at last found what I came to consider to be the very essence of Islamic architecture.
I.M. Pei

Buildings have memories; memories embedded in their volumes and inscribed on their surfaces, reflected in the modifications, alterations, and additions they acquire over time, and recorded in texts or transmitted through tales, songs, or images. Some of these memories are premeditated. They are planted in the design and represent a synthesis of the patron's desire, the architect's imagination, and the builder's capability. They also link the building to the traditions of buildings that preceded it, which endow it with its historical setting and provide the contours of its own narrative. Most memories, however, are spontaneous and circumstantial. Accumulating over time at no set pace, they attach themselves to the building, thickening its narrative and altering it in a variety of unpredictable yet very real ways.

In its very short lifespan thus far, the Museum of Islamic Art (MIA), Doha, has not yet had time to garner many incidental memories, although I am sure it has collected some. Yet I.M. Pei, its architect, has conferred upon it a powerful foundation myth, one that links it to a fabulous literary tradition, even if he did not intend it. Pei has declared that he found inspiration in the ninth-century Mosque of Ibn Tulun in Cairo. The domed cube of that mosque's ablution fountain, with its logical geometry, rotating segments, clean-cut surfaces, and underlying cross-axiality, embodied the essence of Islamic architecture that he was searching for.

His MIA building sublimely captures these architectural qualities while, at the same time, recasting them in a recognisable modern vocabulary that is all Pei's own.

The MIA's formal association with the Mosque of Ibn Tulun, however, opens the door to another dimension of signification that this wonderful building epitomises. The stories preserved in the Arabic sources related to the construction of the Mosque reveal yet another narrative, one that is steeped in the heart of the Arabic and Islamic consciousness. Retelling those tales, with a healthy amount of imagination and a dash of fabrication, allows me to weave the story of the Museum of Islamic Art into their delightful web of fantasies, myths, parables and half-remembered past.

In the good fashion of fables, the story of the Mosque of Ibn Tulun begins with a hidden treasure. One moonlit night, the Amir Ahmad Ibn Tulun went out to the desert with his entourage. Deep in thought, he absentmindedly allowed his horse to wander at will, when the horse suddenly stumbled into a gap in the soft sand. Rising from his fall, the Amir realised that his horse had uncovered an ancient cave, probably Pharaonic, buried in the immense Egyptian desert. Leading his torch-carrying servants down into the cave, Ibn Tulun was struck by the amount of gold and silver coins, and all sorts of precious objects, that filled up the small subterranean room painted with vivid scenes of princely daily life. His mind raced to explain to his dumbfounded followers what had just happened. He hit on a marvellous explanation. God had revealed this treasure to him so that he could spend it on constructing the building that would most glorify His Name. He would build it in his new capital: al-Qata'i'. Thus was created the myth of the Mosque of Ibn Tulun.

With this God-sent fortune, Ibn Tulun wanted to build a mosque that would preserve his memory as a pious, just and generous ruler. He wanted it to be unique but not strange; magnificent but not ostentatious; and monumental but not overpowering. Above all, he did not want to usurp the columns of older temples as was the habit of rulers before him. He agonised over this dilemma, sending out queries to architects and builders. None was able to satisfy his request, until one architect, imprisoned in the horrible jail of *al-mutabbaq* in al-Qata'i' for an inadvertent mishap involving Ibn Tulun, sent word to the Amir that he had a solution.

Released from his cell and brought into the Amir's presence with his hair long and dirty and his clothes in tatters, the architect asked for animal skins upon which to draw his design. And on these, true to his promise, he showed that he could build a mosque with more than a hundred brick pilasters, each equipped with four engaged semi-columns; and that he needed only two porphyry columns for the *mihrab*. And so Egypt acquired its first sublime Samarran mosque.

Egyptian historians of the past, however, did not know that the Mosque of Ibn Tulun had its model in Samarra, the Abbasid capital in Iraq, where Ibn Tulun served before coming to Egypt. They strove to explain its unusual forms and, in the process, concocted fascinating stories, the most inspired of which was the account of the Mosque's spiral minaret: Ibn Tulun, reputed for his poised and serious demeanour, was seen in court one day rolling a piece of paper around his finger. To avoid the appearance of inattentiveness, he told his retinue, 'This is what I was thinking the minaret of my Mosque should look like.' And so the minaret was built like a spiralled cone, exactly like the more famous minaret of al-Mutawakkil in Samarra, constructed a mere twenty-five years earlier and echoed in the contemporary minaret of the Qatar Islamic Cultural Centre in Doha, a stone's throw from the MIA's majestic rotating cube.

Like all legendary buildings, the Mosque of Ibn Tulun is the subject of dreams. One particularly telling dream is attributed to Ibn Tulun himself. While it has been passed down to us in two different forms, the rationale of both is ultimately the same. In the first version, Ibn Tulun sees divine light falling on his city of al-Qata'i' – except for the area of the Mosque. He interpreted his vision negatively to mean that God was not pleased with his Mosque. Why should this be, he complained, when the Mosque was built solely for the Glory of God and only licit funds, the treasure from the cave, were used to finance its construction? A resourceful diviner told him: 'The dream means that the entire city will be destroyed but the Mosque will remain, for did God not say "and when his Lord manifested Himself on the mountain, He shattered it into pieces" (Qur'an 7:143)?' Whenever the Majesty of God descends on something, it crumbles.' Then the historians add: 'This explanation was proven right, for the Mosque is the only structure that remains of Ibn Tulun's capital city.' Another version of Ibn Tulun's dream is that he saw fire coming down from the sky, engulfing the Mosque in its flames. Upon recounting the dream,

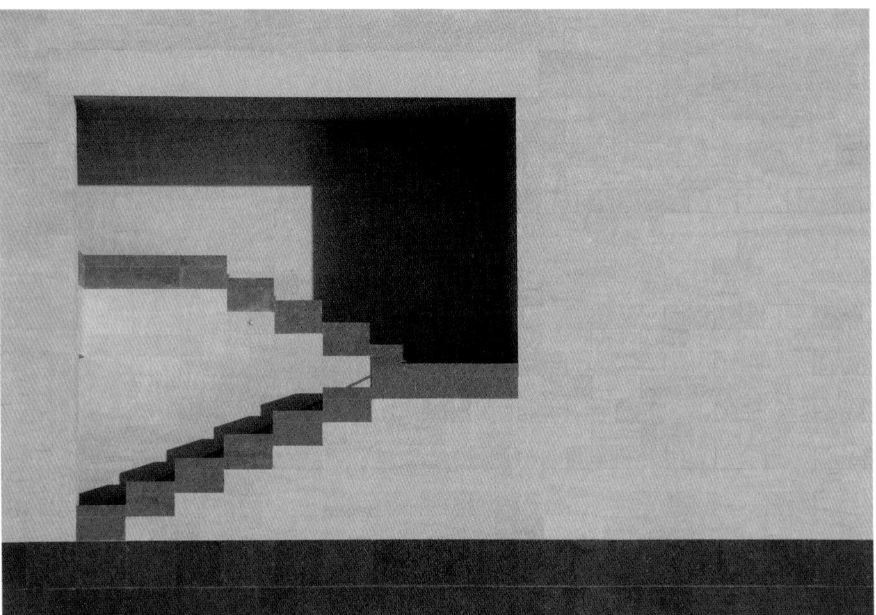

Ibn Tulun was assured that it meant that God had accepted his offering, 'for fire in ancient times used to come down from the sky whenever God accepted an offering, and the proof is the story of Abel and Cain [when God accepted the offering of the burnt lamb]'.

One part of the Mosque that Ibn Tulun built did burn down. The fountain called *al-fawwarah* was destroyed in one hour by a devastating fire a hundred years after its construction. According to historians, it was a marvellous structure: a screened and gilded dome raised on ten marble columns, with sixteen more at its corners, surmounted the marble bowl with the gushing fountain in its centre. Another ornamented dome was used for the call to prayer and a parapet of mahogany surrounded its top. Still a third dome sat at the top of its stairs, which may mean that the *fawwarah* was more than an ablution fountain in the middle of the Mosque's courtyard. After the fire, a new *fawarrah* was built but the Mosque fell into disuse when the Fatimids built al-Qahirah (Cairo). It became a neglected open space where the *Hajj* caravan of the Maghrib stopped on its route to the Holy Land.

It is the second reincarnation of *al-fawwarah*, however, that captured Pei's attention. In the Mamluk period, when the throne was only an assassination away for an ambitious amir, a failed would-be assassin escaped the revenge of a slain sultan's brother and hid in the abandoned Mosque. Scared and constantly moving around in the ruins of the deserted monument, he vowed that if God were to save his life, he would refurbish the Mosque in gratitude. Not only was he saved; fate, with its blind indifference, also made him Sultan. Al-Mansur Lajin, who ruled for only two short years, kept his promise and rebuilt the Mosque, adding the new *fawwarah* that still stands there today. Robust and proportionately tiered, the new *fawwarah* encapsulates the advances in domical engineering achieved in the early Mamluk period, which would ultimately give us the superlative carved stone domes of Mamluk Cairo. With its four openings, four *muqarnas*, squinches, and their corresponding transitional steps on the outside, the *fawwarah* of Sultan Lajin metamorphosed into the Museum of Islamic Art's rotating cube in Doha, in the hands of a modern-day magician of forms. That the transformed shape retains the memories of its origin is stressed by both architect and patron. It is further illustrated by a skilfully doctored image of the Museum with the profile of the *fawwarah* as its reflection on the water of Doha Bay, which was used for the invitation to the Museum's inauguration in November 2008. A literary transposition, as suggested by the foundational anecdotes of the Mosque of Ibn Tulun, could be as fruitful and enriching of the MIA's narrative as the architectural one was of its form.

Pei wanted his building to sit alone in the water. He feared that one day it could be swallowed up by the gigantic towers rising around it – similar to the forest of skyscrapers he witnessed rising on West Bay. Ibn Tulun's Mosque stood on a rocky outcrop, the exaggeratedly named Jebel Yashkur (Mount Yashkur), which rose above its surroundings and which was chiselled by the builders to fit its layout. Both buildings sought and achieved a distinction of site, one floating in full view of the city, the other hovering above its skyline. I am tempted to see in this push the traces of a similarly strong will of the architects, both of whom clearly understood the powerful ability of architecture to immortalise its architects. Pei's steely but infinitely polite determination, served with a disarmingly charming smile, is famous. Ibn Tulun's architect, who was apparently a Christian from the East named Sa'id al-Farghani, seems to have been strong-willed as well. Not only did he dare send a message from his jail to the mighty governor who had imprisoned him, asserting his design expertise, he also delivered. His serene mosque with its brick pilasters and spiralling minaret lasted for more than 1,000 years. And when the Amir forgot to reward him for his architectural feat, he climbed the minaret and requested his compensation in a loud voice, and received it. Here, perhaps, the comparison between the two architects stops. Pei did not need to climb on any imaginary or real minaret. He was amply celebrated for his achievement and a position was endowed in his name for the study of Islamic architecture at the University of Oxford.

Buildings, as Ibn Khaldun noted seven centuries ago, require huge outlays of time, money and manpower that can only be supplied by strong and wealthy patrons. Of course, it helps if divine intervention alleviates the financial burden. Thus, a treasure of buried gold in the past triggered Ibn Tulun's project. Likewise, the bounty of another subterranean source of wealth, gas and oil, fuelled the creation of a new monument to the culture that engendered the old Mosque and countless beautiful objects, a choice selection of which made it to the sanctum of the new Museum. Thus, in inspiration and in artistic refinement, the Museum of Islamic Art in Doha is a worthy heir to the Mosque of Ibn Tulun in Cairo. And like its millennial doppelganger, the Museum's story too is told via dreams and visions, those of the Amir of Qatar, his wife, and his architect. They all used the words 'dream' and 'vision' in expressing their strong desire to create an iconic building for Doha; a building that represents a modern rendering of the rich Islamic architectural heritage. And they realised it. May the MIA, like the Mosque of Ibn Tulun, live to perpetuate these dreams and visions for more than 1,000 years.

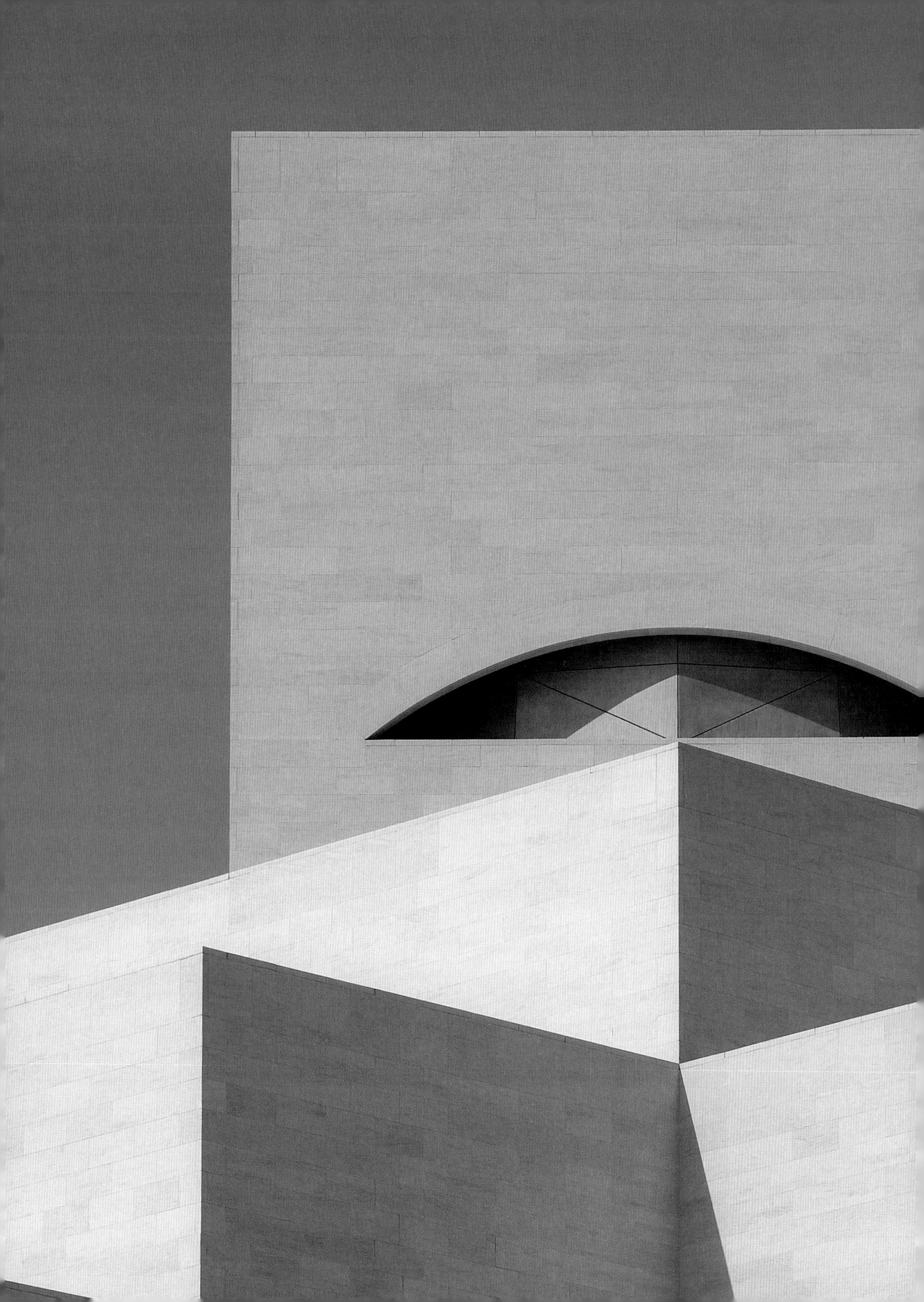

Notes on translation

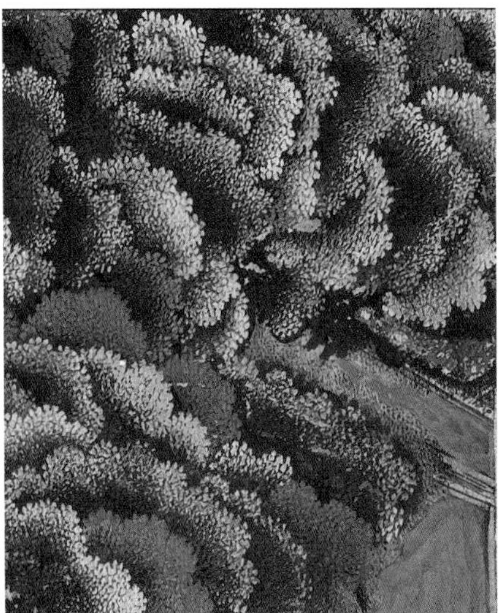

Radwa Ashour, 'An Andulasian Penbox' was translated by Ahdaf Soueif.

Najwa Barakat, 'The Shroud of St Lazarus: A Text' was translated by Abla Sharnoubi.

Jabbour al-Douaihy, 'St Jerome' was translated by Abla Sharnoubi.

Bejan Matur, 'Infinity's Watchman' was translated by Ruth Christie.

Ghassan Zaqtan, 'Laila and the Majnoun' was translated by Ahdaf Soueif.

All other texts were created in English.

Biographies

AHDAF SOUEIF is the author of the best-selling *The Map of Love* (shortlisted for the Booker Prize in 1999 and translated into more than twenty languages), and the much-loved *In the Eye of the Sun* and the collection of short stories, *I Think of You*. Soueif is also a political and cultural commentator. The *London Review of Books* has called her 'a political analyst and commentator of the best kind' and her clear-eyed reporting and analysis is syndicated throughout the world. A collection of her essays, *Mezzaterra: Fragments from the Common Ground*, was published in 2004. Her translation (from Arabic into English) of Mourid Barghouti's *I Saw Ramallah* also came out that year.

Writing in English and Arabic, concerned with both the art of fiction and the state of the world, she works at several crossroads. She has been awarded three honorary DLitts by British universities – having earned her PhD in Linguistics from the University of Lancaster in 1979. She is a Fellow of the Royal Society for Literature, a fellow of the Lannan Foundation for Cultural Freedom and the first recipient of the Mahmoud Darwish Award, 2010. In 2007 Soueif founded Engaged Events, a UK-based charity. Its first project is the Palestine Festival of Literature.

RIZ AHMED is 'consolidating his position as one of Britain's brightest talents' (*Guardian*) in the fields of film, music, and the arts. He has starred in multi-award-winning films such as *The Road to Guantánamo* (Berlin Silver Bear), *Britz* (BAFTA Best TV Drama), *Shifty* (winner of Best Actor, Geneva Film Festival, nominated for Best Actor BIFA Awards), and the BAFTA-winning *Four Lions*. As Riz MC his debut album *MICroscope* was released in 2011 to universal critical acclaim.

SUAD AMIRY is the author of the best-selling *Sharon and My Mother-in-Law* (2005), translated into seventeen languages and awarded the prestigious 2004 Viareggio Prize. Her book *Menopausal Palestine: Women at the Edge* was published in India (2010). Her latest, *Nothing to Lose but Your Life* (2010), has been published in English and Arabic by Bloomsbury Qatar Foundation Publishing. A Palestinian writer and architect who has been living in Ramallah since 1981, she studied architecture at the American University of Beirut, Lebanon; in Michigan, USA; and in Edinburgh, Scotland; and is the founder and Director of the Riwaq Centre for Architectural Conservation in Ramallah. She also serves as the vice-president of the Board of Trustees of Birzeit University.

RADWA ASHOUR's *Granada (Part I)* was awarded the 1994 Cairo International Book Fair Book of the Year Award, while *The Granada Trilogy* took first prize at the Arab Woman's Book Fair in 1995. In 2007 Ashour was awarded the Constantine Cavafy Prize for Literature, and in 2009 the Tarquinia Cardarelli International Criticism Prize. Ashour is an author, translator and scholar. She is co-editor of the four-volume *Encyclopaedia of Arab Women Writers* (2004). Born in Cairo, her works have been translated into several languages. She is professor of English and Comparative Literature at Ain Shams University, Cairo.

TASH AW has won the 2005 Whitbread First Novel Award and the 2005 Commonwealth Writers' Prize for Best First Novel (Asia Pacific region). His novels *The Harmony Silk Factory* (2005) and *Map of the Invisible World* (2009) have been translated into twenty-four languages. He was born and grew up in Malaysia, moving to the UK to attend university. He now divides his time between London and South-east Asia.

NAJWA BARAKAT is the author of six successful novels, and has a background in theatre and film. Born in Beirut, she has worked for various Arabic and European newspapers, radio and TV channels. She has a postgraduate diploma in theatre from the Beirut Fine Arts Institute, Lebanon, and a diploma in cinematic studies from Paris. Her novels include *Bas al-Awadem* (The Bus of Good People) (1996), which was the winner of the 1996 Best Literary Creation prize awarded by the Lebanese Cultural Forum in France. In 1997 she published *Al-Mosta'jira* (The Tenant) in French, which was adapted for the theatre in France. *Ya Salam* (1999) was followed by *Loghat al-Sirr* (The Secret Language) (2004), which was republished in Cairo (2010). Towards the end of 2005, Barakat launched the 'How to write a novel' project, and in 2009 she established 'Muhtaraf: How to write a novel: for literature, theatre and cinema', a permanent workshop designed to find and develop creative young Arab talent.

RUTH CHRISTIE is the translator of novels by Latife Tekin (1993) (with Saliha Paker) and by Selçuk Altun (2008) (with Selçuk Berilgen). She also translated *The Shelter Stories* by Feyyaz Kyacan Fergar (2007). She has translated two selections of poems by Oktay Rifat, one minor and one major (1992 and 2007), and a major selection of poems by Nazim Hikmet (2002). These three works were done in collaboration with Richard McKane. Her translation of Bejan Matur's *In the Temple of a Patient God* was published in 2004. Many of her translations of Turkish poetry have appeared in literary magazines and journals worldwide. Born in Scotland, she studied English Language and Literature at the University of St Andrews, and later Turkish Language and Literature at London University.

WILLIAM DALRYMPLE's highly acclaimed best-seller *In Xanadu* was published when he was twenty-two. He has also published seven books of non-fiction, including *White Mughals* (Wolfson Prize), *The Last Mughal* (Duff Cooper Prize) and most recently, *Nine Lives* (Asia House Literary Award). *City of Djinns* won the Thomas Cook Travel Book Award and the *Sunday Times* Young British Writer of the Year Award. *The Age of Kali* won the French Prix d'Astrolabe.

JABBOUR AL-DOUAIHY has published a series of novels and short-story compilations, and his most recent book, *June Rain* (2006), was shortlisted for the International Prize for Arab Fiction. He is professor of French Literature at the Lebanese University.

JAMES FENTON is the author and editor of many volumes of poetry. A former Oxford

Professor of Poetry, he is the recipient of numerous awards and honours, among them the Queen's Gold Medal for Poetry (2007), and the Whitbread Prize for Poetry (1994). Fenton has also written extensively about art history for *The New York Review of Books*, and his essays were gathered in *Leonardo's Nephew: Essays on Art and Artists*. He has also published a history of the Royal Academy in London, under the title *School of Genius*. He lives in New York.

ADAM FOULDS' first novel, *The Truth About These Strange Times* (2007), won the *Sunday Times* Young Writer of the Year Award and the Betty Trask Award. His long narrative poem *The Broken Word* (2008) was shortlisted for the John Llewellyn Rhys Memorial Prize and the *Sunday Times* Young Writer of the Year Award, and won a Somerset Maugham Award and the 2008 Costa Poetry Award. His second novel, *The Quickening Maze* (2009), was shortlisted for the 2009 Man Booker Prize for Fiction.

PHILIP HENSHER is the author of several novels and a collection of short stories. He is a regular broadcaster and contributes reviews and articles to various newspapers and journals including *The Spectator*, the *Mail on Sunday* and *The Independent*. His latest novels are *The Northern Clemency* (2008), shortlisted for the Man Booker Prize for Fiction and the Commonwealth Writers' Prize (Eurasia Region, Best Book); and *King of the Badgers* (2011).

ERIC HOBSBAWM has been described as the world's greatest living historian. A writer and lecturer whose books include a three-volume history of the nineteenth century (*The Age of Revolution*, *The Age of Capital* and *The Age of Empire*), *Nations and Nationalism since 1780*, and more specialised works in the fields of labour history, he has also written an autobiography, *Interesting Times*. He was born in Alexandria, Egypt, in 1917, and educated in Vienna, Berlin, London and Cambridge. He has been teaching and writing about history since 1947 and has been the recipient of numerous awards, honorary degrees and honorary citizenships. He is President of Birkbeck College, University of London.

SONIA JABBAR is an essayist, journalist, photographer, film-maker, artist and human rights activist whose work has largely addressed conflicts in South Asia.

JAMEEL (Jim) AL-KHALILI's latest book is *Pathfinders: The Golden Age of Arabic Science* (2010).

His previous widely translated popular science books include *Black Holes, Wormholes and Time Machines* (1999), *Nucleus: A Trip into the Heart of Matter* (2001) and *Quantum: A Guide for the Perplexed* (2004). He has also presented a number of science documentaries on TV and radio, including the BAFTA-nominated *Chemistry: A Volatile History* and *Science and Islam*, which appeared on the BBC in 2010. The Baghdad-born scientist, author and broadcaster is professor of physics at the University of Surrey in the UK where he also holds a chair in Public Engagement in Science. He was awarded the Royal Society's Michael Faraday Prize in 2007. He is also Executive Vice President of the British Science Association.

SARAH MAGUIRE has published four highly-acclaimed poetry collections, most recently *The Pomegranates of Kandahar* (2007). *Haleeb Muraq*, poems translated into Arabic by Saadi Yousef, was published by Dar Al Mada in 2003. She is the only living English-language poet with a book in print in Malayalam. Maguire is the founder and director of the Poetry Translation Centre based in London.

JAMAL MAHJOUB is a prize-winning novelist and essayist. His first three novels, *Navigation of a Rainmaker* (1989), *Wings of Dust* (1994) and *In the Hour of Signs* (1996), examine various aspects of Sudan's history and its relationship to Britain from colonial times through independence. *The Carrier* (1998) deals with astronomy, heliocentricity and the role played by Arab scientific work in developments in European thought. His other novels include *Travelling with Djinns* (2003), *The Drift Latitudes* (2006) and *Nubian Indigo* (2006). He is working on a non-fiction account of the situation in Sudan. Born in London and brought up in Khartoum, his fiction is largely concerned with people whose identity is divided between cultures and continents.

BEJAN MATUR is an acclaimed poet whose first poetry book, *Rüzgar Dolu Konaklar* (Winds Howl through the Mansions) (1996), won several literary prizes. She has published numerous poetry books. Her poems have been translated into seventeen languages. A collection of her poems has been published in English under the title *In the Temple of a Patient God*. She writes a column for the Turkish daily, *Zaman*, and runs the Diyarbakır Culture and Arts Foundation (DKSV). Her first prose book, *Dağın Ardına Bakmak* (Looking Behind the Mountain) (2011), about PKK guerrillas, became a bestseller within a week of publication.

PANKAJ MISHRA is the author of *The Romantics: A Novel* (2000), winner of the Los Angeles Times' Art Seidenbaum Award for First Fiction; *An End to Suffering: The Buddha in the World* (2004); and *Butter Chicken in Ludhiana: Travels in Small Town India* (1995). He contributes literary and political essays to various international publications. His most recent book is *Temptations of the West: How to Be Modern in India, Pakistan, Tibet, and Beyond* (2006).

SHIRIN NESHAT is an Iranian-born visual artist and film-maker who has held a number of solo gallery and museum exhibitions internationally. She has won many prizes, including the Golden Lion Award at the Venice Biennale in 1999, and the Lillian Gish Prize in 2006. Her first feature-length film, *Women without Men*, received a Silver Lion Award at the Venice International Film Festival in 2009. She currently lives in New York.

NASSER RABBAT is the Aga Khan Professor and Director of the Aga Khan Program for Islamic Architecture at MIT. He has published many books and scholarly articles, including *The Citadel of Cairo: A New Interpretation of Royal Mamluk Architecture* (1995), *Thaqafat al-Bina' wa Bina' al-Thaqafa* (2002) and *al-Mudun al-Mayyita* (2010). His most recent books include *al-Naqd Iltizaman* (2011), *L'art Islamique à la recherche d'une méthode historique* (2011), and *Architecture as Social History: Building, Culture, and Politics in Mamluk Egypt and Syria* (2010). Rabbat has worked as an architect in Los Angeles and Damascus and regularly consults on architectural and urban design projects in the Islamic world. He contributes articles to various Arabic newspapers, magazines, and blogs, and has been awarded a number of fellowships.

YOUSSEF RAKHA's latest work is the novel *Kitab al-tughra: ghara'ib al-tarikh fi madinat al-marrikh* (The Book of the Tughra). He is the Cairo-born author of *Beirut shi mahal*, nominated for the Lettre Ulysses Award for the Art of Reportage, several other volumes on Arab cities, a collection of short stories, *Azhar al-Shams* (Flowers of the Sun) (1999), and a collection of poems and essays, *Kullu Amakinina* (All Our Places) (2010). He has worked for *Al-Ahram Weekly*, the Cairo-based English-language newspaper, and for Abu Dhabi's *The National*.

MARCUS DE SAUTOY OBE is Professor of Mathematics at the University of Oxford, and a Fellow of New College. He is also the Charles

Simonyi Professor for the Public Understanding of Science. He is the author of *The Music of the Primes*, *Finding Moonshine* and most recently *The Number Mysteries*. His TV shows include *The Story of Maths*, a four-part landmark series for the BBC. In 2009 he was awarded the Royal Society's Michael Faraday Prize.

ANTON SHAMMAS was born in Fassuta in northern Palestine, and currently teaches at the University of Michigan in Ann Arbor, where he has lived since 1987. He has written poetry, fiction, plays and essays in three languages, and has translated extensively from and into Arabic, Hebrew and English. His novel *Arabesques* (1986) was chosen by the editors of the *New York Times Book Review* as one of the best novels published in English in 1988.

KAMILA SHAMSIE is the author of five novels, including *Burnt Shadows*, which was shortlisted for the Orange Prize for Fiction and is being translated into twenty-one languages, as well as *Salt and Saffron* and *Kartography*. Three of her novels have received awards from the Pakistan Academy of Letters. She is a trustee of the Free Word Centre (UK) and on the board of English PEN. She writes comment pieces and reviews for a number of publications, primarily the *Guardian* (UK).

ABLA SHARNOUBI, a British-born Egyptian writer, is currently working on her first novel, which is set in contemporary Cairo. She studied Human Sciences and Music Technology before co-founding an independent music publishing company in London, where she lives and works. She is currently studying for a Master's degree in Creative Writing.

RAJA SHEHADEH's books include the highly praised *Strangers in the House* (2002), *When the Bulbul Stopped Singing: Life in Ramallah Under Siege* (2003) and *Palestinian Walks: Notes on a Vanishing Landscape* (2007), for which he won the Orwell Prize for Political Writing. His latest book is *A Rift in Time, Travels with My Ottoman Uncle*. Shehadeh, who lives in Ramallah, is a founder of the pioneering human rights organisation Al Haq, an affiliate of the International Commission of Jurists.

OLIVER WATSON has been involved with the Museum of Islamic Art, Qatar, since 2003, becoming its Director in 2008, when it opened to the public. He was recently appointed as the first I.M. Pei Professor of Islamic Art and Architecture at the University of Oxford. A specialist in the history of Islamic ceramics, he has also worked at the Victoria and Albert Museum in London, where he was responsible for the new Glass Gallery which opened in 1995, and at Oxford University's Ashmolean Museum.

GHASSAN ZAQTAN is a poet and writer from Palestine. He has published ten volumes of poetry and three novels, and his work has been extensively translated into French, Italian, Norwegian, Chinese and Spanish, Portuguese and English. A selection of his work, translated by Fadi Joudah, will be published in 2012 by Yale University Press. He has promoted Palestinian poetry through his research and editing of *Wave of Modern Palestinian Poetry Anthology* (2008) and *Permanent Visitors of Flame* (2000). He was the editor-in-chief of the PLO's *Bayadir* literary magazine, and editor of *Masharef* literary magazine with the late Palestinian writer Emile Habibi. Zaqtan has also contributed to documentary cinema and his novel *Light Sky* (1992) was performed in the theatre. He has a weekly column in *Al-Ayyam* newspaper, and works as a consultant for the Welfare Association on cultural policy. Zaqtan has lived in Ramallah since his return from the Diaspora in 1995.

SLAVOJ ZIZEK is a philosopher, theologian and art critic, whose numerous publications include *Living in the End Times* (2010), *Parallax View* (2008) and *On Belief* (2004). His work mainly covers German Idealism, cinema theory, and the critique of ideology.

MUIZ ANWAR is a visual communicator whose innovations in contemporary Arabic aesthetics have won him recognition by some of the world's most iconic designers. His work evolves an experimental visual language born from the principles of classical Islamic art and philosophies, which reflect the complex, cultural semiotics and geopolitics of the modern Arab world. After graduating he spent a year interning with prestigious type foundries, Dalton Maag, London, and FontShop International, Berlin, where he began exclusive production of two unique Arabic and Latin typefaces. He has since launched a critically acclaimed magazine, branded national and international arts organisations and festivals and been recognised in digital and print journals across the globe. Anwar now hosts a client portfolio that spans the Americas, Europe, the Middle East, Africa and Asia.

Notes

Ahdaf Soueif, 'Introduction'

1. *Mezzaterra, Fragments from the Common Ground*, London: Bloomsbury, 2004, pp.7, 8.

Kamila Shamsie, 'Notes on a Leaf'

1. Qur'an 6:59; trans. Tarif Khalidi.

Slavoj Zizek , 'Choosing our Fate'

1. Quoted from www.blackwell-synergy.com/doi/abs/10.1046/j.1523-1739.2000.00053.x.
2. See Jean-Pierre Dupuy, *Pour un catastrophisme eclaire*, Paris: Editions du Seuil, 2002.
3. Fethi Benslama, *La psychanalyse a l'epreuve de l'Islam*, Paris: Aubier, 2002, p. 320.
4. Peter Hallward, *Damming the Flood*, London: Verso Books, 2007, p. 13.
5. Citation for the '*Abyssinian slave*' hadith, please see: Libcom.org, 'The Zanj Slaves Rebellion, AD 869-883', http://libcom.org/library/zanj-slaves-rebellion-ad-869-883.

Suad Amiry, 'Aniconism, Huntresses and Men's Jewellery'

1. 'Persian Rugs: The O'Connell Notes' website: (http://www.persiancarpetguide.com/sw-asia/Rugs/Persian/Yazd_Rugs/Safavid_Silk_Metal_Boucle_Figural_Panel.htm).
2. (www.themodernapprentice.com).

Sonia Jabbar, 'Heart of Empire'

1. Anne-Marie Schimmel, *The Empire of the Great Mughals*, Reaktion Books, London, 2004. pp.180-1.
2. Ebba Koch, *The Complete Taj Mahal*, Thames & Hudson, London, 2006. p.18.
3. June 1631: temporary burial in Burhanpur; December 1631 (1041 AH): brought to and buried in Agra; January 1632 (1041 AH): exhumed and buried in a small domed building on the Taj construction site; May 1633: exhumed and buried on a white marble platform of the mausoleum. Ibid.
4. See the beautifully illustrated Milo Cleveland Beach, Ebba Koch and Wheeler M. Thackston, *The King of the World: The Padshahnama : An Imperial Mughal Manuscript from the Royal Library, Windsor Castle*, Thames & Hudson, London, 1997.
5. Francois Bernier, *Travels in the Mogul Empire 1656-1668*, (Reprint) Asian Educational Service, New Delhi, 1996. pp.11-3.

6. Abraham Eraly, *Emperors of the Peacock Throne; The Saga of the Great Mughals*, Penguin, New Delhi, 1997, p.356.

7. Waldemar Hansen, *The Peacock Throne; The Drama of Mogul India*, Motilal Banarasidass, New Delhi, 1972, p.420.

8. Niccolao Manucci, *Storia do Mogor, or Mogul India 1653-1708*, John Murray, London, 1907, p.431.

9. Hansen, op cit., p.485.

Anton Shammas, 'The Nightmare of the Translator'

1. Rafael Alberti's 'The Ballad About the One Who Never Went to Granada', translated by Rachel Severin and Alia Persico-Shammas, by request.

William Dalrymple, 'The Coronation Portrait'

1. Translation of Zafar poem by Ahmed Ali.

Nasser Rabbat, 'MIA and the Memory of Ibn Tulun'

1. Qur'an 7:143; trans. M. M. Pickthall.

Object directory

from the Museum catalogue

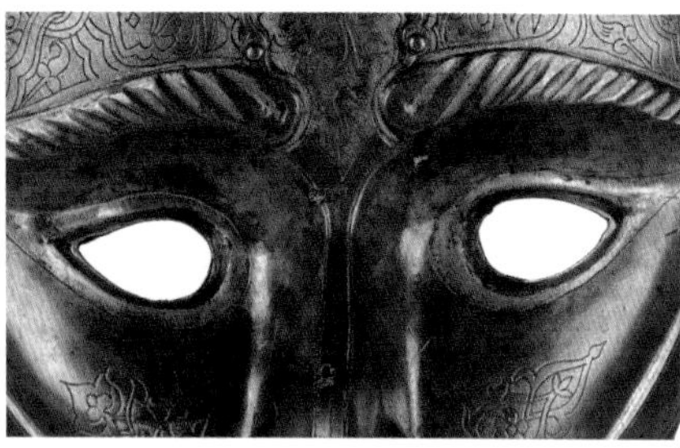

p: 18, 21

War Mask

Steel with gold inlay
Eastern Turkey or Western Iran
15th century (9th-10th centuries AH)
MW.6

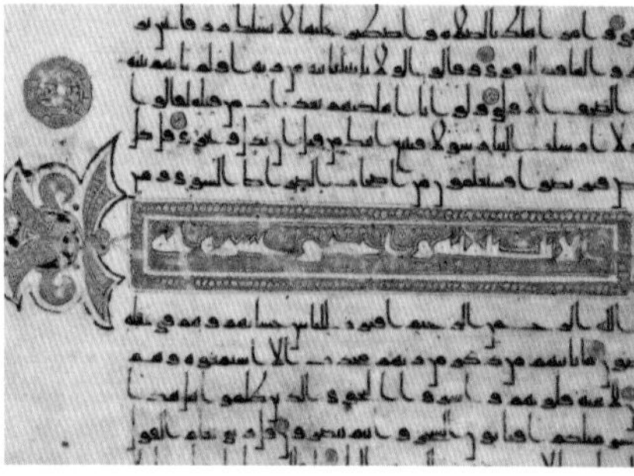

p: 22, 25, 28, 30

Qur'an in Kufic script

Ink and gold on parchment
North Africa or Near East
Early 10th century (4th century AH)
MS.620

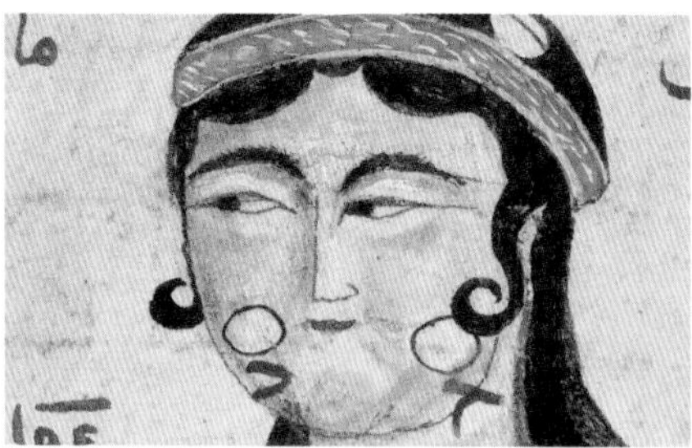

p: 32, 35, 37, 38

Book of Fixed Stars

Text by: Abul-Husayn Abd al-Rahman ibn Umar ibn Muhammad al-Sufi.
Copied and illustrated by:
Ali ibn Abd al-Jalil ibn Ali ibn Muhammad.
Ink on paper
Iraq (Baghdad)
February–March 1125
(Muharram–Safar 519 AH)
MS.2

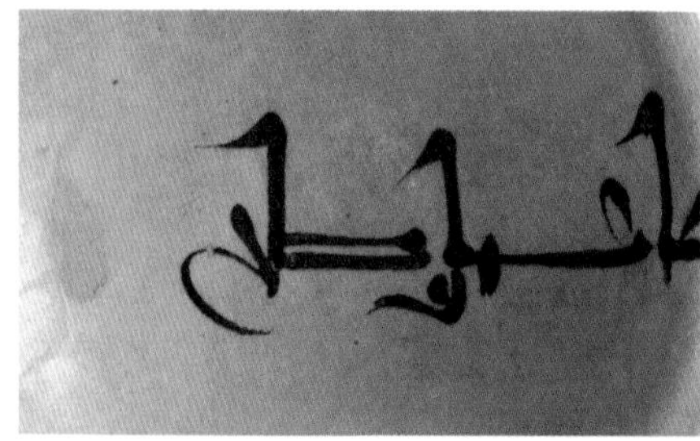

p: 10, 40

Bowl

Iraq (probably Basra)
9th century (3rd century AH)
PO.31

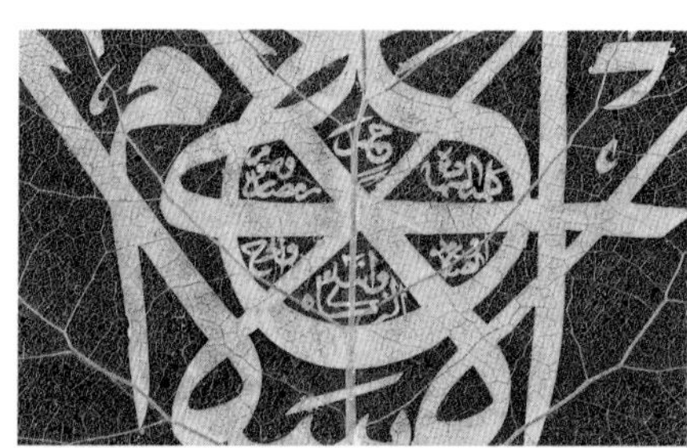

p: 46, 49, 52

Calligraphic Compositions

Natural leaf and gold

Turkey

20th century (14th century AH)

MS.161-3

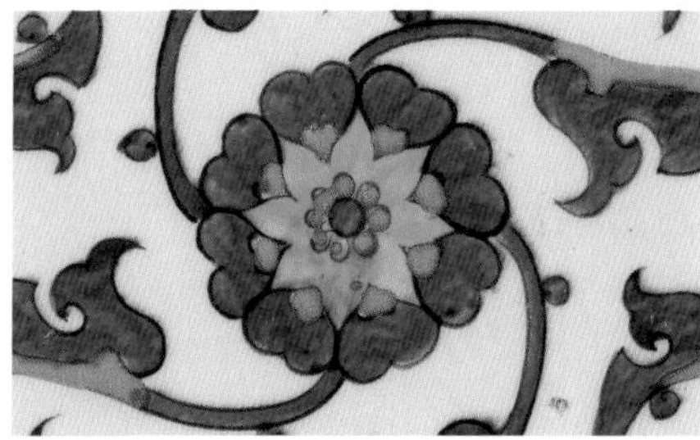

p: 60

Iznik Tile

Fritware, underglaze painting

Iznik, Turkey

c.1560 (c.967 AH)

PO.316

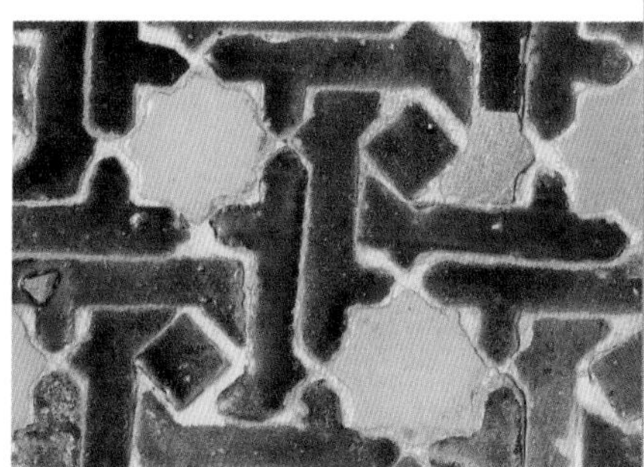

p: 54

Glazed Mosaic Tile

Earthenware, glaze

Spain

14th century (8th century AH)

TI.45

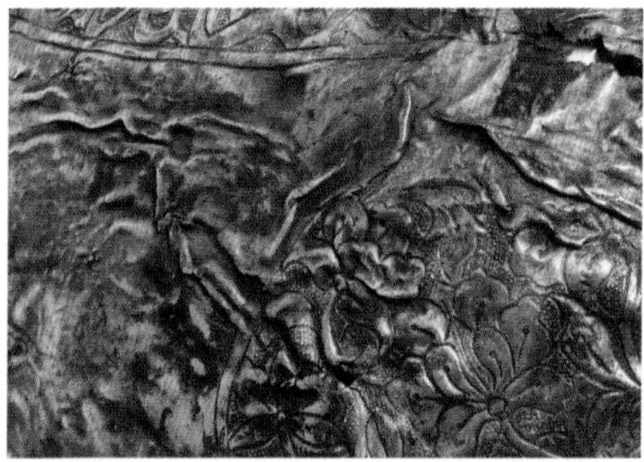

p: 62, 66

Silver Vase

Silver

Iran

14th century (8th century AH)

MW.212

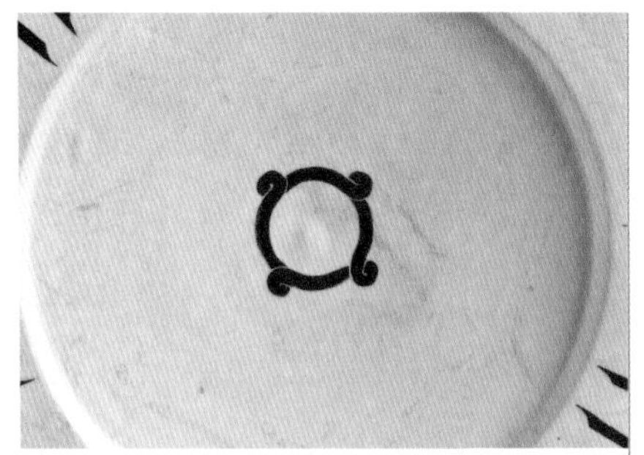

p: 68

Dish

Earthenware, slip painting

Iran or Central Asia

10th century (4th century AH)

PO.24

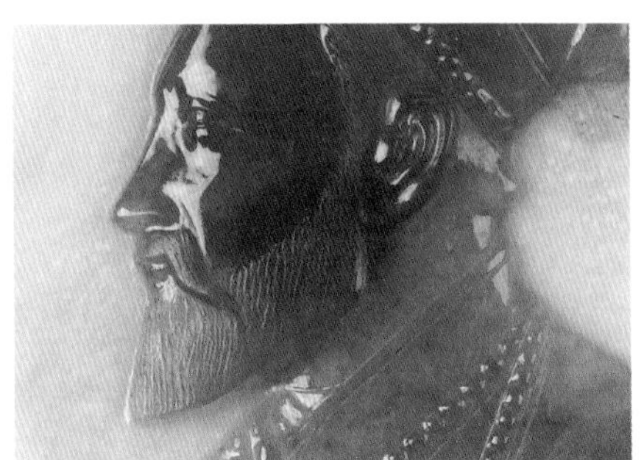

p: 84, 89

Cameo portrait of Emperor Shah Jahan

Sardonyx, bloodstone

India

1630-40 (1040-50 AH)

HS.4

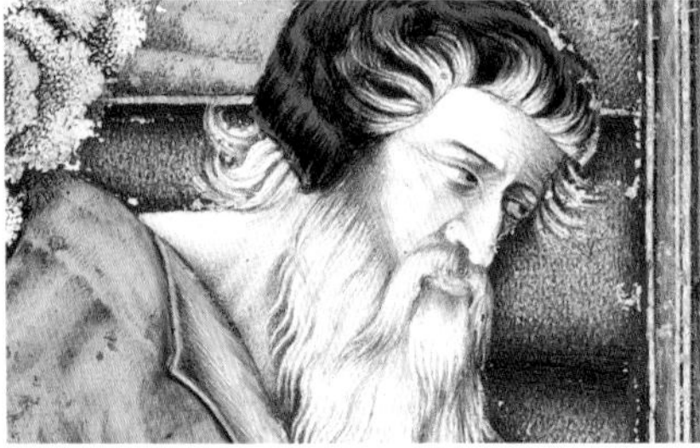

p: 76, 83, 134, 137, 140, 192, 197, 238

Portrait of St Jerome Representing Melancholy

by Farrukh Beg

Opaque watercolour, ink and gold on paper

India

Miniature: 1615 (1024 AH)

Album page mounted: c.1640 (c.1049 AH)

MS.44

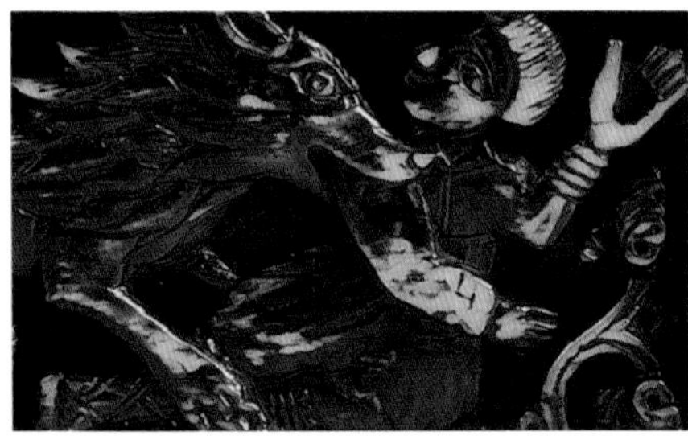

p: 90, 93, 96-7

Penbox

Ivory, brass

Spain

December 1003–January 1004

(Rabi' al Awal 394 AH)

IV.4

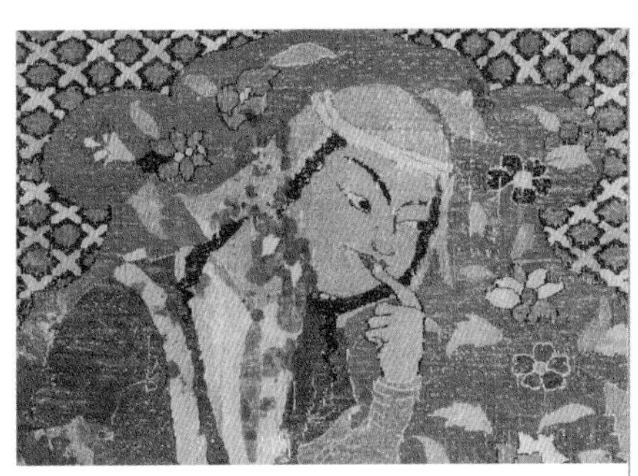

p: 98, 102, 105

Leila and Majnoun Tapestry

Silk tapestry

Iran (probably Kashan)

Late 16th-early 17th century

(Late 10th-early 11th century AH)

CA.1

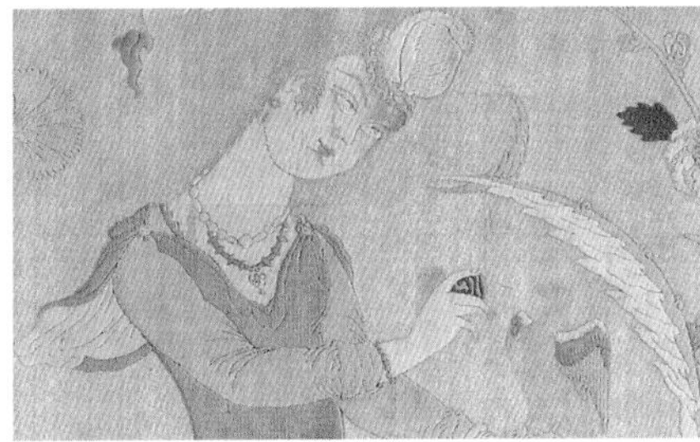

p: 114-5, 117

Safavid Silk and Velvet Panel

Voided silk velvet, metal thread and bouclé

Iran

Early 17th century (11th century AH)

TE.204

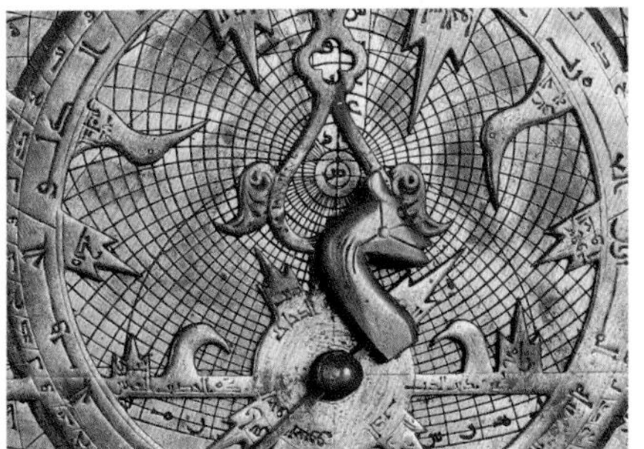

p: 118, 133

Planispheric Astrolabe

by Hamid ibn al Khadir al Kujandi

Brass

Iran [Rayy] or Iraq [Baghdad]

984-85 (374 AH)

SI.5

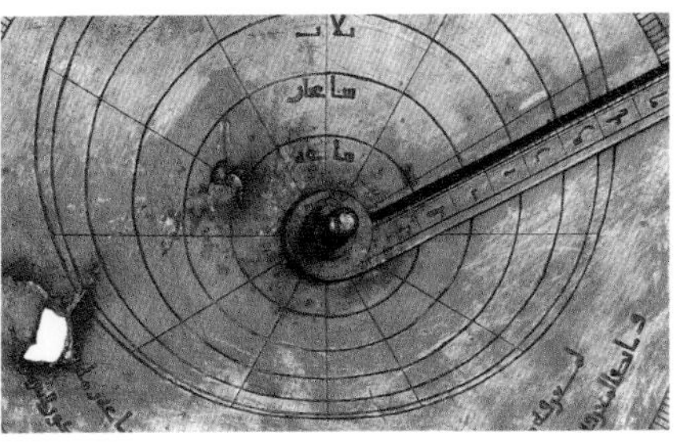

p: 142, 146, 149

Mathematical and Astronomical Instrument

Signed by Nastulus

Brass

Iraq (Baghdad)

Late 9th-early 10th century

(4th century AH)

MW.278

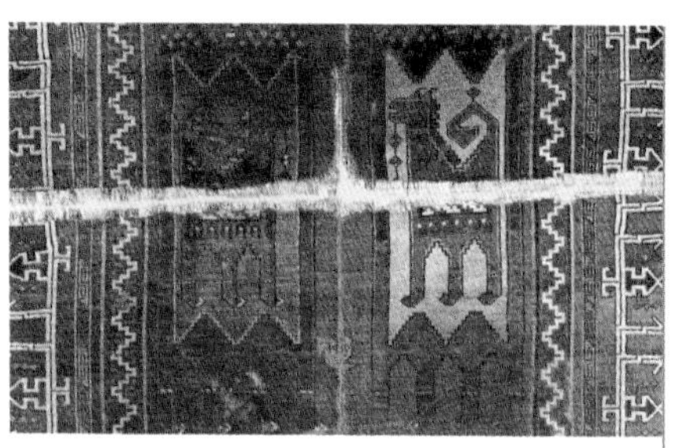

p: 150, 153, 156

Four-animal Carpet

Wool

Turkey

14th century (8th century AH)

CA.77

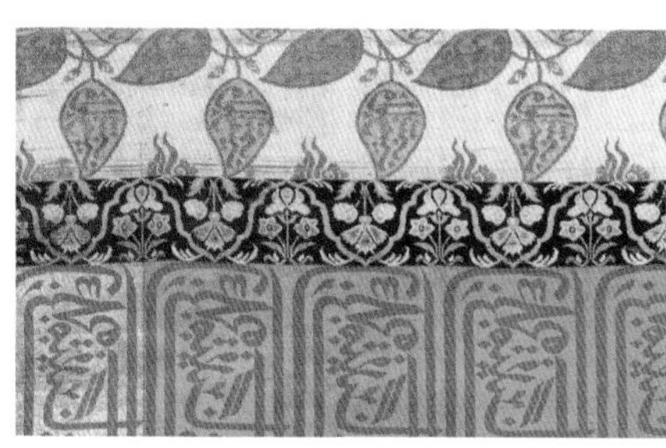

p: 163, 166

Tomb Cover with Reversed Inscriptions

Silk, precious metal thread

Iran

17th or 18th century

(12th or 13th century AH)

TE.27

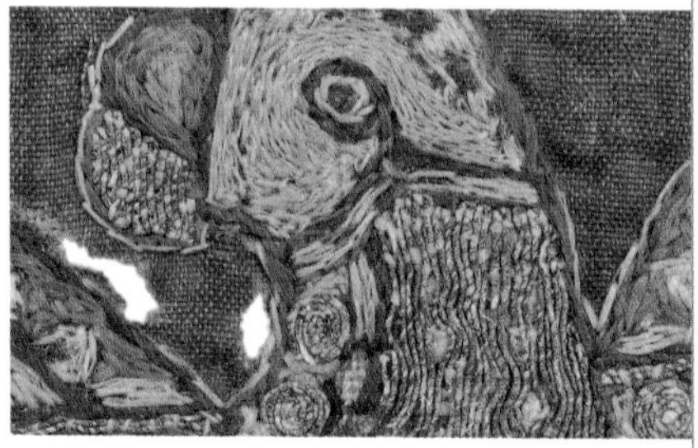

p: 158

Textile Fragment from
the Shroud of St Lazarus

Silk taffeta embroidered with silk and gilded leather substrate wound around silk core

Spain

c.1007 (c.397 AH)

TE.150

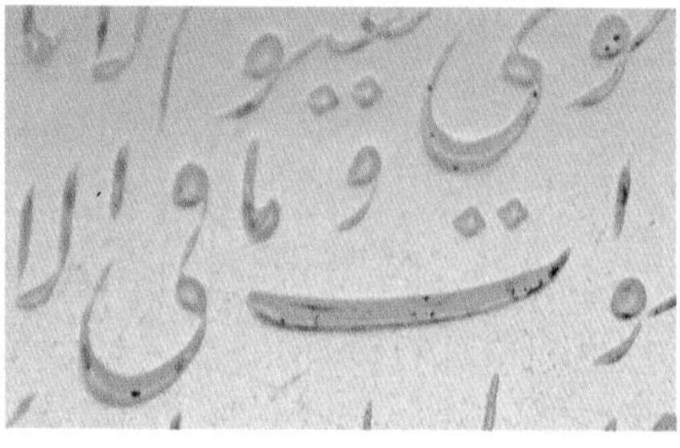

p: 168, 175

Calligraphic Jade Pendant (haldili)

Jade (nephrite)

India

1631-32 (1041 AH)

JE.85

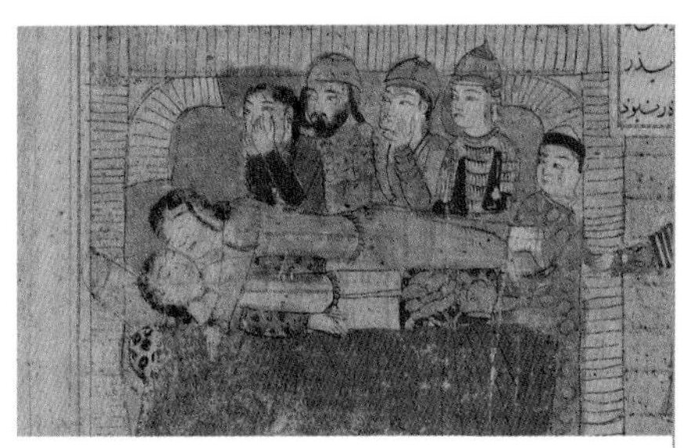

p: 176

Jarira dies on the body of her son Farud

Illustrated page from the Shahnameh

Calligraphy by:

HASAN BIN MUHAMMAD BIN ALI BIN HUSAYNI

Ink and pigments on paper

Iran (Shiraz)

1341 (741 AH)

MS.355

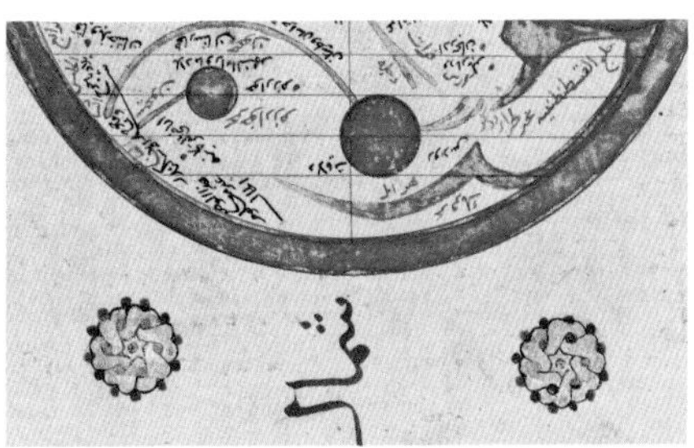

p: 184

Map of the World

Opaque watercolour and ink on paper

Egypt or Syria

Probably 15th century

(Probably 9th-10th century AH)

MS.228

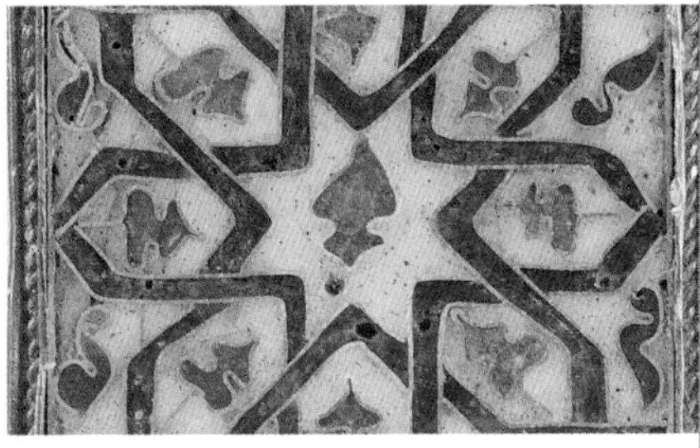

p: 183

Belt Buckle

Gold, enamels

Spain (Granada)

14th century (8th century AH)

JE.210

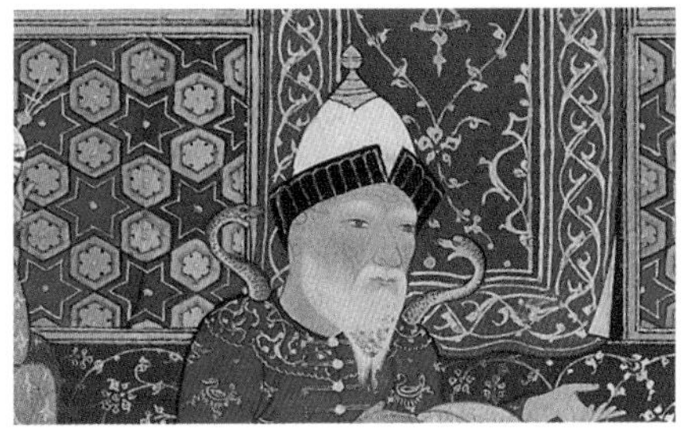

p: 189, 190

The Nightmare of Zahhak

Page from the Shahnameh of Shah Tahmasp

Mir Musavvir

Opaque watercolour, ink and gold on paper

Iran (Tabriz)

c.1525-35 (c.931-41 AH)

MS.41

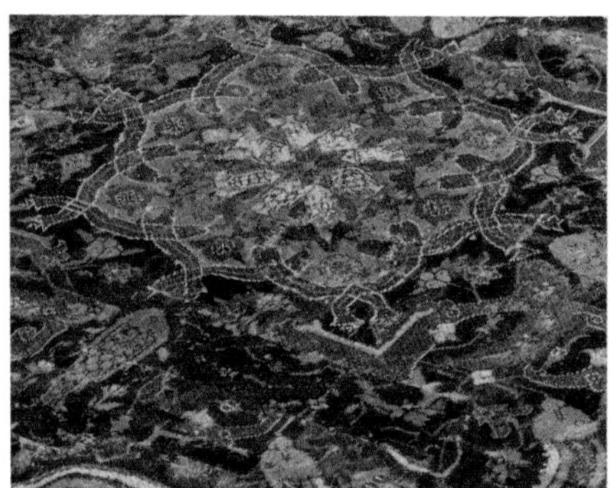

p: 8-9, 198, 201-4, 209

The 'Hyderabad' Carpet

Wool, cotton
India (Hyderabad)
17th century (11th-12th centuries AH)
CA.017

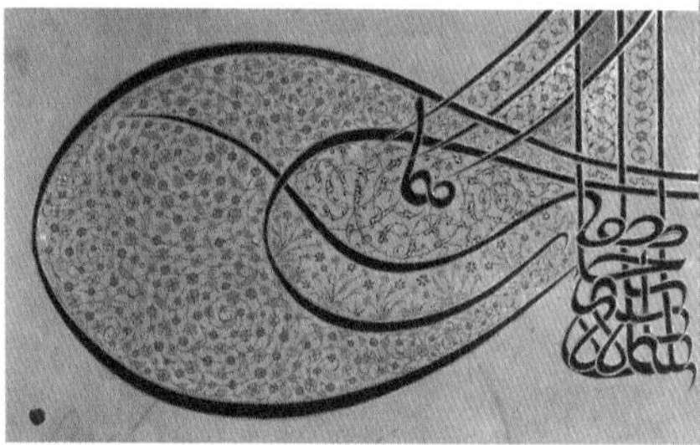

p: 210

Imperial Decree Ferman of Sultan Sulayman the Magnificent

Ink, pigments and gold on paper
Turkey
1559 (966 AH)
MS.1

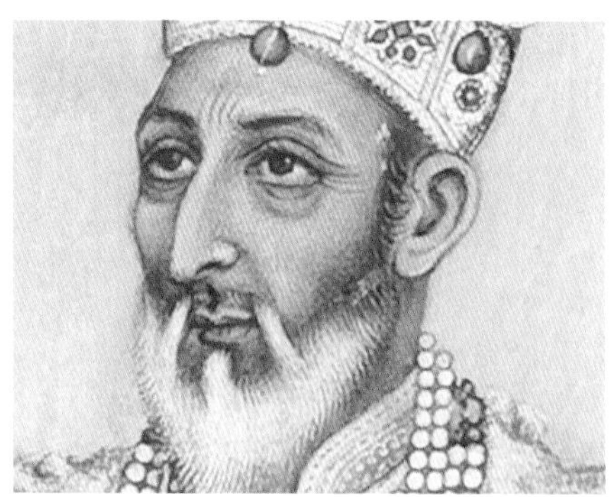

p: 218, 221

Portrait of Bahadur Shah II, the last Mughal Emperor

Opaque watercolour and gold on paper
India, Delhi
1838-89 (1254 AH)
MS.56

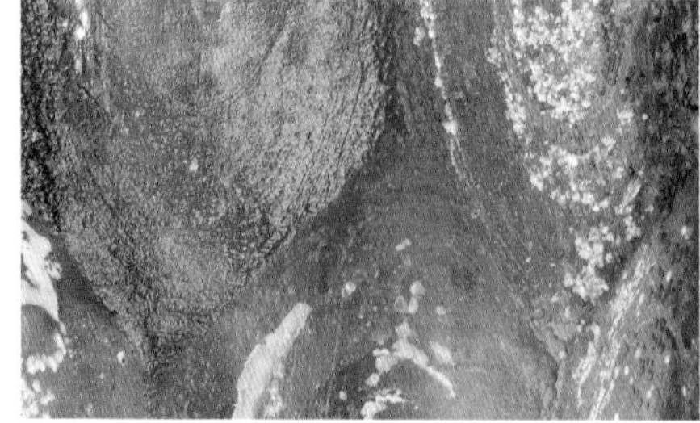

p: 226, 229

Glass Document Holder

Glass
Iran
6th-8th century (1st-3rd century AH)
GL.119

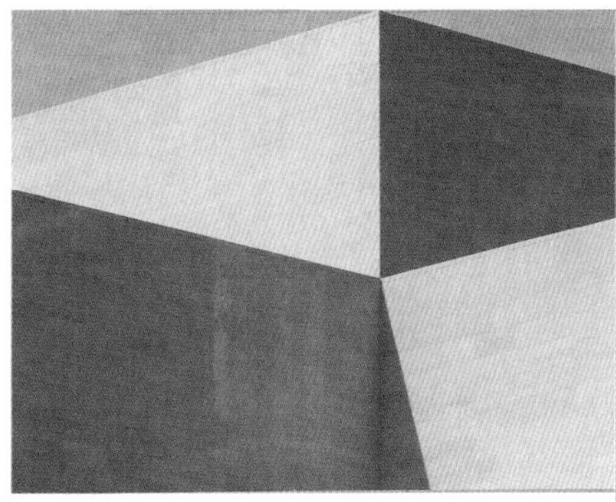

p: 6, 10, 17, 59, 108, 180, 230, 234, 237

Museum of Islamic Art

by I.M. Pei

Limestone

Doha

Opened 2008

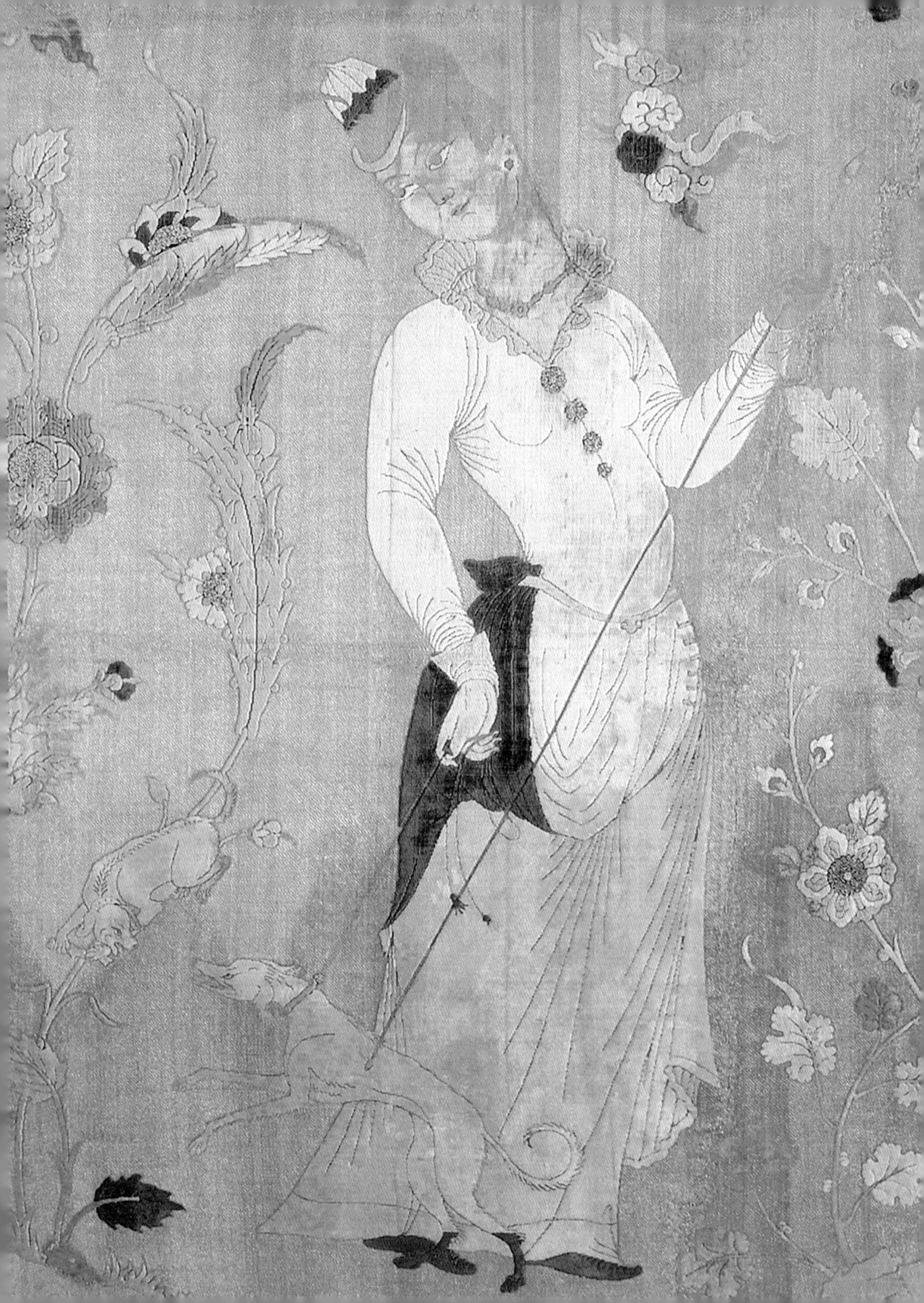